T0325555

Islamic Banking

Islamic Banking

How to Manage Risk and
Improve Profitability

AMR MOHAMED EL TIBY

WILEY

John Wiley & Sons, Inc.

Published by John Wiley & Sons, Inc., Hoboken, New Jersey.
Published simultaneously in Canada.

For general information on our other products and services or for technical support, please contact our Customer Care Department within the United States at (800) 762-2974, outside the United States at (317) 572-3993 or fax (317) 572-4002.

Wiley also publishes its books in a variety of electronic formats. Some content that appears in print may not be available in electronic books. For more information about Wiley products, visit our web site at www.wiley.com.

Library of Congress Cataloging-in-Publication Data:

El Tiby, Amr Mohamed, 1956–
  Islamic finance : how to manage risk and improve profitability / Amr Mohamed El Tiby.
      p.   cm. – (Wiley finance ; 640)
  Includes bibliographical references and index.
  ISBN 978-0-470-88023-4 (hardback); ISBN 978-0-470-93010-6 (ebk);
  ISBN 978-0-470-93008-3 (ebk); ISBN 978-0-470-93011-3 (ebk)
    1. Banks and banking–Islamic countries.   2. Risk–Islamic countries.   I. Title.
  HG3368.A6E47 2011
  332.1–dc22

                                                                      2010028557

Printed in the United States of America

10 9 8 7 6 5 4 3 2 1

To my mother,
To the soul of my father,
To my wife and children
Mohamed, Nada, and Khaled

Contents

List of Tables

Foreword

As many would say that the worst of the financial crisis is now behind us, it is indeed an opportune time for the expert materials (such as this book) on the issues of risk and profitability, particularly with reference to the Islamic financial services industry.

As is well known in the Islamic banking and finance industry, Islamic banking refers to a system of banking or banking activity that is consistent with the principles of Islamic law (*shari'ah*) and its practical application through the development of Islamic economics.

Islamic banking arguably emerged (and many view it) as a viable alternative model to conventional banking. The Islamic financial services industry, while still at a growing stage compared with its conventional counterpart, is progressing with a consistent pace.

Banks, conventional as well as Islamic, are subject to a wide range of risks in the course of their operations. Islamic banks, however, face an additional set of unique risks that arise from the shari'ah-compliant financing structures that they employ. I hope readers will have a better understanding of the risks associated with Islamic banking after reading this book.

There has been a growing amount of capital availability with the Islamic banks and they have been aggressively looking for new investment opportunities.

The supply of funds coincided quite naturally with the demand for infrastructure projects in the Middle Eastern Muslim countries. As a result, not only were Islamic banks able to participate in large-scale projects, but also innovation and financial engineering in refining the Islamic financing techniques experienced exponential growth. Put differently, Islamic banks now participate in a wide financing domain stretching from simple shari'ah-compliant retail products to highly complex structured finance products, which range from power projects and water desalination plants to roads, bridges, and other infrastructure projects. In sum, Islamic modes of financing are now being used for short-, medium-, and long-term project financing and hedging.

As for the role of Islamic banks in economic development, Islamic banks, while functioning within the framework of shari'ah, can perform a crucial task of resource mobilization. Their efficient allocation on both PLS (Musharaka and Mudaraba) and non-PLS (trading and leasing) based modes can strengthen the payments systems, and can thereby contribute significantly to the economic growth and development in their respective jurisdictions.

In order to ensure the maximum role of Islamic finance in economic development, it is necessary to create an environment that could provide an incentive for Islamic banks to earmark more funds toward the development of micro, small, and medium-size enterprises.

Islamic Finance: How to Manage Risk and Improve Profitability, written by a seasoned banker and scholar, Mr. Amr Mohamed El Tiby, is therefore timely and a truly welcome addition to the growing literature on the subject.

I sincerely congratulate Mr. El Tiby for this fine, aspiring contribution to the field of Islamic banking and finance.

ADNAN AHMED YOUSIF
President & Chief Executive
and Board member of Al Baraka Banking Group in Bahrain
and the Chairman of the Board of Union of Arab Banks

The global economic crisis brought to the fore the inadequacy of conventional banking regulations in general and their capital adequacy in particular in relation to the risks associated with their business; both aspects require serious reconsideration. Bankers, supervisors, and regulators across the globe are evaluating the causes and subsequences of the global economic crisis and the credit crunch facing banks. A better understanding of the role and importance of a solid regulatory framework and its weaknesses and strengths is crucial to ensure a safe and sound financial system.

Islamic banks were the least affected by the credit crunch due to their asset-based nature of operations. However, they still face many challenges; many bankers as well as regulators are assessing Islamic banks' robustness. The Islamic financial system, while still in its infancy if compared to the conventional financial system, has proven to have solid foundations. *The Banker's* third annual survey in 2009 of the top 500 Islamic financial institutions worldwide shows growth of assets at an extremely healthy rate of 28.6 percent to reach assets of $822 billion in 2009 compared to $639 billion in 2008, whereas in conventional banking the rate of growth of assets of the top 1,000 world banks has declined from 21.6 percent in 2008 to 6.8 percent in 2009 (*The Banker* 2009).

The book also explores the regulatory framework of the Islamic financial institutions, the regulatory issues and concerns, and the challenges facing the Islamic financial industry. It is important to note here that while much has been achieved in the regulatory framework of Islamic banks, much remains to be done.

The book has four parts: Part One provides an introduction and history of the development of Islamic banks. Part Two reviews the nature of risk in Islamic banks and Islamic financial instruments. It highlights the critical roles of regulation and supervision and sound corporate governance. Part Three considers the regulatory framework for both the Islamic and conventional banks. Part Four discusses corporate governance features specific to Islamic finance. A concluding chapter provides a summary and perspectives.

PART ONE: UNDERSTANDING THE ORIGINS

Part One consists of two chapters:

Chapter 1 gives an introduction and a brief overview of the book's contents.

Chapter 2, History and Development of Islamic Banking, offers a review of the historical background of Islamic banking, starting from the early days of Islam until now. The development of the modern Islamic banks is divided into four periods, beginning in the late nineteenth and early twentieth centuries. Each of the four periods is associated with a specific set of social and economic conditions and factors, which contributed collectively to the reviving and development of the Islamic financial system. This chapter will also show the development of the Islamic regulatory bodies and the supervisory agencies that support the Islamic financial system, as well as the development of Islamic banks in five countries: Egypt, Iran, Pakistan, Sudan, and Malaysia.

PART TWO: RISK IN ISLAMIC BANKING

Banks, conventional as well as Islamic, are subject to a wide range of risks in the course of their operations. In general, banking risk falls into four categories: financial, operational, business, and event risk. Islamic financial institutions face a unique mix of risks and risk-sharing arrangements resulting from the contractual design of the financing instruments, which is based on the principles of *shari'ah*; the nature of the liability base and the unique relationship between the bank and the Investment Account Holders (IAH); the liquidity infrastructure and constraints; and the overall legal framework and environment. Institutions offering Islamic financial services (IIFS) are set on different foundations from the conventional financial institutions. The first priority of IIFS is to adhere to shari'ah rules and principles, which take priority over profit.

IIFS are required to abide by the following ideals: (1) promotion of fairness in transactions and the prevention of an exploitative relationship, (2) sharing of risks and rewards between principals in all financial/commercial transactions, (3) the need for transactions to include elements of materiality leading to a tangible economic purpose, (4) the prohibition of interest, and (5) the prohibition of financing activities that are *haram* (forbidden, meaning anything that is against shari'ah), as all transactions must be legitimate and comply with the shari'ah rules and principles. Therefore, Islamic modes of finance, such as *murabaha* and profit and loss sharing (*mudarabah/musharakah*), display unique risk characteristics that must be accounted for in the calculation of capital adequacy requirements and in the development of the risk-management framework.

Part Two consists of four chapters:

In **Chapter 3**, The Nature of Risk in Islamic Banking, we explore the different types of risk that face banks, and the unique risks associated with Islamic banks in particular.

Chapter 4, The Inherent Risk in Islamic Banking Instruments, reviews and explains the basis and unique characteristics of the finance instruments used by Islamic banks, as well as compares and contrasts them with those used by conventional banks.

The chapter reviews the risks associated with the financial instruments used in Islamic banks and how such instruments operate. In addition, it will show the underlying fundamental differences in financial instruments between Islamic and conventional banks.

Chapter 5, Operational Risk in Islamic banking, discusses one of the most important risks that Islamic banks face. It explores and explains why Islamic banks have higher operational risk exposure than conventional banks. The chapter discusses three types of operational risk: (1) shari'ah noncompliance risk, (2) fiduciary risk, and (3) legal risk.

Chapter 6 is dedicated to the Islamic capital market. In it, we discuss the importance and role of capital market. We also delve into the Islamic bond market, referred to as *sukuk*. The chapter concludes with a look at the challenges and obstacles facing the development of the Islamic capital market.

PART THREE: CAPITAL ADEQUACY

The capital adequacy standard (CAS) is based on the principle that the level of a bank's capital should be related to and consistent with the bank's specific risk profile. The determination of the capital adequacy requirement (CAR) is based on the components of risk, namely credit, market, and operational risk. The Islamic banks' characteristic of mobilizing funds in the form of risk-sharing investment accounts, together with the materiality of financing transactions, impacts the overall risk of the balance sheet, and subsequently, the assessment of the capital adequacy requirements.

The nature of risk in Islamic banks differs from conventional banks because of the differences in the nature of assets between the two. Whereas the assets in conventional banks are based on debts, the assets in Islamic banks range from trade finance to equity partnership. Therefore, some of the Islamic banks' instruments carry additional risks that are not applicable to conventional banks. Subsequently, the calculation of risk weights for Islamic banks is different than it is for conventional banks.

Part Three has three chapters:

Chapter 7, The Importance and Role of Capital, sheds some light on and reviews the notion of capital. In this review, we follow two approaches: (1) the importance and role of capital in banking, and in Islamic banking in particular; and (2) historical reviews of the capital adequacy regulations and an examination of the different views regarding the necessity of banking regulations.

Chapter 8 pertains to The Regulatory Framework of the Conventional Banking System: Basel I and II. The regulatory framework of Islamic banking and the work of the Islamic Financial Services Board (IFSB) and the Accounting and Auditing Organization for Islamic Financial Institutions (AAOIFI) are mainly drawn upon the work and regulatory framework of The Basel Capital Adequacy Accord I and II, which were issued by the Basel Committee on Banking Supervision (BCBS). Therefore, I found it necessary, in order to better understand the Islamic regulatory framework, to dedicate this chapter to these two accords. The discussion in this chapter focuses on the historical background of Basel I and II, and provides an overview of the framework and regulatory bodies involved, namely, The Bank for International Settlement and the Basel Committee on Banking Supervision. **Chapter 9** looks at the regulatory framework for Islamic financial institutions, which includes the three pillars: (1) minimum capital requirements, (2) supervisory review process, and (3) market discipline. This chapter is dedicated to the first pillar of the capital adequacy framework for Islamic financial institutions, which is the minimum capital requirements. We examine the background and development of such regulations and the salient differences between Islamic and conventional banks, as well as how Islamic banks function within the conventional regulatory environment. This chapter also offers a recommendation to adjust the capital adequacy formula to account for the risk associated with the assets funded by IAH funds.

PART FOUR: CORPORATE GOVERNANCE

In the last few years, most countries across the globe have witnessed great difficulties in their banking systems—to the extent of the collapse of major banks in the United States and Western Europe. The year 2008 witnessed the collapse of Lehman Brothers, the largest investment bank in the United States, in addition to 130 local banks during 2009, and 42 local banks in the first quarter of 2010. Some other major banks were bailed out by their governments to save them from falling down. In some countries, like the United Arab Emirates, central banks had to step in to alleviate depositors' fears by issuing laws to guarantee all individual deposits for three years. Subsequently, the banking crisis has severely affected the whole economy and was one of the main factors for the international economic crisis we are now facing. The fact that all these problems arose, despite implementing global standards and regulations by the financial systems in these countries, has raised the importance of the issue of corporate governance.

Banks are extremely important to the development of the economy. In their role of collecting and utilizing funds, banks help in maintaining market stability and in providing low-cost capital, which stimulates growth in the economy. Corporate governance in such banks is a major element to this development. In addition, good corporate governance is considered an integral part of the institutional foundation of an economy and as a way to minimize the systemic risk in the financial system.

Part Four consists of four chapters:

Chapter 10, The Supervisory Review Process and Issues, focuses on the supervisory review process as one of the main contributing factors to the safety and soundness of the financial system. This chapter discusses the supervisory review process in Islamic banking, as well as issues in Islamic banking and Islamic windows with regard to this process. The relationship between risk analysis and bank supervision is also addressed.

Chapter 11, Corporate Governance in Islamic Banking, is dedicated to the issue of corporate governance in banks, and in Islamic banks in particular. It demonstrates the different models of corporate governance, as well as discusses in detail the corporate governance standards for Islamic banking and the recently established Shari'ah Governance System, which was issued by the IFSB in December 2009. This was done to further strengthen the existing standards and deepen the understanding of Islamic corporate governance for supervisors and stakeholders. The chapter continues to focus on the specific aspects of corporate governance that are unique to Islamic banks and Islamic windows, including the very important issue of Investment Account Holders (IAH) and Profit Sharing Investment Accounts (PSIA).

Chapter 12, Market Discipline and Transparency in Islamic Banking, examines transparency and disclosure requirements, which are major factors in the safety and soundness of any financial system. In Islamic banks, these are yet to be sufficiently developed, as there are major inconsistencies in the transparency and disclosure requirements across the different Islamic systems. This chapter shows the importance of market discipline in enforcing transparency. The main objective of this chapter is to examine market discipline, transparency, and disclosure of data in Islamic banking and to show how this differs from in conventional banks.

Chapter 13, Challenges Facing Islamic Banking and Recommendations, looks at the future challenges facing Islamic banking. It also presents conclusions and recommendations that aim to further enhance and strengthen the regulatory framework to ensure the development of a sound financial system. In addition, the chapter offers recommendations to adjust the capital adequacy formula—both the standard and the supervisory formulas—to take into consideration the risk assets that are funded by the unrestricted and restricted PSIA funds.

Acknowledgments

I would like to thank each and every person at John Wiley & Sons who gave me support: Bill Falloon, Meg Freeborn, Claire Wesley, and Tiffany Charbonier.

Special thanks go to Mr. Adnan Ahmed Yousif, President & Chief Executive and Board member of Al Baraka Banking Group and the Chairman of the Board of Union of Arab Banks. Special thanks go to Mr. Mohammad Nasr Abdeen, Chief Executive Officer of Union National Bank, for his continuous guidance and support.

Special thanks go to Dr. Wafik Grais, Senior Advisor of The World Bank, for his guidance. Special thanks go to Sir Howard Davies, The Director of London School of Economics, and to Dr. Hazem El Beblawi, Advisor to Arab Monetary Fund, and Dr. Jamal Sanad Al-Suwaidi, Director General of The Emirates Center for Strategic Studies and Research.

Special Thanks go to Mr. Ismail Hassan Mohammad, the former Governor of the Central Bank of Egypt. Special thanks go to Mr. Ashraf El-Ghamrawi, Board member of Al Baraka Islamic Bank. I would like to thank Dr. Adel A. Beshai and Dr. William M. Mikhail for their moral support.

Introduction

Demonstrating courage and tenacity, El Tiby has taken up the challenge of putting together a book on Islamic finance. *Islamic Banking: How to Manage Risk and Improve Profitability* provides a well-documented review of Islamic finance for specialists looking for a reference document as well as non-specialists seeking a comprehensive introduction to the topic. El Tiby brings to the table a thorough knowledge of the theory and practice of Islamic finance. This book provides an interesting historical overview of the origins of Islamic finance and its more recent developments, offering a historical depth that is not usually found in contemporary writings.

In focusing on risks faced by institutions offering Islamic financial services (IIFS), El Tiby highlights the role of regulatory framework, transparency, and corporate governance. The author has appropriately devoted a chapter to operational risk, as it is one of the areas where the specificity of Islamic finance is most obvious. The chapter on Islamic capital markets provides a good overview that will benefit readers wishing to refresh their knowledge on the subject. This book thoroughly covers capital adequacy issues, often dealt with by local regulators, the IFSB and AAOIFI. El Tiby brings together the conventional approach to capital adequacy as developed by the Basel Committee for Banking Supervision, and its adaptation to Islamic finance, developed most notably by the IFSB. *Islamic Banking: How to Manage Risk and Improve Profitability* is a worthwhile addition to the literature on Islamic finance.

DR. WAFIK GRAIS
Senior Advisor, Financial Sector Group, World Bank

PART One

Understanding
the Origins

CHAPTER 1

Introduction to Islamic Banking

The guiding principles of Islamic banking have existed throughout Islamic history, yet modern Islamic banking has been around for a relatively short time. During the time of the Ottoman Empire, which dominated the Muslim world from 1299 to 1922, an interest-based banking style was introduced to the Islamic world in order to finance the expenditure of the large expansion of the empire. Most Islamic jurists at this time thought of it as a contradiction to the Islamic principles that prohibit usury (*riba* in Arabic). The Hebrew word for usury is *neshek*, meaning literally "a bite" to indicate the pain inflicted upon the debtor. Usury is interpreted in the Quran and the Bible as *any* interest charged on loans, as opposed to the modern definition of usury as the charging of unreasonable or relatively high rates of interest.

The mid-twentieth century writing on Islamic finance has given rise to practical discussions on the subject, which has in turn raised the issue of replacing conventional financial practices with alternatives that are in compliance with Islamic law. *Shari'ah* denotes the Islamic law that governs all aspects of Muslims' lives. It is derived from the Quran and the *sunnah*, which is the sayings and examples set by the Prophet Mohammed. The development of modern Western banking goes back to the mid-seventeenth century, when development in mathematics and statistics provided powerful tools for financial mathematical science. These tools were developed over 300 years, and as a consequence, we have a robust interest-based financial system in place. At the same time, the legal and regulatory framework for the Western banking model has come a long way.

In addition, the last four decades have witnessed an increasing role of international independent regulators for conventional banks, such as the Bank for International Settlements (BIS) and the Basel Committee on Banking Supervision in enhancing the safety and soundness of the financial system. Although they do not have formal supranational supervisory authority, all banks across the globe are voluntarily following their regulations, seeking international recognition. Capital adequacy regulations have received large attention and were developed from the early years of the twentieth century, whereas other regulatory issues—such as risk management standards and best practices, market discipline, and corporate governance—have received increasing global attentions in the last four decades. Capital adequacy regulations became one of the most important developments in the banking industry and elements of bank soundness. Kevin Dowd describes capital adequacy regulations in the following words: "One of the more important developments in 20th century central banking is the rise of capital adequacy regulations—the imposition by regulators of minimum capital standards on financial institutions" (Dowd 1999).

Unfortunately, the Ottoman Empire, did not give priority or attention to developing the financial system that is based on the shari'ah rules and principles. In recent times, there were early experiments with Islamic banking in Pakistan in the late 1950s. In Egypt, Mit Ghamr Local Savings Bank was the first successful modern experience in the world; it was established in 1963 as an undercover endeavor for fear of being viewed as a form of Islamic fundamentalism. The bank was closed in mid 1967, and its operations were taken over by The National Bank of Egypt, which employed interest-based transactions. Starting from the mid 1970s, and as a result of the sharp increase in oil prices that brought large wealth to the Middle East, the demand for shari'ah-compliant solutions, as an alternative to the conventional financial solutions, has tremendously increased. While the Islamic financial services have developed in fast pace starting in the 1970s, the regulatory bodies and the regulations governing Islamic financial institutions have not developed as fast as the industry itself.

In recent years, there were many efforts exerted by Islamic financial regulatory bodies like the Islamic Financial Services Board (IFSB) and Accounting and Auditing Organization for Islamic Financial Institutions (AAOIFI) to develop regulatory framework for Islamic financial institutions, which includes capital adequacy standards, risk management framework, and corporate governance standards. Another goal of organizations such as these was to harmonize Islamic financial practices like financial reporting, accounting treatments, and disclosure requirements with the internationally accepted standards and practices. Those efforts are aiming for enhancing and strengthening the regulatory framework in order to ensure a safe and sound Islamic financial system and to smoothly and effectively integrate and harmonize the Islamic financial system and practices with the international financial system and practices.

Despite all those efforts, there are still many issues that need to be further developed and resolved. The first issue is the lack of standard practices and rules. Islamic financial systems in different parts of the world differ in their accounting operations and financial reporting. In addition, Islamic banks operating in one country may have different interpretations to the same issue due to the fact that banks have their own shari'ah boards that may have different views. And some shari'ah boards impose a stricter interpretation than others.

The second issue is the ambiguity regarding how Islamic financial institutions operate and how they should be regulated. The issue that is raised is related to the supervisory authorities and the regulatory frameworks that govern and regulate the conventional banking system—mainly, whether they are competent to regulate Islamic banks or whether there should be separate supervisory authority and a different regulatory framework for Islamic financial institutions.

Third, there are funding and liquidity problems caused by Islamic banks' inability to borrow at interest on the inter-bank market or hedge against interest-rate risks through derivatives. It is harder to match assets and liabilities for fear that they will be unable to meet demands for withdrawing deposits. In addition, Islamic banks usually do not have discount window of lender of last resort as an option that is offered by the central banks to conventional banks (O'Sullivan 1996).

Fourth, one of the major obstacles that faces the development of Islamic banks is the lack of transparency and disclosure of information to both investment account holders and the supervisory authorities. Most central banks in the Americas, Europe, and the rest of the world either decline to furnish data or are unable to calculate shari'ah-compliance assets within their nations (Divanna 2007).

Finally, corporate governance issue in Islamic banking is one of the serious issues that need to be carefully considered. The investment account holder's right and the nature of their relationship with Islamic banking is one of the topics that is unique to Islamic banks.

A better understanding of the nature of risk in Islamic banking is crucial in setting solid and sound regulatory framework. There are four major factors that affect the risk in Islamic banks and make it different than conventional banks.

1. The Islamic banks' basic foundations, which set its priorities as the promotion of fairness in transactions and the prevention of an exploitative relationship, sharing of risks and rewards between principals in all financial/commercial transactions, the need for transactions to include elements of materiality leading to a tangible economic purpose, the prohibition of interest, and the prohibition of financing activities that do not comply with the shari'ah rules and principles.
2. The nature of the relationship between the bank and the customers. Islamic banks' modes of finance are mainly asset backed, which involves

a great deal of contracts between the two parties. Such arrangements increase the legal risk in both the drafting stage and the enforcement in case of legal dispute. Also, the actual possession of the assets involved increases the operational risk carried out by Islamic banks.

3. The profit and loss sharing arrangement between the bank and the customer on both sides of the balance sheet, which represents unique risk characteristics.
4. The liquidity constraint that faces Islamic banks as they are unable to borrow in the market, as well as the very limited scope of their secondary market and the absence of the lender of last resort option.

The Capital Adequacy Standards for Islamic banks that were set by the Islamic Financial Services Board (IFSB) are mainly drawn on the work of Basel II. The IFSB has taken into consideration, on the one hand, the unique risk characteristics in the utilization of funds in the asset side of the balance sheet. And on the other hand, they have examined the nature and role of capital and the unique relationship between the bank and the Investment Account Holders (IAH) in the mobilization of funds. One of the major conceptual differences between the capital adequacy requirements in Islamic banks and conventional banks is that assets funded by the IAH funds are not subject to capital charge.

The nature of the relationship between the Islamic bank and the IAH is unique and raises a very serious concern when it comes to corporate governance. The concern arises from the fact that while IAH are exposed to loss of their capital, they do not have any governance right. Once the IAH enter into a contract with the bank, the control over the investment decisions is completely transferred to the bank. There is complete separation between the capital providers and the management. The IFSB has issued two standards, one for corporate governance and the other for the Shari'ah Governance System. Corporate governance issue for Islamic windows is another area of concern. Apart from the issues that face pure Islamic banks, such as fairness and transparency, balance sheet segregation is an additional issue that is unique to Islamic windows. It is crucial to ensure that the funds that are raised by the Islamic windows are completely separated and are not in any form mingled in the banks' conventional activities.

CHAPTER 2

History and Development of Islamic Banking

The history of Islamic banking goes back to the birth of Islam. This chapter contains three sections:

1. The first section addresses Islamic banking activities during the early days of Islam.
2. The second section examines the modern history and development of Islamic banking starting from the late nineteenth century and continuing through to the present date.
3. The third section highlights the development of Islamic banking in Egypt, Iran, Pakistan, Sudan, and Malaysia. The reasons for choosing these countries is that Egypt, pioneered by Mit Ghamr Local Savings Bank, which was established in 1963, is said to be a milestone in the development of modern Islamic banking because it has proved that *shari'ah* rules and principles are sufficient to meet the financial needs of the Muslims of today. Iran, Pakistan, and Sudan are three countries that have begun to completely transform their banking systems to Islamic. Malaysia is said to be the largest country to embrace Islamic banking and is considered the largest Islamic financial center in the world.

THE EARLY DAYS OF ISLAM

The first organized Islamic financial institution is *Baitul Mal*, which translates to "House of Money" and was established in the early days of Islam. Originally, administration of taxes, distribution of *zakat* (wealth tax), and managing government expenditures were the main function of Baitul Mal. During the time of the Prophet Mohammed (*pbuh*) and Abu Bakr Al Sidiq, the first of the Rashidun caliphate, all revenues received were distributed immediately; therefore, there was no need for a permanent Baitul Mal. The actual establishment of Baitul Mal as an organized financial institution is attributed to Omar Bin Al Khatab, the second caliph. During this period, there was a large increase in state revenue from the concord territories that needed to be managed. A central treasury was established in Medina, headed by Abdulla bin Arqam as treasury officer, and provincial treasuries were also set to manage the province revenues and expenditure and to remit the net proceeds to the central treasury. For bookkeeping and accounting, a separate accounts department was established.

The major sources of funding for Baitul Mal were revenues from concord territories, zakat (wealth tax applied at the rate of 2.5 percent on all Muslims), *jizia* (tax due from non-Muslims for providing protection), and *kharaj* (land tax). Secondary sources of funding included *sadaqah* (donations) and any funds or properties with no owners or legal heirs. On the expenditure side, and apart from the state expenses such as payment of salaries and other expenditures, Omar Bin Al Khatab introduced the first of what we now call Social Security. This included providing income to the poor, elderly, orphaned, widowed, and disabled, as well as unemployment insurance, retirement pensions, and public trusteeship.

During this time, allowance to non-Muslims and relief from jizia were also first applied. During the early days of Islam, some banking activities took place in the form of custody of money and precious items and remittances. As mentioned by Haron and Shanmugam (1997), Az Zubair ben Al Awwam was the first person to apply the Islamic principle of *qard*, or loan, in the history of Islamic banking. Abdallah ben Az Zubair received cash in Mecca and wrote to his brother in Iraq, who repaid the depositors when they arrived in Iraq.

During the period of the Muslims ruling, which lasted for almost 12 centuries from the early days of Islam until the collapse of the Ottoman Empire in 1922, there was a large spread, in many parts of the world, of the Islamic principles (*shari'ah*) that govern all aspects of the lives of Muslims, including the core principles of financial and commercial activities. The Islamic Empire, within the first 100 years of the death of the Prophet Muhammed (*pbuh*), was larger than the Roman Empire, reaching Spain in the west and India in the east. In addition, this era witnessed flourishing economic and commercial activities, as well as with the sciences, particularly at the golden era of the Abbasid Caliphate from 750 to 1258. Despite the availability of all elements needed, Muslims failed to establish and develop a financial system that caters for the financial needs of both Muslims and non Muslims. It was not until the seventeenth century when the conventional interest-based financial system was established in Europe as a result of the economic and commercial activities revival as well as the development in mathematics and statistics, which provided powerful tools for financial mathematical science.

THE MODERN ISLAMIC BANKING SYSTEM

The start of the Islamic banking system as we now know can, to a large extent, be attributed to the wave of reform thoughts and ideas that took place in the late nineteenth and early twentieth centuries in what was known as the Islamic resurgence movements. During this time, Muslim thinkers and reformers revived and encouraged the ideas of reapplication of Islamic principles to all aspects of life and that adherence to *shari'ah* principles is essential for Islam and Muslims. One of the main issues that concerned Muslim scholars was how to eliminate *riba* from their lives and how they could make their financial dealings compliant with their *shari'ah*. Rashid Rida (1865–1935) was a Syrian scholar and jurist who joined Jamal Al Din Al Afghani (1838–1897) and Mohamed Abdu (1849–1905) in their newspaper *Al-Urwa al-Wuthqa* and the later-launched *Al Manar* weekly news paper in Cairo, where they published articles that discussed the legitimately of interest. This period has also witnessed thinkers such as Hassan Al Banna (1906–1949), the founder of the Muslim Brotherhood (the foremost of Egypt's resurgent Islamic Organization), Sayed Qutb (1906–1966), one of the foremost figures in modern Sunni Islamic revivalism and the thinker of the Muslim Brotherhood in Egypt, and Syed Abul Ala Mawdudi (1903–1979), a Sunni Pakistani journalist, the founder of Islamic revivalist party *Jamaat-e-Islam* and a major Islamic thinker and revivalist leader. Their ideas and writings on how to reestablish the Islamic state and how to reinforce Islamic *shari'ah* into all aspects of Muslims lives, have helped in enhancing the awareness of the importance of establishing the Islamic financial system in Muslims' minds.

   Islamic banking, as an institution, has only been around for almost 70 years, whereas the idea of interest-free banking has been around for as long as the inception of Islam. The first attempt to establish an interest-free bank, which ended unsuccessfully, was in the mid 1940s in Malaysia. The idea was to invest pilgrims' savings in real estate and plantations in accordance with *shari'ah* principles. The second experiment was in the 1950s in the rural areas of Pakistan, and unfortunately, it did not continue. In 1962, the Malaysian government set up the Pilgrim's Management Fund to help prospective pilgrims save and profit from their money. The most successful and innovative experiment, however, was the establishment of Mit Ghamr Local Savings Bank in Egypt in 1963. It was marked as a milestone in the evolution of the modern Islamic banking system. Although the bank provided basic banking services such as deposit accounts, loan accounts, direct investment, and social services, it was sufficient to meet the needs and requirements of the surrounding community. The bank provided clear evidence that there are *shari'ah*-compliant financial solutions alternative to the conventional banking system and that these rules and principles are still applicable to meet the modern-day business and financial needs of the Muslim community. This was the most important contribution in recent history that moved the concept of Islamic banking forward.

The history of modern Islamic banking can be divided into four periods:

1. The establishment period.
2. The spread period.
3. The international recognition period.
4. The evaluation period.

TABLE 2.1 The Development of Islamic Banking from 1965 to Present

The Period	Date	Characteristics
Establishment	1965–1976	Major activities across the Muslim world in the area of research in all fields that concern Muslims' daily lives. The establishment of Muslim organizations to promote cooperation and support among Muslim countries. The establishment of several Islamic banks across the Muslim world.
The Spread	1977–2002	Fueled with the sharp increase in oil prices and huge wealth in the Middle East. The establishment of hundreds of Islamic banks across the globe. The transformation of the Financial System to complete Islamic banking in Iran, Sudan, and Pakistan.
The International Recognition	2003–2009	The global acceptance of Islamic banks by the Western and Recognition American regulators. The growing interest of international banks in Western Europe, the United States, and Japan in Islamic Finance.
The Evaluation	2009–present	The large, healthy gross of Islamic assets compared to the large decline in the conventional bank assets during the global crisis. Islamic banks were the least affected by the global crisis.

The first period, which lasted from 1965 until 1976 and witnessed many Islamic activities across the Muslim world, set the ground for establishing the Islamic financial system. In 1965, Al Azhar Al Sharief in Egypt established the Islamic Research Academy, which consists of 50 members out of whom 30 are Egyptian and 22 are from other Islamic countries. The members are experts in different fields such as medical sciences, engineering, astronomy, law, and political and economic science. In addition, there is a group of scholars who are experts in *shari'ah*. The objective of the Academy is to research the issues that are of interest to and encountered by Muslims in their daily lives (Gomaa 2006).

In the early 1960s, the Ministry of Endowments in Egypt established the Supreme Council for Islamic Affairs, which consists of several committees with large groups of expertise in all fields (Gomaa 2006). The objective of the council is to establish and develop the cultural and religious relationship between Egypt and the rest of the world, and to provide services for Islam and Muslims regarding their conduct, beliefs, and culture. The council publishes educational periodicals in Arabic and other languages, provides simple interpretation and translation for the Quran, and publishes encyclopedias in all the Islamic sciences.

During this period, many conferences were held including the Conference of the Finance Ministries of Islamic Countries in Karachi in 1970. The first international conference for Islamic economics was held in 1976 in Mecca under the patronage of King Abdul Aziz University, which is considered to be the first scientific conference in the Islamic economy. The late King Faisal Bin Abdul Aziz is considered to have made major contributions toward the development of Islamic economics by initiating the establishment of the Organization of Islamic Conferences (OIC). In 1969, the organization was established upon a decision of the historical summit, which took place in Rabat, Kingdom of Morocco, as a result of the criminal arson of Al-Aqsa Mosque in occupied Jerusalem. The organization, with its 57 members from all over the world, is considered the second largest intergovernmental organization after the United Nations. The second OIC conference of foreign ministers was held in Karachi, Pakistan, in December 1970.

A third meeting for the foreign ministers of Islamic countries was held in Benghazi, Libya, in March 1973, where they examined the proposal for establishing The Islamic Development Bank. Subsequent meetings were held, and finally, the draft to create the Islamic Development Bank (IDB) was approved. The bank was officially established in October 1975, with founding members from 22 Islamic countries. The bank's main office is located in Jeddah, Kingdom of Saudi Arabia. It has two regional offices in Rabat, Kingdom of Morocco, and another in Kuala Lumpur, Malaysia. The bank was established for the purpose of promoting the economic and social development and progress in accordance with *shari'ah* principles for all member and Muslim countries.

The functions of IDB, as stated in its 1994 annual report (Meenai 1989), are as follows:

> *The functions of the bank are to participate in equity capital and grant loans for productive projects and enterprises, besides providing financial assistance to member countries in other forms for economic and social development. The bank is also required to establish and operate special funds for specific purposes, including a fund for assistance to Muslim communities in non-member countries, in addition to setting up trust funds. The bank is authorized to accept deposits and mobilize financial resources by way of appropriate modes of financing. It is also charged with the responsibility of assisting in the promotion of foreign trade, especially in capital goods, among member countries, providing technical assistance to member countries, extending trading facilities for personnel engaged in development activities in Muslim countries to conform to the* Shari'ah. *(Meenai 1989)*

This period also witnessed the establishment of several Islamic banks in the Arab world: Nasser Social Bank in Egypt in 1971; Dubai Islamic Bank, established in Dubai, United Arab Emirates, in 1975 by a group of businessmen from several countries as the first private Islamic bank in the world; Faisal Islamic Bank in Egypt in 1977; and Faisal Islamic Bank in Sudan in 1977—both as private banks. In 1977, the government of Kuwait set up the Kuwait Finance House.

The second period, which spanned from 1977 until 2002, was fueled by the sharp increase in oil prices that brought large wealth to the Middle East and the spread of Islamic banks across the Islamic and non-Islamic countries. During this period, more than 100 Islamic banks were opened and operating across the world. In addition, conventional banks started to provide and offer *shari'ah*-compliant products and services through dedicated departments in what became known as *Islamic windows*. This period also witnessed the full transformation of the banking system in Iran, Sudan, and Pakistan to the Islamic banking system. The transformation of the financial system was done rapidly in both Iran in August 1983 and Sudan in July 1984. In Pakistan, however, it was a gradual process that started in 1947, was formalized in the late 1970s, and was generalized in mid 1985.

The third period, in my view, seems to have stretched from 2003 until the middle of 2009. There are two major distinctive features in this period:

1. The global acceptance of the *shari'ah*-compliant financial solutions by the regulatory authorities in Western Europe and the United States, particularly by the Financial Services Authority (FSA), the single financial regulator in the United Kingdom.
2. The growing interest and involvement of the international financial giants in Western Europe, Japan, and the United States in Islamic financial transactions. These include ANZ Grindlays, Citibank, Union Bank of Switzerland (UBS), Credit Swiss, and HSBC. Japanese banks have also become involved in Islamic transactions. The Industrial Bank of Japan (IBJ) has established an Islamic portfolio for *Mudarib*. The Bank of Japan and the Japan Bank of International Cooperation, both of which are government agencies, have joined the IFSB as observers.

During this period the Financial Services Authority (FSA) in the United Kingdom authorized three wholly Islamic banks initiated by Middle Eastern investors and institutions to meet the increasing demand for *shari'ah*-compliant financial solutions. This demand was a result of the sharp increase in oil prices that led to excessive liquidity in the Middle East and the emerging need for alternative assets. The three banks authorized by the FSA are the Islamic Bank of Britain in 2004, the European Islamic Investment Bank in 2006, and the Bank of London and the Middle East in July 2007. The first one has retail activity nature of business, and the other two are wholesale activity nature of business. The SFA has also authorized one Islamic hedge fund manager and is considering an application from the first wholly Islamic *Takaful* providers. *Shari'ah*-compliant products and services are not only attractive to 1.6 billion Muslims across the globe, but also to non-Muslims. Out of the top 15 countries in the volume of Islamic assets, the United Kingdom comes in tenth with *shari'ah*-compliant assets of $10.4 billion (Timewell and Divanna, 2007).

The fourth period, also in my opinion, seems to have begun sometime in the middle of 2009, when bankers, supervisors, and regulators across the globe were evaluating the causes and consequences of the global economic crises and the credit crunch facing banks. Despite the fact that it is still early to come to concrete conclusions, many bankers as well as regulators are evaluating the fact that Islamic banks were the least affected by the credit crunch due to its asset-based nature. *The Banker*'s third annual survey in 2009 of the world's top 500 Islamic financial Institutions shows growth assets at an extremely healthy rate of 28.6 percent to reach assets of $822 billion in 2009, compared to $639 billion in 2008. In conventional banking, the rate of growth of assets of the top 1,000 world banks declined from 21.6 percent in 2008 to 6.8 percent in 2009 (*The Banker* 2009).

REGULATORY AGENCIES FOR ISLAMIC
FINANCIAL SERVICES

The regulatory bodies and regulations of Islamic finance have not developed as fast as the industry itself. In recent years, there were many efforts to standardize Islamic financial regulatory practices in terms of accounting, corporate governance, capital adequacy requirements, and risk management standards.

On a local prospective, Islamic financial institutions are regulated and supervised by the regulatory and supervisory authority in their respective countries. In all countries, except for Malaysia, at the bank level, each bank has its own *Shari'ah* Supervisory Board that advises on transactions and performs supervisory functions. Malaysia is the only country where the government has one single *Shari'ah* Supervisory Board for all Islamic banks in the country.

On a global perspective, the Islamic financial industry is supported by several international bodies. In this section, we will discuss four: (1) Islamic Financial Services Board (IFSB), (2) Accounting and Auditing Organization for Islamic Financial Institutions (AAOIFI), (3) Islamic International Rating Agency (IIRA), and (4) International Islamic Financial Market (IIFM).

The Islamic Financial Services Board (IFSB) is based in Kuala Lumpur, Malaysia, and it began its operations on March 10, 2003. It functions as an international standard-setting body of regulatory and supervisory agencies that have a vested interest in ensuring the soundness and stability of the Islamic financial services industry, which is defined broadly to include banking, capital market, and insurance. The IFSB members include 49 regulatory and supervisory authorities in addition to the International Monetary Fund, World Bank, Bank for International Settlements, Islamic Development Bank, Asian Development Bank, and Islamic Corporation for the Development of Private Sector, and 138 market players and professional firms operating in 39 countries. The IFSB objectives can be classified into three major groups: (1) the prudential and regulatory perspective, (2) the coordination and harmonization among all different groups, and (3) the training and research area.

Prudential and regulatory perspective:

- To promote the development of a prudent and transparent Islamic financial services industry through introducing new, or adapting existing, international standards consistent with *shari'ah* principles, and recommending these for adoption.
- To provide guidance on the effective supervision and regulation of institutions offering Islamic financial products and to develop for the Islamic

financial services industry the criteria for identifying, measuring, managing, and disclosing risks, taking into account international standards for valuation, income, and expense calculation and disclosure.

Coordination and harmonization:

- To liaise and cooperate with relevant organizations currently setting standards for the stability and the soundness of the international monetary and financial systems and those of the member countries.
- To enhance and coordinate initiatives to develop instruments and procedures for efficient operations and risk management and to encourage cooperation among member countries in developing the Islamic financial services industry.

Training and Research:

- To facilitate training and personnel development in skills in areas relevant to the effective regulation of the Islamic financial services industry and related markets.
- To undertake research into and publish studies and surveys on the Islamic financial services industry. And to establish a database of Islamic banks, financial institutions, and industry experts.

The IFSB has so far issued 12 standards and guiding principles to regulate the Islamic financial services industry. These standards cover the areas of risk management, capital adequacy, corporate governance, the supervisory review process, market discipline and transparency, governance for the Islamic collective investment scheme, the *shari'ah* governance system, the development of the Islamic capital market, and the conduction of business. Additionally, several standards were issued to regulate Islamic *Takaful*.

The second body supporting the Islamic finance industry is the Accounting and Auditing Organization for Islamic Financial Institutions (AAOIFI). The AAOIFI is an international Islamic independent, nonprofit organization that focuses mainly on the area of accounting and auditing. The AAOIFI prepares accounting, auditing, governance, and *shari'ah* standards, which are globally acceptable. It was established by an agreement of association signed by Islamic financial institutions on February 1990 in Algeria and was registered on March 1991 in Manama, the Kingdom of Bahrain. The organization is supported by 200 institutional members from 45 countries including central banks, Islamic financial institutions, and international Islamic banking and finance industries across the globe. The objectives of AAOIFI are to develop and disseminate accounting and auditing thoughts relevant to Islamic financial institutions and their applications. This includes holding seminars, publishing periodical newsletters, as well as carrying out and commissioning research. The other objectives of AAOIFI are to prepare, promulgate, interpret, review, and amend accounting and auditing standards for Islamic financial institutions (AAOIFI 2008). AAOIFI plays a crucial role in harmonizing the Islamic financial institutions practices with the internationally accepted practices.

The third body supporting the Islamic finance industry is the Islamic International Rating Agency (IIRA), based in Manama, Kingdom of Bahrain, and established in July 2005 to provide capital markets and the banking sector in Islamic countries with a rating spectrum that encompasses the full array of capital instruments. It also aims to enhance the level of analytical expertise in those markets. The IIRA is sponsored by multilateral development institutions, leading banks, other financial institutions and rating agencies and has a board of directors and a completely independent rating committee. The IIRA, in its aim to become the principal reference for credit ratings in relation with *shari'ah*, has set seven objectives:

1. To develop methodologies and benchmarks for issue/issuer ratings.
2. To provide independent assessment and opinions on the likelihood of timely payment of financial obligations by sovereign, corporate, banks, and financial institutions and securities issued by government, corporate, banks, and financial institutions.
3. To provide independent opinion on the level of compliance with the rules and principles of *shari'ah*.
4. To assess the governance system adopted by corporate, banks, and financial institutions.
5. To disseminate and publish information and data relating to business enterprises for the development of a sound and efficient capital market.
6. To offer research, analysis, and evaluation of sectors, industries, and entities.
7. To encourage and promote a sound disclosure framework and a higher level of transparency in the Islamic financial systems (IIRA).

The fourth body is the International Islamic Financial Market (IIFM), which is an international nonprofit institution, founded with the collective efforts of the central banks and monetary agencies of Bahrain, Brunei, Indonesia, Malaysia, Sudan, United Arab Emirates, Pakistan, and the Islamic Development Bank based in Saudi Arabia. It was established by an agreement on November 13, 2001, and began its operations on April 1, 2002, with its headquarters in the Kingdom of Bahrain. The main objective of the IIFM is to establish, develop, promote, and regulate an international financial market based on the *shari'ah* rules and principles. The IIFM is working to promote five areas:

1. In the regulatory area, the IIFM works to bring Islamic Financial Market participants into a common understanding through establishing links between them and the regulatory bodies on the Islamic capital and money market segment of the industry.
2. Wider *shari'ah* acceptance.
3. Provide recommendations, guidelines, and best practices regarding primary and secondary market issues to all members.
4. Provide unified documentation frameworks and product development, which would help in reducing the cost and improve the transactional securities for its members.
5. Encourage and facilitate knowledge sharing across the industry and the world through different activities such as conferences and publications (International Islamic Financial Market 2008).

THE SPREAD OF ISLAMIC BANKING

In this section, we discuss the development of Islamic banks in five countries—Egypt, Iran, Sudan, Pakistan, and Malaysia. The reason for choosing these countries is that Egypt, with its pioneer experiment in early 1963, is said to be the milestone in the history of modern Islamic banking. Iran, Sudan, and Pakistan are the three countries that started the process of transforming the financial system to a purely Islamic one. Malaysia has had the most successful experiment in developing Islamic banks. It has adopted a well-balanced approach to develop the Islamic Financial System in parallel to the conventional financial system. They have succeeded to make the two systems complement each other.

Egypt

The most important event in the history of modern Islamic banking was the successful experiment of Mit Ghamr Local Savings Bank in the Nile Delta of Egypt in 1963. Before we go into the experiment, we need to shed some light on the political atmosphere in Egypt from the time of President Gamal Abdel Nasser to the time of President Anwar Al Sadat, because it had a serious effect on both the establishment and development of Islamic banks in Egypt.

In 1954, Egypt witnessed a change in the political atmosphere when the Muslim Brotherhood group was accused of the attempted assassination of Gamal Abdel Nasser. The Muslim Brotherhood was abolished and thousands of its members were imprisoned and punished. Again in 1965, they were accused of an attempted *coup d'etat* and many of them were imprisoned. In 1966, Sayyid Qutb—the most influential thinker of the Brotherhood—was executed by Nasser's regime. As a result of the change in the political environment and the hostile attitude of the regime toward Islamic activities, the bank was established by Dr. Ahmed Al Najjar, an economist and social activist, as an undercover endeavor with private initiatives, and it later gained large support from customers. The bank adopted some ideas from the German Savings Banks with the principle of rural banking, within the general framework of *shari'ah* rules and principles. The bank's depositors' base increased from 17,560 in 1963 to 251,152 in 1967. Similarly, its deposits increased from LE 40,944 in 1963 to LE 1,828,375 in 1967 (Haron and Shanmugam 1997). In 1967, the bank was shut down and its operations were undertaken by The National Bank of Egypt.

In 1970, the new regime of Anwar Al Sadat, the successor of the late president Nasser, anticipated the threat by the powerful political groups at this time mainly the leftist group and the group that still have loyalty to Nasser's regime. In its effort to emphasis control and protection, the regime started to Islamitize the political, economic, and social life of Egypt. In regard to the social life, this was evident in the extreme focus on Islamic activities in the media and in the political front, particularly in the form of support given to Islamic groups in the universities (Heikal 1983).

In 1971, the establishment of Nasser Social Bank by the new regime of Anwar Al Sadat revitalized the idea of interest-free banking. The bank was government-owned, and subsequently, three new banks were granted licenses to operate: Faisal Islamic Bank, Islamic International Bank for Investment and Development, and Egyptian Saudi Finance Bank. Faisal Islamic Bank in Egypt was established by a special act called Law No. 48/1977 for the establishment of Faisal Islamic Bank, and Decree No. 77/1977 of the Ministry of *Awkaf* (Endowment). The bank received special privileges that facilitated its operations, such as exemption from the laws governing foreign exchange and from the laws regulating labor, employment, wages, salaries, remunerations, pension, medical treatment, and social insurance. Another development in the Egyptian Islamic banking system is the establishment of Islamic windows in conventional banks, which provided banking products and services based on the shari'ah principles.

The Islamic Republic of Iran

The Islamic banking system in Iran was born as a result of the Islamic Revolution in 1979. In June 1979, the banking system, which consisted of nearly

35 private and government banks, was nationalized by the Revolutionary Council. Through amalgamations and consolidations, the number of existing banks was reduced to six commercial banks and three specialized banks, in addition to the establishment of 22 provincial banks.

The transformation of the entire conventional banking system to Islamic was on a gradual basis that lasted for six years. A comprehensive legislation was prepared to bring the entire operations of the banking system to comply with shari'ah principles. The proposal was submitted to the Revolutionary Council in 1982 and was passed by the Parliament in 1983 as the law for usury. The new law required banks to convert their interest-based deposits to interest-free deposits within one year and to convert their entire operations to comply with shari'ah principles, as per the set guidelines, within a transition period of three years. In March 1985, all banking transactions were strictly based on shari'ah principles.

The shari'ah interpretation to riba in the Iranian Islamic banking system has removed the obstacle of banks to finance government based on predetermined and fixed interest rates. According to their interpretation, there are four conditions to be met in order for riba to exist, which are:

1. Indebtedness
2. Debtor independent from the creditor
3. The determination of premium over the principal amount
4. The actual receipt of such premium

Because all banks are government owned as a result of the nationalization process that took place, the second condition is not met. Subsequently, banks being fully dependent on the government were able to finance the government using interest-bearing modes. Applying the same methodology and interpretation on financial transactions, all loans between either two companies or two branches of a same company are not considered *riba* if they have the same shareholders (Lewis and Algaoud 2001).

Pakistan

The idea of Islamic banking in Pakistan goes back to the early days of the independence. Muhammad Ali Jinnah, the founder of Pakistan, in his speech on the occasion of the opening ceremony of the State Bank of Pakistan (SBP) on July 1, 1948, said:

> *I shall watch with keenness the work of your Research Organization in evolving banking practice compatible with Islamic ideas of social and economic life. The economic system of the West has*

created almost insoluble problems for humanity and to many of us appears that only a miracle can save it from disaster that is not facing the world. It has failed to do justice between man and man and to eradicate friction from the international field. On the contrary, it was largely responsible for the two world wars in the last half century. The Western world, in spite of its advantages, of mechanization and industrial efficiency is today in a worse mess than ever before in the history. The adoption of Western economic theory and practice will not help us in achieving our goals of creating a happy and contended people. We must work our destiny in our own way and present to the world an economic system based on true Islamic concept of equity of manhood and social justice. We will thereby be fulfilling our mission as Muslims and giving to humanity the message of peace which alone can save it and secure the welfare, happiness and prosperity of mankind.

In 1977, Pakistan initiated the first attempt to Islamitize the banking system. The process started with a presidential request to the Council of Islamic Ideology (CII) to prepare a plan to eliminate interest from the banking system. In 1980, the CII presented its report and recommended a gradual process that includes three phases.

1. Phase one started from July 1980 by eliminating interest from all specialized institutions, such as National Investment Trust (NIT), Investment Corporation of Pakistan (ICP), and Housing Building Finance Corporation (HBFC).
2. The second phase started in July 1981, by dedicating separate counters in all national commercial banks to mobilize deposits based on profit and loss sharing arrangement parallel to the conventional system.
3. During the third phase that started in 1984, the SBP issued circular No. 13 of 1984 to eliminate *riba* from the banking system and on January 1, 1985, federal and provincial governments, public sector corporations, and public and private joint stock companies were obliged to only finance through interest-free modes (Akhtar 2007), and in July 1985, all commercial banks were made interest free.

The first attempt of 1980 was faced with difficulties in implementation, particularly when the Federal Shari'ah Court considered that some processes and products are not in compliance with shari'ah. There were some important lessons that emerged from the 1980 attempt, which were supported in the relaunch of Islamic Banking in Pakistan. The first lesson is that flexibility and evolutionary process are key elements to effective accommodation of any changes in the system. The second lesson is that all stakeholders need to be well prepared and equipped before launching the new system (Akhtar 2007).

The government and the SBP's major concern was the stability and efficiency of the banking system; therefore, in September 2001, they decided that the transformation of the banking system should be made gradually and in phases, and that Islamic banks will operate side by side with the conventional banks. In December 2001, the SBP introduced an Islamic banking policy that encouraged the parallel development of the Islamic and conventional banking system in a gradual and steady fashion. Also, in order to further strengthen the new direction, the SBP established a comprehensive shari'ah-compliance mechanism to promote confidence in the system, which is based on three pillars:

1. Shari'ah board at SBP to approve guidelines and policies and to set the criteria for advisors.
2. Shari'ah advisors in all banks to provide guidance to banks and build confidence in clients.
3. Shari'ah audit system.

The SBP also issued detailed criteria for establishing full-fledged Islamic commercial banks in the private sector. In January 2002, the SBP issued the first Islamic commercial banking license to Al Meezan Investment Bank (MBL). In June 2002, all formalities related to the acquisition of Société Générale-Pakistan bank by the MBL was completed and the bank started with a network of five branches across the country (SBP 2003). In addition, nine model agreements and contracts for Islamic financing instruments and shari'ah audit guidelines were introduced by the SBP and reviewed and approved by the SBP Shari'ah Board (Akhtar 2007).

Sudan

Sudan is the third country that attempted to convert its banking system fully to comply with shari'ah. The Sudanese experience cannot be considered as a rich experience. The decision to transform the banking system to Islamic in 1983 was made by the late President Jaafar Mohammad Numeiri. He decided that all banks must operate according to shari'ah rules. In 1984, the government issued the civil administrative act that prohibited the use of interest across the whole economy. In 1985, upon the collapse of the government of Numeiri, there was a hostile attitude toward Islamic activities, and many banks reverted to the conventional practices while the others were operating under great pressure (Bashir 1999). It was not until 1989, when the military overthrew the government, that the whole economy was transferred to comply with shari'ah. In 1993, in order to ensure strict adherence to the shari'ah rules, the government established the shari'ah High Supervisory Board (SHSB). As we can see, the Sudanese experience cannot be considered as rich of an experience as that of Malaysia or Pakistan.

Malaysia

The roots of Islamic banking in Malaysia go back to the late 1960s, with the Malay Muslim civil disturbances. During that time, the Malay Muslims were against the dominance of the commercial sector by the Chinese Malaysians and also against the increased influence of Western tradition in the social life, which contradicts and violates the Muslim culture (Venardos 2007).

The first attempt to establish Islamic banks was made by Bumiputera Economic Congress in 1980, when they requested that the government permit the pilgrimage board to establish Islamic banks. In 1981, participants in a seminar held in the National University of Malaysia requested the government to issue a law to allow Islamic banks in Malaysia. In July 1981, the government appointed a steering committee to study the operations of Faisal Islamic Bank in Egypt and Sudan. The committee presented its favorable recommendations to the prime minister of Malaysia in 1982. The Malaysian Islamic system started with the Islamic Banking Act (IBA) that came into effect in April 1983. The Act empowered Bank Negara, the Central Bank of Malaysia, to supervise and regulate Islamic banks. The first Islamic bank, Bank Islam Malaysia Berhad (BIMB), began its operations in 1983. The bank promotes shari'ah-compliant products through its large network and subsidiaries.

The Islamic banking system in Malaysia is aggressive compared to other Islamic countries and is supplemented by the Islamic financial market and the Islamic stock market. To further support the new Islamic banks and to provide them with tools for liquidity requirements and channels to invest their excess funds, the government issued Government Investment Certificates (GIC) according to the Government Investment Act 1983. In 1996, the Banking and Financial Institutions Act of 1989 (BAFIA) was amended to allow conventional banks to offer shari'ah-compliance products to its customers through Islamic windows.

In May 1997, the National shari'ah Advisory Council (NSAC) on Islamic banking and *Takaful* was established by the Central Bank of Malaysia. The objectives of the NSAC, being the highest shari'ah authority, are to provide BNM with advice on Islamic banking and *Takaful* issues and provide Islamic banks and *Takaful* companies with shari'ah advisory regarding their products and services.

Malaysia, in its aspiration to become an international Islamic financial center, granted three new licenses in 2004 to Islamic financial institutions—namely, Kuwait Financial House, Al Rajhi Banking and Investment Corporation, and a consortium of Islamic financial institutions, which consists of Qatar Islamic Bank, RUSD Investment Bank, and Global Investment House.

The Malaysian Islamic model has successfully incorporated Islamic banking into the conventional financial system and harmonized its practices with Western practices. There is no attempt to dissolve the conventional banking system or to fully transform the entire system to an Islamic model. Malaysia believes that the Islamic system should be recognized as a tool for effective financial practice. The system was supported by government promotions for its products. In addition, universities and research centers were opened up to inform and educate the population about this new model of finance. The results were extremely positive to both Western and Eastern investors (Zaher and Hassan 2001). The successful growth of Islamic banking in Malaysia is due to the following factors: (1) support of the monetary authorities represented by the Ministry of Finance and The Central Bank, such as the establishment of the Islamic inter-bank money market, (2) coming up with new products and services such as the introduction of mortgage bonds, and (3) providing the right environment in terms of attractive fiscal incentives and political stability, which are needed for growth (Al Omar and Abdel Haq 1996).

SUMMARY

The roots of Islamic banks goes back to the early days of Islam, yet its real birth can be attributed to the reform period that started in the late nineteenth century and early twentieth century by pioneer Islamic thinkers and reformers. The development of Islamic banks can be divided into four periods starting from 1965 until the present. The first two periods can be considered as the establishment and spread of Islamic banks in the Muslim world. These two periods have witnessed large activities across the Muslim world, which has helped in setting the ground for the gross of Islamic banks. It has also witnessed the emerging of Islamic banks as an alternative to the conventional banking system. The third period has witnessed awareness and growing interest of Islamic banks in Western Europe, the United States, and Japan. The fourth period, which started during the global economic crisis, is considered the first real testament to the strength of the Islamic banking system. The solid performance of the Islamic banks during the crisis is the best proof that the basics and foundations of Islamic banks are solid and sound.

The Islamic financial system is supported by several regulatory and supporting agencies that exert great efforts to support the system. While much has been done on the regulatory front, there is still much to come.

The Malaysian experience with Islamic banks is a model to emulate. They have succeeded in building a very solid and sound Islamic banking system on par with the conventional banking system. They have managed to make these two systems complement each other. The success of the Malaysian model is mainly attributed to the support of the government and regulatory agencies with regard to establishing an environment conducive to growth and the promotion of its products. Also, universities and research centers have played a very important role in educating the population about this new model of finance

The purpose of Part One is to discuss the origins of Islamic banking. It is important to understand that Islamic banks have solid, traceable roots, and that they are not just a passing financial trend. It is also important to understand the major fundamentals and principles that form the basic foundations and govern Islamic banks. The fact that Islamic banks are set on a different foundation than the conventional banks exposes Islamic banks to a different set of risks during their course of business. Therefore, Part Two will be dedicated to understanding the nature of risk in Islamic banks and how it differs from the conventional banks.

Risk in Islamic Banking

CHAPTER 3

The Nature of Risk in Islamic Banking

B anks, conventional as well as Islamic, are subject to a wide range of risks in the course of their operations. In general, banking risk falls into four categories: financial, operational, business, and event risk. Islamic financial institutions face a unique mix of risks and risk-sharing arrangements resulting from the contractual design of instruments based on the principles of shari'ah, liquidity infrastructure, and the overall legal governance.

Institutions Offering Islamic Financial Services (IIFS) are set on different foundations from conventional financial institutions. The generating of profit in IIFS takes second place to adherence to shari'ah. IIFS are required in all their operations and dealings to fully comply with the following ideals:

- Promotion of fairness in transactions and the prevention of any exploitative relationship.
- Sharing of risks and rewards between the different partners in the transaction.
- The prohibition of interest, this means that transactions need to include elements of materiality that leads to a tangible economic purpose.
- Fair distribution of risk and rewards among all stakeholders.
- The prohibition of financing activities that contradicts the shari'ah rules and principles, which are known in Arabic as *haram*.

Therefore, Islamic modes of finance such as *murabahah* and profit and loss-sharing, or *mudarabah* and *musharakah*, display unique risk characteristics that need to be accounted for in capital adequacy requirements and a risk management framework (Haron and Hock 2007).

Islamic banks face two types of risk while conducting their operations: (1) risks similar to conventional banks, and (2) unique and specific risks that arise due to particular requirements necessary to comply with shari'ah principles. The prohibition of interest and the requirement of materiality of the financing transaction form determine the type and nature of the instruments that can be utilized by IIFS and their associated risk. In addition, IIFS face constraints in managing liquidity, as they cannot use any interest-bearing instruments characteristic of the money market.

Risk is inherent in banking and unavoidable; therefore, the task of risk management is to manage the different types of risk at acceptable levels and sustainable profitability. This task requires the continual identification, quantification, managing, and monitoring of risk exposure, which in turn requires sound policies, adequate organization, efficient processes, skilled analysts, and elaborated computerized information systems. In addition, risk management requires the capacity to anticipate changes and act in such a way that a bank's business can be structured and restructured to profit from the changes or at least to minimize losses. The role of a regulatory authority is not to impose ways of how business should be conducted. Instead, it should focus on maintaining prudent oversight of a bank by evaluating the risk composition of its assets and by insisting that an adequate amount of capital and reserves are available to safeguard solvency (Greuning and Iqbal 2008).

In a document issued in 2005, the IFSB set 15 principles for Islamic financial institutions (other than *takaful* institutions) on risk management. The objectives of these principles are to ensure that Islamic banks comply with the shari'ah rules, particularly the prohibition of interest, apply shari'ah compliant risk mitigation techniques, and complement the Basel Committee on Banking Supervision's guidelines on risk management to cater to the specific needs and unique nature of the risks facing Islamic financial institutions. The first principle for general requirements (as shown in Table 3.1) sets the

TABLE 3.1   IFSB Principle for General Requirement

Principle 1.0:	IIFS shall have in place a comprehensive risk management and reporting process, including appropriate board and senior management oversight, to identify, measure, monitor, report and control relevant categories of risk and, where appropriate, to hold adequate capital against these risks. The process shall take into account appropriate steps to comply with shari'ah rules and principles and to ensure the adequacy of relevant risk reporting to the supervisory authority.

Source: Islamic Financial Services Board (2005b).

ground rules for an effective risk management framework that takes into account the unique characteristics and the nature of risk in Islamic finance.

The purpose of this chapter is to review banking risk and the inherent risk associated with Islamic finance, along with the associated risk management principles.

BANKING RISK AND THE INHERENT RISK ASSOCIATED WITH IIFS

In general, risk associated with banks—both Islamic and conventional—falls into four main categories: financial, operational, business, and event risks. Each of these four categories is further divided into subcategories, as shown in Table 3.2. The effect and impact of each type of risk differs depending on whether it is applied to conventional or Islamic banks. It is also important to note that there are some types of risks that are applicable to Islamic banks, only due to the unique nature of its operations. Along with each type of risk, we will demonstrate the IFSB risk management principles associated with it.

Financial Risk

The sub categories of financial risk are credit risk, equity investment risk, market risk, liquidity risk, and rate of return risk (displaced commercial risk).

Credit Risk   Credit risk is defined as the risk of counterparty failure to meet their obligations in a timely manner or the deterioration of the borrower's repayment capacity. Credit risk is the most common source of risk in Islamic and conventional banks and the major reason for bank failure. Therefore,

TABLE 3.2 Islamic Banking Risk

Financial Risks	Operational Risks	Business Risks	Event Risks
Credit risk	Legal risk	Country risk	Banking crisis
Equity investment risk	Failure risk	Withdrawal risk	Exogenous
Market risk	Fiduciary risk	Settlement and prepayment risk	
Liquidity risk	Shari'ah-compliance risk	Volatility risk	
Rate of return risk		Reputation risk	
		Equity	

one of the primary concerns of a supervisor is to ensure that banks have a well-articulated and implemented credit policy in place.

The management of credit risk usually needs to have three sets of policies (Greuning and Iqbal 2007): (1) The first set of policies is designed to limit or reduce credit risk through examining concentration, diversification, lending to connected parties, and sector/region risks. (2) The second set of policies is used to measure the risk by classifying the assets that carry risk into different risk classes. (3) The third set of policies aims to ensure that banks maintain adequate provisions to absorb loan losses.

There are two approaches that are applied in measuring credit risk: (1) The first is the traditional approach that assigns the counterparty into a rating class corresponding to a probability of default. (2) The second approach is the advanced credit Value-at-Risk (VAR) method. Both approaches share basic principles, which include estimating the expected loss on an exposure or a portfolio of exposure owing to specified events (default, rating downgrade, nonperformance, a specified covenant in the contract, etc.), and calibrating unexpected losses (losses that exceed a specified number of standard deviations from the mean) that may occur at some probability level. Expected losses are provisioned for and regarded as expense that is deducted from income, while unexpected losses are backed up by capital allocation.

The calculation of both expected and unexpected losses in an individual loan require an estimate of probability of default or probabilities of rating downgrades from one rating class to a lower class. Other shared principles include potential credit exposure at default or at the time of rating transition, and loss-given default or reduction in the value of the asset following a rating transition. The measurement of these three components of credit risk and the calculation of unexpected losses are the fundamental requirements of Basel II (Sundararajan 2007).

The level of provisions assigned by the bank is usually related to how the collection and recovery system is developed. In countries where the system is highly effective, the provisions are smaller than in countries where the systems are not very effective. There are two approaches adopted to deal with loss assets: (1) the British approach, where the assets are kept in the banking books until all efforts are exhausted, subsequently making the reserves appear higher than they are in actuality, and (2) the U.S. approach, which is more conservative and involves the writing off of all loss assets against the reserves, subsequently making the reserves appear lower than they are in actuality.

In Islamic finance, credit risk exposure arises in connection with:

- The accounts receivable in murabahah contracts, where the bank delivers the assets but does not receive the payments. And in nonbinding murabahah, if the customer does not accept the assets that have already been purchased by the bank.

- Counterparty risk in salam contracts, the accounts receivable, and counterparty in itisna contracts if the bank fails fully or partially to deliver the assets.
- Lease payments receivable in ijarah contracts, and sukok held to maturity in the banking book.
- When the bank acts as rab el mal in mudarabah investment, and has no control over the transaction, assessing credit risk becomes difficult.

A detailed explanation of the risk inherent in the Islamic instruments will be discussed in the next chapter. The Capital Adequacy Standard for Institutions Offering only Islamic Financial Services referred to as The Standard issued in 2005 by the Islamic Financial Services Board (IFSB) measures credit risk according to the Standardized Approach of Basel II (IFSB 2005a).

Credit risk management in Islamic banks is more complicated than conventional banks due to many reasons, such as the case of default by the counterparty and the fact that Islamic banks are prohibited from charging any accrued interest or imposing any penalty, except in the case of deliberate delay. During this delay, the bank's capital is stuck in nonproductive activity, and the bank's investors/depositors do not earn any income. Also, in the case of negligence or misconduct of the *Mudarib* or *Musharakah* partner, the bank has to go into a more complicated recovery process than what would be applied in conventional banks. In Islamic banking, it became common practice to request additional collateral from the customers for risk mitigation purposes, which in turn has its own difficulty, particularly in the case of liquidating or trying to sell.

The IFSB has set four key principles of credit risk and credit risk mitigation, as shown in Table 3.3. The principles aim to ensure that all banks have in place a clear and sound lending strategy that complies with and takes into consideration the credit exposure at all stages of the financing agreement. Also banks should have in place a well-articulated credit policy that includes the proper risk assessment and due diligence review prior to deciding on granting any credit facility. Banks should have effective methodologies for measuring and reporting credit risk exposure. In addition, banks should have shari'ah-compliant credit risk mitigation techniques in place.

Equity Investment Risk   One of the unique risks associated with the Islamic banks is the equity investment risk, as conventional banks do not enter into such transactions, which involve investing in equity-based assets. Islamic banks are exposed to two different types of risk while holding the equity instruments, depending on the purpose of the instruments: (1) The first type

TABLE 3.3 IFSB Principles for Credit Risk

Principle 2.1	Islamic financial institutions shall have in place a strategy for financing, using the various Islamic instruments in compliance with shari'ah, whereby they recognize the potential credit exposures that may arise at different stages of the various financing agreements.
Principle 2.2	Islamic financial institutions shall carry out a due diligence review in respect of counterparties prior to deciding on the choice of an appropriate Islamic financing instrument.
Principle 2.3	Islamic financial institutions shall have in place appropriate methodologies for measuring and reporting the credit risk exposures arising under the use of an Islamic financing instrument.
Principle 2.4	Islamic financial institutions shall have in place shari'ah-compliant credit risk-mitigating techniques for each Islamic financing instrument.

Source: Islamic Financial Services Board (2005b).

of risk, which is our concern in this part, arises as a result of the holding of equity for the purpose of investment. In this case, the instruments are mainly based on mudarabah and musharakah contracts. (2) The second type of risk arises as a result of the holding of equity for trading or liquidity purposes, which are dealt with under market risk.

Islamic banks, while investing in mudarabah and musharakah instruments, are not only exposed to high market, liquidity, and credit risk, but they also are exposed to high volatility in gains as well as to loss of capital. Through such instruments, the investments, however, contribute significantly to the bank's earnings. The IFSB, in the guidelines for risk management (2005b), has broadly defined equity investment risk as "the risk arising from entering into a partnership for the purpose of undertaking or participating in a particular financing or general business activity as described in the contract, and in which the provider of finance shares in the business risk."

The involvement in the management of investment during the life span of the contract represents the major difference between mudarabah and musharakah. In mudarabah, the bank as the capital provider (*rab el mal*) is considered to be a silent partner with no control power over the management, whereas the other partner as mudarib has the full power to manage the investment. In the case of failure, the bank will bear all the losses while having no power to influence the other party to take the necessary remedial measurements when needed. In addition, this gives rise to moral hazard problems, because the other partner may have a high-risk appetite and take excessive risk, while the bank may not have the same risk appetite.

In musharakah, however, both the bank and the other party are partners investing their funds together; therefore, the capital of the other party is also at risk, which will result in reduction of the moral hazard problem. The bank, in this type of contract, has the option to be a silent or an active partner. Due to the unique features of the equity investments contracts and the high risk associated with them, banks are required to take the necessary measurements prior to and during the life span of the contract.

While performing the risk evaluation of the project, a set of measurements should be adhered to:

- Exercise extreme precaution and due diligence in evaluating the investment and its associated risk as well as the investment partners' profile to protect the funds of the IAHs. This due diligence should include examination of the past records of the partners, the profile of the management team and their credibility and reputation, the quality of the business plans, and the human resources capacity of the project.
- Examine the legal and regulatory environment that affect the performance of the equity investment.
- Proper management of the project from its inception through close monitoring at all stages, proper financial disclosure, transparency in reporting, and supervision for the risk-mitigation techniques that are applied.
- Be prepared with alternative plans for fluctuations and variations in cash flow and for implementing an exit strategy when needed.

There are three risk management principles with regard to this type of risk as shown in Table 3.4:

1. To ensure that all banks have an effective risk management system and reporting process in place.
2. To ensure that banks will assess the potential impact of their methods through proper and consistent valuation methodology, and that there will be a clear understanding and mutual agreement between the two parties on the terms and conditions of the contract, the methodology of risk evaluation, and the bases of profit calculations and allocations.
3. To ensure that banks have well-articulated and effective exit strategies in place. Such strategies should have the approval of the shari'ah board for extension and redemption conditions.

TABLE 3.4 IFSB Principles for Equity Investment Risk

Principle 3.1	IIFS shall have in place appropriate risk management and reporting processes in respect of the risk characteristics of equity investments, including mudarabah and musharakah investments.
Principle 3.2	IIFS shall ensure that their valuation methodologies are appropriate and consistent, and shall assess the potential impacts of their methods on profit calculations and allocations. The methods shall be mutually agreed between the IIFS and the mudarib and/or musharakah partner.
Principle 3.3	IIFS shall define and establish the exit strategies in respect of their equity investment activities, including extension and redemption conditions for mudarabah and musharakah investments, subject to the approval of the institution's shari'ah board.

Source: Islamic Financial Services Board (2005b).

Market Risk   Market risk is defined as the risk of losses in on-and-off balance sheet positions arising from unfavorable movements in market price (IFSB 2005b). IIFS are exposed to a higher market risk than conventional banks due to the asset-backed nature of their finance instruments. Market risk rises in many of the Islamic finance contracts; some examples are:

- *Ijarah*: in case the lessee defaults, then the IIFS have to either re-rent or dispose of the asset at the market price, which may be lower than the agreed upon price or rent.
- *Ijarah Montahiya Beltamaluk* (IMB): if the lessee defaults, there is a risk on the carrying value of the leased asset, which is taken as collateral if the market price is lower than the book value.
- *Salam*: commodity price fluctuations on the long position exist until the final disposal.
- *Parallel Salam*: if the bank fails to deliver the items and needs to buy the same, at a higher price, from the market to meet its obligations.
- Foreign exchange: fluctuations arising from foreign exchange spot rate changes in cross-border transactions and the foreign currency receivables and payables.

Conventional banks are exposed to these risks in the positions that they hold in financial instruments. These positions are held to secure a short-term profit from price or interest-rate variations, or to hedge against risk in other elements of the trading books. IISF, according to shari'ah principles, are not allowed to earn returns from speculative transactions or transactions connected to future events, such as hedging against risk or other derivatives. Trading books in Islamic banks are limited to traded equities, commodities, foreign exchange positions, and various forms of *Sukok*. IIFS carry out many asset-based transactions in which they take ownership of physical assets as co-investors. Therefore, the risk is common to an entire class of assets or liabilities in case of economic changes or external events (systemic risk, e.g., changes in stock-market sentiment, interest rates, and currency or commodity markets).

Market risk can be measured by the traditional exposure indicators, such as:

- Net open position in foreign exchange.
- Net position in traded equity.
- Net position in commodities.
- Rate-of-return gap measured by currency of denomination.
- Various duration measures of assets and liabilities in the trading books.

Islamic banks are also exposed to markup and benchmark risk. In conventional banking, interest-rate risk in the banking books is a consequence of mismatches between assets and liabilities. As a result, the rate payable on liabilities exceeds the rate receivable on assets, which leads to an "interest-rate squeeze" that may jeopardize its profitability and viability. In Islamic banks, there is no interest; instead, there are returns receivable based on a markup nature as on *Mudarabah* assets or *Ijarah* rentals that are fixed in advance, while the returns to the PSIA holders follow current market expectations. The result, as in conventional banks, is a similar kind of squeeze that leads to displaced commercial risk (Archer and Abdel Karim 2007).

In general, rate-of-return risk results from risk of reduction in the value of a fixed-interest asset due to a rise in interest rates, risk of an interest rate mismatch between fixed-rate assets and floating-rate liabilities or vice versa. This results in a profit and cash-flow squeeze, and possible loss due to a change in the margin between domestic rates of return and the benchmark rates of return. This occurs when some Islamic banks use an external benchmark to price the markup in murabahah contracts such as the London Inter-Bank Offered Rate (LIBOR), which may not be closely linked to the domestic return. If domestic monetary conditions change requiring adjustments in returns on deposits and loans, but the margin between the external benchmark and domestic rates of return shifts, there could be an impact on asset return (Sundararajan 2007).

TABLE 3.5 IFSB Principles for Market Risk

Principle 4.1   IIFS shall have in place appropriate framework for market risk
                       management (including reporting) in respect of all assets held,
                       including those that do not have a ready market and/or are
                       exposed to high price volatility.

Source: Islamic Financial Services Board (2005b).

The IFSB has set a guiding principle, as shown in Table 3.5, to ensure
that IIFS have an effective market risk management framework and reporting
mechanism in place.

Liquidity Risk   Liquidity is considered to be one of the major causes of bank
failure. It plays a crucial role in mitigating the expected and unexpected balance sheet fluctuations and providing funds for growth. It represents a bank's
ability to accommodate the redemption of deposits and other liabilities and
to cover the demand for funding in the loan and investment portfolio. The
amount of liquid or readily marketable assets that a bank should hold depends on both the stability of its deposit base structure and the potential for
rapid expansion and growth of its asset and investment portfolio. In general, a bank will need lower liquidity if the deposit base is large, with low
concentration nature and an asset portfolio that consists mainly of short- to
medium-term loans. A higher liquidity will be needed if the major portion of
the asset portfolio consists of large long-term loans and the deposit base has
a high concentration nature. In addition, a bank will need higher liquidity if
there are indications of withdrawal of large corporate deposits or of small
deposits, as well as of borrowers using large funds already committed by the
bank (Greuning and Iqbal 2008).

Liquidity risk is interpreted in many ways. The IFSB has defined liquidity
risk as the potential loss to IIFS arising from their inability either to meet
their obligations or to fund increases in assets as they fall, without incurring
unacceptable costs or losses. It can also be defined as the risk that arises
from either excess liquidity or shortage of liquidity in cases of difficulty
of trading an asset, difficulty in obtaining funding at a reasonable cost,
and nonavailability of liquid assets to meet liabilities. Liquidity risk can be
measured by the standard measure of liquidity gap for each maturity bucket
and in each currency, or by the share of liquid assets to total assets or liquid
liabilities. Liquidity risk, as it applies to Islamic banking, can be of two
types: (1) lack of liquidity in the market, where the illiquid asset makes it
difficult for banks to meet their liabilities and financial obligations, and (2)

lack of access to funding, where banks are unable to borrow or raise funds at a reasonable cost when needed.

As required by the IFSB (2005b), Islamic banks need to have effective liquidity management policies in place. These policies need to be set bearing in mind the unique nature of its business and the capital market environment. They also must ensure the following:

- The active involvement of the board of directors in setting in place an effective strategy that implements sound processes to measure and monitor liquidity.
- Effective monitoring and reporting system in place.
- Sufficient funding capacity that includes the shareholders' ability and willingness to provide additional capital as deemed necessary.
- Effective liquidity crises management in place and access to fixed assets liquidity.

Liquidity measurement is determined by constructing maturity ladders based on appropriate time bands. The excess or shortfall in any period is the difference between the expected cash inflow and outflow, which is called the net funding requirements (NFR). Subsequently, the management of the bank will decide on how to close the gap through asset management, liability management, or both.

Liquidity risk is one of the most critical risks facing Islamic banks for several reasons. The first is the limited availability of shari'ah-compatible instruments similar to those available to conventional banks, namely the inter-bank market and the secondary market debt instruments. The prohibition of borrowing on the basis of interest and the absence of an active inter-bank money market have restricted Islamic banks in their ability to manage their liquidity position effectively. The second reason is attributed to the limited scope and restrictions imposed in the secondary market transactions. This is because shari'ah principles impose restrictions on the trading of financial claims unless such claims are linked to a real asset. The third reason is that Central banks discount window, as the lender of last resort option that is available to conventional banks is not available to Islamic banks. This is because Islamic banks cannot borrow based on interest. Fourth, certain characteristics of shari'ah-compliant instruments available to Islamic banks give rise to liquidity risk. For example, the cancellation risk in murabahah or the inability to trade murabahah or *Bay' al Salaam* contracts, which can only be traded at par. There is also the illiquidity of commodity markets and the prohibition of secondary trading of salam or istisna contracts. Finally, Islamic banks are obliged to maintain a high level of idle cash as they can only invest a small portion of the large current account portfolio they hold

TABLE 3.6 IFSB Principles for Liquidity Risk

Principle 5.1	IIFS shall have in place a liquidity management framework (including reporting) taking into account separately and on an overall basis their liquidity exposures in respect of each category of current accounts and unrestricted investment accounts.
Principle 5.2	IIFS shall assume liquidity risk commensurate with their ability to have sufficient recourse to shari'ah compliant funds to mitigate such risk.

Source: Islamic Financial Services Board (2005b).

due to the limited liquid short-term shari'ah-compliant instruments available to them (Greuning and Iqbal 2008; Iqbal and Mirakhor 2007).

The IFSB has also set two principles for liquidity risk management, as shown in Table 3.6: (1) The first principle requires IIFS to have an effective liquidity management framework and reporting mechanism in place. The framework should be designed to facilitate both the overall exposure and the separate category exposure of current accounts and unrestricted investment accounts. (2) The second principle is to encourage banks to adequately measure their liquidity risks with relation to their ability to raise funds in order to mitigate this type of risk.

Rate-of-Return Risk (Displaced Commercial Risk)   Displaced Commercial Risk occurs when IIFS tend to increase the rate of return to investment account holders (IAHs) as an incentive to keep their funds in the institution. This is taken from its share of profit as *Mudarib*. The rate of return to the client is smoothed at the expense of the profit attributable to the shareholders. The Accounting and Audit Organization for Islamic Financial Institutions (AAOIFI) has identified displaced commercial risk as the risk when an Islamic bank is under pressure to pay its investors or depositors a rate of return higher than what should be payable under the actual terms of the investment contract. This occurs when a bank underperforms during a certain period and is unable to generate adequate profit for distribution to the Investment Account Holders. An extreme example is the case of the International Islamic Bank for Investment and Development in Egypt, which distributed all of its profits to investment account holders and nothing to shareholders from the mid to late 1980s. And in 1988, the bank distributed to its depositors an amount exceeding its profit, and the difference appeared in their balance sheet as loss carried forward. This risk may severely affect the bank's solvency in extreme cases.

There are three main differences between interest-rate risk in conventional banks and rate-of-return risk in Islamic banks (Greuning and Iqbal 2008):

1. Uncertainty is higher in Islamic banks because their investments are a mix of markup based and equity based, whereas conventional banks have less uncertainty in the rate of return on investment because they offer a blend of interest-based and fixed-income securities.
2. Rate of return on deposits in Islamic banks is not predetermined, whereas the interest rate is fixed in conventional banks.
3. The return on equity investments is not determined until the end of the project.

There are two internationally accepted standard practices to mitigate this risk. The first is to maintain a reserve called Profit Equalization Reserve (PER), which is created by setting aside a portion of gross income before allocating the bank's own share as Mudarib. The reserve is used as a tool to align the rate of return offered by Islamic banks to the market rate of return offered by conventional banks in order to eliminate or at least reduce the sharp fluctuations of returns on investment deposits and to prevent future shocks. The basis of computing this reserve should be predefined, reviewed, and approved by the board of directors before entering into a contract with the depositors and IAH. The second practice is to maintain an Investment Risk Reserve (IRR) that is funded by setting aside a portion of the income of investors-depositors after allocating the bank's share to be utilized to offset the risk of future investment losses. The basis of calculation and the terms and conditions of this reserve should be reviewed and approved by the board of directors (AAOIFI 2008).

Although the practice of maintaining these two types of reserves is becoming common and is in alignment with prudent risk management, yet some criticisms have been raised, particularly with regard to governance issue, which need to be tackled. First, there is the limited disclosure of such reserves and the lack of transparency, which negatively affect the credibility of the bank. Second, investment account holders do not have the right to influence the use of such reserves and to verify the exposure of the overall investment. Third, such reserves are in favor of the long-term investors at the expense of the short-term investors. Finally, it is sometimes requested that investment account holders waive their rights to these reserves. In light of these criticisms, it is strongly important for Islamic banks that are maintaining such reserves to standardize the practice, and to fully and clearly disclose the basis of computing such reserves. Also, the rights of investment

TABLE 3.7 IFSB Principles for Rate of Return Risk

Principle 6.1	IIFS shall establish a comprehensive risk management and reporting process to assess the potential impacts of market factors affecting rates of return on assets in comparison with the expected rates of return for investment account holders (IHA).
Principle 6.2	IIFS shall have in place an appropriate framework for managing displaced commercial risk, where applicable.

Source: Islamic Financial Services Board (2005b).

account holders to these reserves should be clearly stated and explained to the depositors. The short-term depositors may feel that maintaining such reserves is against their interest, seeing as how they are subsidizing long-term depositors. Therefore, Greuning and Iqbal (2008) suggest that only long-term depositors should bear the cost of such reserves and not the short-term depositors.

The IFSB has set two principles for rate of return risk, as shown in Table 3.7: (1) The first principle is to ensure that IIFS have in place an effective risk management and reporting framework to assess and mange the effect(s) of the market elements on the rate of return to meet the IAH expectations and to be in a competitive position with the conventional banks. (2) The second principle is to encourage banks to effectively manage their displaced commercial risk to be able to compete with conventional banks.

Operational Risk

Operational risk is defined in Basel II as "the risk of loss resulting from inadequate or failed internal processes, people, and systems or from external events. This includes legal risk, but excludes strategic and reputation risk" (BCOBS 2004). Operational risk is significant in Islamic banks due to the specific contractual features of their mode of finance and the legal environment.

In Islamic banking, operational risk may arise due to many reasons, such as:

- The cancellation risk in nonbinding murabahah and istisna contracts.
- An inadequate internal control system to detect and manage potential problems in operational processes and back-office functions.
- The potential difficulties in enforcing Islamic financial contracts in a broader legal environment.

- The risk of noncompliance with shari'ah requirements, which may impact the income of the bank as all income from such activities will be considered null.
- The risk of misconduct and negligence in managing the investment portfolio. In such a case, the bank will have to bear all losses and mudarabah will become a liability on the bank, which will negatively affect the bank's capital adequacy and solvency.
- The risk arises from the need to maintain and manage commodity inventories. This will include the possible loss due to inadequate inventory system. Also the additional cost of inventory.
- The potential costs and risks in monitoring equity-type contracts and the associated legal risks.
- The increasing use of structured financial transactions, particularly that the securitization of assets originated by the bank may expose the bank to legal risk (Sundararajan 2007).

In general, operational risk can be divided into four categories:

1. Operational risks that are somewhat similar to risks at conventional banks. These include all types of risk such as misconduct and having an inadequate internal control system.
2. Risk related to the asset-based and the contractual nature of the financial instruments used by Islamic banks. This gives rise to risk associated with the shari'ah-compliant products, where the bank is exposed to risk in the drafting and execution of the contracts. Also, Islamic banks due to the asset-backed nature of the finance instruments carry more physical assets in their balance sheet than conventional banks. This leads to additional risk associated with the cost, control, and management of the inventory. In addition, the operational risk associated with information technology in Islamic banks is far higher than conventional banks as the software is not yet fully developed and standardized.
3. Shari'ah-compliance risk, which consists of two types of risk: (1) risk relating to potential noncompliance with shari'ah rules and principles in the bank's operations, and (2) risk associated with mudarabah contracts and the possibility of misconduct. In cases of misconduct or negligence by the mudarib, the funds invested by the fund providers become a liability of the mudarib.
4. Legal risk, which is defined in Basel II as "including, without being limited to, exposure to fines, penalties, or punitive damage resulting from supervisory actions, as well as private settlements" (BCOBS 2004). Legal risk that arises from uncertainty in interpreting and enforcing contracts that comply with shari'ah is very significant in Islamic banks.

TABLE 3.8 IFSB Principles for Operational Risk

Principle 7.1	IIFS shall have in place an adequate system and controls, including shari'ah Board/Advisory, to ensure compliance with shari'ah rules and principles
Principle 7.2	IIFS shall have in place appropriate mechanisms to safeguard the interests of all fund providers. Where IAH funds are commingled with IIFS' own funds, IIFS shall ensure that the bases for asset, revenue, expense, and profit allocations are established, applied, and reported in a manner consistent with IIFS' fiduciary responsibilities.

Source: Islamic Financial Services Board (2005b).

IFSB has set two principles for managing operational risk, as shown in Table 3.8:

1. To ensure that IIFS have sufficient resources and an adequate system and control in place to mitigate this type of risk. In addition, all banks must appoint a shari'ah board to ensure that all operations are conducted in compliance with shari'ah rules and principles.
2. To ensure adequate measurements are in place to protect the interests of the depositors and shareholders.

In addition, the IIFS need to exercise their fiduciary responsibility toward the unrestricted account holders. The IIFS need to establish the bases of allocation of revenues, expenses, and profit, as well as disclose these in a transparent fashion in case of investments funded by a shared pool. Operational risk will be discussed in detail in Chapter 5.

Business Risk

Business risk is associated with the bank's business environment, including macroeconomic and policy concerns, legal and regulatory factors, and the overall financial infrastructure, such as payment systems and auditors. Business risks are mainly comprised of six types of risk:

1. Volatility risk that results from fluctuations in the exchange rate of currencies.
2. Equity risk that arises from depreciation of investments due to stock market dynamics.

3. Settlement and prepayment risk. Settlement risk is when counterparty does not deliver security or its value in cash as per the agreement set when the security is traded, after counterparty has delivered security or cash as per the agreement. Prepayment risk is the risk of loans, particularly mortgage loans, being prepaid before maturity due to a drop in interest rates.
4. Withdrawal risk, where banks are faced with large withdrawals of customer deposits. The risk may arise due to many reasons, such as loss of trust or confidence in the bank and higher rate of return offered by other banks or windows in conventional banks.
5. Country risk resulting from potential volatility of foreign assets due to political or financial events in a particular country.
6. Reputation risk is the risk that results in damaging the reputation of the institution due to irresponsible act or behavior of the management. Reputation risk is a risk that is applicable to Islamic banks as well as for conventional banks. The loss of trust in any financial institution, whether conventional or Islamic, will have a profoundly negative effect on the financial system as a whole. The Islamic financial industry, being in a premature stage in comparison to the conventional banking system, is exposed to higher reputation risk with a far more severe impact than the conventional banking system. The major cause of this risk is the inconsistency in the standards and practices among different Islamic banks in different jurisdictions due to the different interpretations of shari'ah rules and principles. In addition, some shari'ah boards are stricter than others in the different interpretations of terms and conditions in the Islamic financial contracts.

Event Risk

Event risk includes all types of exogenous risks that could jeopardize the bank's operations or undermine its financial condition and capital adequacy. Such risk includes political events, contagion due to the failure of a major bank or a market crash, banking crises, natural disasters, and civil wars. This risk is unpredictable, and in most cases, unexpected until immediately before the event occurs. Banks, therefore, need to maintain a cushion of capital to prepare for this type of risk.

SUMMARY

Risk is unavoidable in both conventional as well as Islamic banks. The nature of risk, however, is different in Islamic banking because of its unique foundations. The basic principles that form the foundations of Islamic banks are: the promotion fairness, risk and reward sharing, the prohibition of interest, the materiality of all transactions, and the prohibition of transactions that are not in compliance with shari'ah rules and principles. In addition, the Islamic modes of finance are asset backed, which exposes Islamic banks to a unique set of risks.

As risk is unavoidable, the role of risk management in banking is crucial to manage the different types of risk at acceptable levels. A sound risk management framework should ensure on going identification, quantification, managing, and monitoring of risk exposure. Such framework would require sound policies, efficient processes, skilled analysts, and elaborated computerized information systems. It will also requires the empowerment to effect changes and makes bank's business ready for restructuring as deemed necessary in order to profit from the changes or at least to minimize losses.

Islamic banks are exposed to two sets of risk: (1) risk that is similar to conventional banks, and (2) risk that is concerned with adherence to certain principles. Banking risk in both Islamic and conventional banks can be divided into four categories: (1) financial risk, (2) operational risk, (3) business risk, and (4) event risk.

Financial risk includes credit risk, equity investment risk, market risk, liquidity risk, and rate-of-return risk (displaced commercial risk). Credit risk is similar to conventional banking, but credit-risk management and recovery processes are far more complicated in the Islamic banking system than in conventional banks. Equity investment risk is unique to the Islamic banks, because conventional banks do not enter into equity-based assets transactions. There are two types of equity investment risk: (1) the type that arises as a result of holding of equity for the purpose of investment, and (2) the type that arises as a result of holding equity for trading or liquidity purposes, which are dealt with under market risk. Islamic banks are exposed to a higher market risk than conventional banks due to the asset-backed nature of their finance instruments. Also, Islamic banks carry out many asset-based transactions with physical assets, so the risk is common to an entire class of assets or liabilities in case of economic changes or external events. Liquidity risk is considered one of the most severe risks facing Islamic banks. There are many reasons for this, such as the unavailability of instruments that comply with shari'ah principles, the limited scope of the secondary market, and the absence of the lender of last resort. Displaced commercial risk is a risk that is also unique to Islamic banks; it arises when the banks decide to smooth the rate of return to the clients in an attempt to motivate them to keep their money in the bank. Maintaining Profit Equalization Reserve (PER) and Investment Risk Reserve (IRR) are the two risk mitigation techniques that are globally accepted.

Operational risk in Islamic banks can be classified into four categories:

1. Operational risks that are similar to conventional banks, which includes all types of risk: misconduct, inadequate internal control system, and so forth. Also, the operational risk associated with information technology in Islamic banks is far higher than in conventional banks, as the software is not yet fully developed and standardized.
2. Risk related to the asset-based and contractual nature of the financial instruments used by Islamic banks, which includes the risk involved in the drafting and execution of the contracts and the risk associated with carrying more physical assets in their balance sheet than conventional banks.
3. The shari'ah-compliance risk, which consists of risks relating to potential noncompliance with shari'ah rules and principles in the bank's operations and risk associated with Mudarabah contracts and the possibility of misconduct.
4. Legal risk, which arises primarily out of uncertainty in interpreting and enforcing contracts that comply with shari'ah.

Business risk is associated with the bank's business environment, including macroeconomic and policy concerns, legal and regulatory factors, and the overall financial infrastructure. Business risks include: volatility risk, equity risk, settlement and prepayment risk, withdrawal risk, country risk, and reputation risk.

Event risk includes all types of exogenous risks that could jeopardize the bank's operations or undermine its financial condition and capital adequacy in case it occurs.

Now, as we begin to understand the overall risk associated with Islamic banking operations, we need to also examine the inherent risk in the Islamic banking instruments, which is covered in Chapter 4.

CHAPTER 4

The Inherent Risk in Islamic Banking Instruments

Shari'ah-compliant products on both sides of the balance sheet carry different types of risk than the conventional counterparty. The unique nature of risk inherent in the shari'ah-compliant products arises due to three main factors:

1. The asset-backed nature of the shari'ah finance instruments as banks need to have actual possession of the asset.
2. The profit- and loss-sharing concept in the musharakah contracts.
3. The profit-sharing and loss-bearing concepts in the mudarabah contracts in both sides of the balance sheet.

This chapter will review the specific risk characteristics, mainly credit, market, displaced commercial risk, and operational risk specific to each of the shari'ah-compliant products: *murabahah*, *salam* and parallel *salam*, *istisna* and parallel *istisna*, *ijarah* and *ijarah muntahia bittamleek*, *mudarabah*, and *musharakah*.

MURABAHAH

Murabahah is one of the most predominantly used contracts in Islamic finance. It is a contract referring to a sales contract, whereby the IIFS sell to a customer at an agreed profit margin, plus cost, a specified kind of asset that is already in their possession. Murabahah for the Purchase Orderer (MPO) is a contract that refers to a sales contract, whereby the IIFS sell to a customer at cost, plus an agreed profit margin, a specified kind of asset that has been purchased and acquired by the IIFS based on a promise to purchase (PP) from the customer. The promise to purchase can be binding or nonbinding. The actual sale of the asset is a necessary condition in order for murabahah to comply with shari'ah.

The main characteristics of the murabahah contracts that make them different from the conventional banking loans are as follows:

- The contracts are backed and securitized by real assets, which is the major difference in the mode of finance between Islamic and conventional banks. This feature results in a lower risk exposure for Islamic banks.
- A murabahah contract is a sales contract that takes into account a higher price for the deferment of payment, whereas a loan is an increase in debt for the purpose of deferment.
- In case of default, Islamic banks are only entitled to the value of the assets, and in case of late payments, there are no penalties or other liabilities to be charged to the customers. IIFS, however, are permitted to charge late payment fees and penalties in the case of a customer who is financially sound but delays payment for unjustified reasons (SBP 2003). This is in contrast to the conventional banks, where interest keeps accruing in cases of default and penalties are imposed with regard to late payments.

Credit Risk

The IIFS are exposed to credit risk similar to conventional banks which is the risk of losses in the event of default or deterioration of the customer capacity for repayment. The measurement of credit risk is also similar to conventional banks where there are mainly two methods: (1) the traditional approach of assigning a risk rating to each category related to its probability of default; (2) Value-at-Risk (VaR), which is a more advanced approach. Both approaches are based on the measurement of the expected losses in a portfolio or exposure and the unexpected loss. For the expected loan losses, banks need to make sufficient provisions, which are deducted from income as expenses; and for unexpected losses, to be accounted for and absorbed by capital.

Market Risk

IIFS are exposed to market risk resulting from murabahah and nonbinding MPO. The risk arises in these two types of contracts when the customer cancels the agreement to purchase and the IIFS needs to sell the assets, as they may incur losses if the market price is lower than the actual price. Additionally, the IIFS may bear additional cost for marketing, disposing or cost related to holding it (such as warehousing and insurance). In the case of binding MPO, the IIFS is only exposed to credit risk.

Operational Risk

There are mainly two types of operational risk related associated with murabahah contracts:

1. The acceptability and tolerance of the murabahah across different jurisdictions. For example, there may be a need to adjust the information technology systems for a particular jurisdiction to cope with the systems employed across jurisdictions.
2. The nature of Islamic banking transactions, which involve the need to actually purchase the asset before selling it to the customer, raises legal complications and requirements. In the drafting stage, the transition stage, or the final stage, it is necessary to ensure that the contracts properly match the commercial intent of the transactions in order to establish clarity and understanding among both parties (Archer and Haron 2007).

SALAM AND PARALLEL SALAM

Salam is a contract that refers to an agreement to purchase, at a predetermined price, a specified kind of commodity (physical product that can be traded on a secondary market such as agriculture and mineral products and precious metals) not available with the seller. The commodity is to be delivered on a specified future date and in a specified quantity and quality. The purchase price could be paid in full by the IIFS as the buyers upon the execution of the salam contract or within a maximum two to three days as tolerated by its Shari'ah Supervisory Board (SSB). The commodity may or may not be traded over the counter or on an exchange.

Parallel salam is a back-to-back-contract that allows the IIFS to enter into a second salam contract with a third party, acquiring a specified kind of commodity that is similar to the commodity specified in the first salam contract with the IIFS. Parallel salam is considered as a tool to hedge price risk on the original Salam contract and to protect and save the cost associated with the delivery of the commodity. It is very important to note that salam and parallel salam contracts are neither interconditional nor interdependent. From a legal view, they are two separate and independent contracts and therefore IIFS cannot offset credit exposures between the two contracts.

Credit Risk

The IIFS are exposed to credit risk in salam and parallel salam contracts similar to murabahah and all other sales-based contracts in Islamic banking.

Ultimately, this is the risk of losses in the event of default or deterioration of the customer capacity for repayment. The measurement approaches for credit risk in murabahah are also applicable for salam and parallel salam. Credit risk may lead to loss of all or part of the capital invested if the IIFS makes the full payment of the contract and the commodity is not delivered—resulting in a mismatch in the specification and quality required by the customer—and if there is a delay in the delivery. The IIFS may be able to recover all or part of the capital invested through claims against advance payment (*urboun*) or financial guarantee.

Market Risk

IIFS are exposed to market risk, because of the salient feature of the contract, if the supplier under the salam contract is unable to deliver the commodity under agreement and the IIFS has to purchase the commodity from the market in order to meet their delivery obligations. The IIFS are exposed to price risk when the market price that has to be paid exceeds the amount paid under the salam contract.

Operational Risk

The nature of salam and parallel salam contracts as forward contracts exposes Islamic banks to three types of risk:

1. In the case of early delivery of the commodity, IIFS will bear additional costs such as warehousing, insurance, or even damage if they are unable to sell the goods immediately after delivery. This is because the IIFS has to accept the delivery of the goods even if it comes early, as long as it meets the specifications.
2. In the case of commodity that is not as per the specification required, the IIFS has to either accept it as per the original price or decline the delivery. With regard to accepting the commodity, the IIFS either needs to request that the customer accept the goods with this specification at the originally agreed price under a parallel salam, or sell it at a lower price.
3. In the case of the inability to deliver the commodity in time in salam with parallel salam, the IIFS may be exposed to legal risk if the customer does not agree to reschedule the delivery date.

ISTISNA AND PARALLEL ISTISNA

Istisna is a contract that refers to an agreement to sell a nonexistent asset to a customer, which is to be manufactured or built according to the ultimate buyer's specifications and is to be delivered on a specified future date at a predetermined selling price. As opposed to salam, where payment needs to be made in full by the IIFS upon the execution of the contract, an istisna contract has flexible payment modes where payment can be paid as per the agreement between the two parties. The IIFS may decide to manufacture or build the asset on its own or may decide to engage the service of a third party (IFSB 2005).

Parallel istisna is a second type of istisna contract, whereby the IIFS decide to engage a third party to manufacture or build a specified kind of asset that corresponds to that of the commodity specified in the first contract. Parallel istisna is also considered as a tool to hedge price risk on the original istisna contract. Similar to salam and parallel salam contracts, the two istisna contracts are neither interconditional nor interdependent. From a legal view, they are two separate and independent contracts, and therefore, IIFS cannot offset credit exposures between them.

Credit Risk

IIFS is exposed to credit risk in one of the following three cases:

1. The risk of a customer who is unable to honor the payment obligation for deferred installments or progress billing (loss of amount receivable) when the work is already in progress. This case occurs when the repayment capability depends on the customer strength and cash flow from other sources other than the asset in concern. This category is known as full recourse istisna.
2. The limited and nonrecourse istinsa, where the repayment capability depends in full or in part on the revenue generated by the asset in concern. In this case, the IIFS faces revenue risk arising from the asset ability to generate revenue and not from the creditworthiness or the cash flow of the customer.
3. The full or limited and nonrecourse parallel istisna; in both cases, the IIFS may be exposed to completion risk when an advance payment has to be paid by the IIFS and the subcontractor does not complete the work. In addition, payment made by the IIFS may not be recovered.

Market Risk

The IIFS are exposed to price risk in istisna with parallel istisna if the customer defaults on the contract and the IIFS have to find another purchaser. In most cases, IIFS sells the subject of the contract to another customer at a lower price. The IIFS should ensure the recovery of losses incurred by the customer.

Operational Risk

Istisna and parallel istisna are forward contracts, in which two contracts are involved. The first contract is the istisna between the IIFS and the customer to supply a constructed asset, such as a building or ship, for the customer. The second contract is the parallel istisna between the IIFS and the subcontractors in order to have the asset constructed. In this type of contract, the IIFS are exposed to various types of operational risk.

There are four types of risk that Islamic banks may face in such contracts:

1. In the case of delay from the subcontractor in the parallel istisna, the IIFS will not be able to deliver on time to the customer, and subsequently, the IIFS may have to pay late payment penalties.
2. In the case of excess in the cost over the original agreed budget under parallel istisna, the IIFS may have to fully or partially absorb the additional cost unless it is agreed with the customer under the istisna contract.
3. In case of the failure of the subcontractor under parallel istisna in meeting the predetermined specifications and the quality standards stipulated under the istisna contract, the IIFS may face legal risk unless all parties involved reach an agreement for settlement, which may involve price reduction.
4. The IIFS may face the risk of the subcontractor not completing the work. In such an event, and taking into consideration the technicality of the subject under manufacturing, the IIFS will have to start a process to seek a new contractor to complete the work, which is time consuming and generally very costly. Therefore, it is crucial for the IIFS to exercise due diligence in appointing a well-qualified team or consultant to assess the subcontractor before entering into such contracts.

IJARAH AND IJARAH MUNTAHIA BITTAMLEEK

Ijarah contract refers to an agreement made by the IIFS to lease an asset to a customer for an agreed period against specified installments of the lease rental. The asset in consideration will either be in the IIFS' possession before entering into the contract or may be acquired before it is delivered to the customer. In the later case, the customer may decide on the specifications of the asset.

It commences with a promise to lease that is binding on the part of the potential lessee prior to entering into the contract. *Ijarah muntahia bittamleek* or *ijarah wa iqtina* is a form of lease contract that offers the lessee an option to own the asset at the end of the lease period either by purchase of the asset through a token of consideration, payment of the market value, or by means of a gift contract. The IIFS resume all liabilities related to the leased asset, which include maintenance, security, and normal causes that are not due to the negligence or misconduct of the lessee (IFSB 2005).

Credit Risk

In such contracts, the IIFS are exposed to credit risk if the customer (lessee) is unable to serve the lease rental when it is due. The credit risk with respect to rental proceeds is mitigated by the possession of the asset by the IIFS as collateral. In all types of assets, particularly in the case of movable assets and assets that are used for the purpose of residency, it is difficult for the IIFS to repossess the asset.

Market Risk

IIFS are exposed to market (price) risk if the customer defaults, as they have to either re-rent or dispose of the asset at the market price, which may be lower than the agreed price or rent. Also, the risk exists if the customer, under IMB, decides not to continue with the contract or not to take ownership of the asset at the end of the contract period and the market price is lower than the book value of the asset. In both cases, the risk is partially mitigated by the value of the asset and the *hamish jiddiyyah* (advance payment) paid by the customer.

Operational Risk

Theijarah as an operating lease contract and ijarah muntahia biṭṭamleek as a lease-to-purchase contract expose IIFS to additional unique operational risks due to the nature of these contracts. There are mainly three situations that cause these types of risks:

1. The IIFS may be exposed to both the risk of loss of the lease income and legal risk if the asset is used in activities that are not in compliance with shari'ah principles. The IIFS are then not only exposed to nonrecognition of the lease income, but there will also be a need to find a new lessee. In addition, the IIFS are exposed to legal risk with respect to enforcement of their contractual right to repossess the asset. Such legal procedures are lengthy and time consuming, particularly when the asset is a house where the lessee enjoys protection as a tenant.

2. The IIFS may also be exposed to risk if the asset is damaged by the lessee, and the lessee refuses to fix it. In that case, the IIFS need to take legal action to repossess the asset and recover the damage.
3. If the asset is severely damaged or destroyed as a result of causes not related to the lessee, the bank is required to provide an alternative asset in order for the lessee to continue to pay the rental for the remaining period. This risk may be mitigated through insurance (Archer and Haron 2007).

MUDARABAH

Mudarabah contracts are the cornerstone of Islamic banking. Mudarabah is a profit-sharing and loss-bearing contract; and it may be used on both sides of the balance sheet assets and liabilities. It is a contract between the capital provider as *rab al mal*, whereby the capital provider would contribute capital to an enterprise or activity that is to be managed by the entrepreneur as *mudarib*. Profit generated by that enterprise or activity is shared in accordance with the terms of the mudarabah agreement, while losses are to be borne solely by the capital provider unless the losses are due to the mudarib's misconduct, negligence, or breach of the terms and conditions of the contract. Mudarabaha at the funding side of the balance sheet in the form of profit-sharing and loss-bearing investment accounts are the equivalent to interest-bearing deposit accounts in conventional banks. There are two types of mudarabah contracts, restricted and unrestricted:

1. Restricted Investment Accounts: The account holders authorize the IIFS to invest their funds based on mudarabah or agency contracts with certain restrictions as to where, how, and for what purpose these are to be invested.
2. Unrestricted Investment Accounts: The account holders authorize the IIFS to invest their funds based on mudarabah or *wakalah* (agency) contracts, without laying any restrictions. The IIFS can commingle these funds with their own funds and invest them in a pooled portfolio.

In these types of contracts, IIFS are exposed to displaced commercial risk and operational risk.

Displaced Commercial Risk

This risk arises when the IIFS encourage their investment account holders by increasing the rate of return to keep the funds. Therefore, the IIFS give away a portion of their share of profit. The rate of return to the customer is smoothed at the expense of profit normally attributed to the IIFS' shareholders.

This risk arises as a result of (1) rate-of-return risk that occurs when funds are placed in assets with long-term maturity, and the rate of return is no longer competitive with other alternative investments; and (2) when a bank underperforms during a certain period and is unable to generate adequate profit for distribution to the account holders.

There are two standard practices to mitigate this risk:

1. To maintain a Profit Equalization Reserve (PER), which is funded by setting aside a portion of gross income before deducting the bank's own share as agent. The reserve is used as a tool to align the rate of return offered by Islamic banks to the market rate of return offered by conventional banks, by eliminating or at least reducing the sharp fluctuations of returns on investment deposits and preventing future shocks. The basis of computing should be predefined, reviewed, and approved by the board of directors before the contract with the IAH.
2. To maintain an Investment Risk Reserve (IRR) that is funded by a portion of the income of investors-depositors after allocating the bank's share to offset the risk of future investment losses. The basis of calculation and the terms and conditions should be reviewed and approved by the board of directors (AAOIFI 2008).

Operational Risk

In this case, investors, as rab al mal, share the profit and bear all losses without having any control or governance right over the management. Mudarabah at the asset side of the balance sheet gives rise to two major concerns:

1. The moral hazard problem that may rise if the IIFS management decides to take excessive risk in their investment of such funds, which is not in line with the investor's expectations.
2. The corporate governance issue that arises from the fact that while they bear the risk of loss of their investment, IAH have no governance right over the management decisions and subsequently, their interest may be jeopardized. The IIFS are fully responsible for managing the funds in a shari'ah-compliance activity and providing returns competitive to the conventional banks. Therefore, IIFS are exposed to the risk of investors withdrawing their funds in case IIFS cannot meet the demands of the IAH in terms of competitive returns on their investments. They are also

exposed to the risk that funds under mudarabah will be considered as a liability of the IIFS if there is proof of misconduct or negligence while managing the investments that may lead to solvency problems.

With mudarabah contracts at the asset-side of the balance sheet, the entrepreneur as mudarib has complete control over the management of the project, and the IIFS as rab al mal have a supervisory role but no control over the management decisions. The IIFS share the profit generated with the entrepreneur at an agreed profit ratio. In case the project incurs losses, the entrepreneur will not bear any losses, and the IIFS will have to bear all the losses. This situation, in addition to the risk of capital loss, gives rise to a moral hazard, particularly if the bank does not receive periodical and accurate information from the entrepreneur. Therefore, the bank, in addition to the due diligence performed before granting the funds, needs to exercise extra precautions against the problem of information asymmetry during the life span of the project in order to protect their interests.

MUSHARAKAH AND DIMINISHING MUSHARAKAH

Musharakah is a contract between the IIFS and a customer whereby the IIFS contribute capital to an enterprise, whether existing or new, or to ownership of a real state or moveable asset, either on a temporary or permanent basis. Profit generated by the enterprise or real state or asset is shared in accordance with the terms of the musharakah agreement, while losses are shared in proportion to each partner's share of capital.

Diminishing musharakah is a form of partnership in which one of the partners promises to buy the equity share of the other partner gradually until the title to the equity is completely transferred to the buying partner. The transaction starts with the formation of a partnership, after which buying and selling of the other partner's equity take place at market value or at the price agreed upon at the time of entering into the contract. The buying and selling process is independent of the partnership contract and should not be stipulated in the partnership contract, since the buying partner is only allowed to give a promise to buy. It is not permitted that one contract be entered into as a condition for concluding the other (IFSB 2005).

Credit Risk

Musharakah is the shari'ah mode of finance alternative to the term or installment loan mode of finance in conventional banking. The IIFS are exposed to two types of credit risk while entering into musharakah contract or transactions: (1) capital impairment risk, where they can lose their share in capital invested in the project, and (2) credit risk with regard to the customer's repayment capacity. While entering into diminishing musharakah, the IIFS are exposed to credit risk with regard to the ability and willingness of the partner to meet his commitment to purchase the agreed shares. In addition, the capital invested by the IIFS is subject to capital impairment risk in case the value of the musharakah assets declines.

Operational Risk

Operational risk in such contracts and transactions is attributed to either inadequate due diligence in the pre-establishment stage or to insufficient management during the life span of the project. Inadequate due diligence while appraising the activity and the creditworthiness, soundness, and reliability of the customer, may be a result of the lack of technical expertise and experience, particularly in the new line of business or activities. During the life span of the contract, the risk may arise if the IIFS do not exercise adequate monitoring of the financial performance and control over the management. It is crucial to receive sufficient and timely financial information to enable the IIFS to take corrective measurements at the right time as deemed necessary.

SUMMARY

We have now reviewed the credit, market, and operational risks in six major instruments: (1) murabaha, (2) salam and parallel Salam, (3) ijara and ijarah muntahiya bul tamalum, (4) istisna and parallel istisna, (5) mudaraba, and (6) musharaka and diminishing musharaka. The unique nature of risk in Islamic banking instruments is attributed to the fact that Islamic finance instruments are asset backed. It is also attributed to the unique relationship between Islamic banks and the IAH. This relationship is based on either profit sharing or loss bearing, as in mudarabah contracts, or on the profit and loss sharing, as in musharakah contracts. Displaced commercial risk is a risk that is unique to Islamic banks. This risk arises when banks decide to smooth the rate of return to customers. The only acceptable risk-mitigation techniques for this type of risk are the Profit Equalization Reserve (PER) and Investment Risk Reserve (IRR).

The contractual arrangements that govern the Islamic finance instruments expose Islamic banks to higher operational risk than conventional banks—not to mention the premature stage of the Islamic banks in terms of technology systems and legal infrastructure. Therefore, I find it necessary to dedicate Chapter 5 to a discussion of operational risk in Islamic Banking.

CHAPTER 5

Operational Risk in Islamic Banking

Operational risk is defined in Basel II as "the risk of loss resulting from inadequate or failed internal processes, people, and systems or from external events. This includes legal risk, but excludes strategic and reputation risk" (BCOBS 2004). IFSB had adopted the same definition with some changes to cater to the unique nature of Islamic banking operations. Operational risk as per IFSB is defined as

> *the risk of loss resulting from inadequate or failed internal processes, people, and systems or from external events, which includes but is not limited to, legal risk and* Shari'ah *compliance risk. This definition excludes strategic and reputation risk. (IFSB 2005a)*

As mentioned in earlier chapters, operational risk is significant in Islamic banks due to the specific contractual features of their mode of finance and the premature Islamic legal infrastructure. Its importance is also due to the nature of the business, which must be conducted as per the shari'ah rules and principles.

In this chapter, we focus on three types of operational risk: (1) the risk related to noncompliance with shari'ah principles, (2) the risk associated with the IIFS' fiduciary responsibilities toward all fund providers, and (3) legal risk. Shari'ah noncompliance risk is unique and significant in Islamic banking, as it leads to loss of confidence in the bank and the whole system on the part of the depositors. This, in turn, leads to withdrawal of funds by depositors, loss of income, and reputation risk, which threaten the overall business. Fiduciary and legal risks are significant, as we will see later in this chapter, due to the premature stage of the Islamic banking system.

NONCOMPLIANCE WITH SHARI'AH RULES AND PRINCIPLES

The prime principle of Islamic banks is to provide shari'ah-compliant products and services to customers. Customers, while dealing with Islamic banks, place their full trust and confidence in the bank in this regard. The above fact makes it crucial for Islamic banks to place shari'ah-noncompliance risk as a top priority.

There are two types risk associated with shari'ah:

1. The risk that arises from the different interpretations of shari'ah rules in the different jurisdiction. This risk is the result of the existence of different shari'ah supervisory boards, which leads to nonstandard of practice, financial reporting, auditing, and accounting principles across the board.

2. The IIFS' failure to comply with shari'ah rules and principles (which is our concern in this chapter). In extreme cases, the IIFS is exposed to reputational and insolvency risk as customers lose confidence and trust and will consequently withdraw their funds and cancel their contracts with the bank. Also, the IIFS is exposed to loss of income, as all transactions or contracts that are done in a noncompliant manner will be considered null and income will be illegitimate.

Shari'ah noncompliance risk is defined by the IFSB as "the risk that[that] arises from IIFS' failure to comply with the *Shari'ah* rules and principles determined by the *Shari'ah* Board of the IIFS or the relevant body in the jurisdiction in which the IIFS operates" (IFSB 2005b). The IFSB, in its risk management principles for operational risk, has requested IIFS to (1) maintain an adequate system and control, which includes the assigning of a shari'ah supervisory board to ensure that IIFS comply with shari'ah rules and principles at all times while conducting its operations and activities; (2) that all contract documentation, including all terms and conditions that govern the relationship between the bank and the customer, to be fully in compliance with shari'ah rules and principles; and (3) that a shari'ah compliance review be conducted at least annually by an adequate third party to ensure that the nature and execution of all transactions are legitimate and comply with shari'ah rules and principles.

It is important to note that Islamic finance contracts have many requirements and conditions that need to be fulfilled by the IIFS in order to comply with shari'ah rules and principles. Some of those requirements are as follows:

- In murabaha and ijarah contracts, the asset in concern must exist and be owned by the IIFS. In addition, there is no penalty, fees or extra charges to customers in case of rescheduling or extending the period of the contract due to genuine reasons.

- In salam and istisna contracts, there is no interdependent or inter-conditional between salam and parallel salam or istisna and parallel istisna. Also, there are no penalty, fees, or extra charges to customers in case of late delivery of the commodity under salam contract. With regard to istisna contracts, the asset in consideration may not exist upon enter-ing into the contract and the contract may stipulate penalty conditions.
- In musharakah and mudarabah contracts, the funds need to be invested in shari'ah-compliant activities and there is no capital guaranteed. Also, in diminishing musharaka, the purchase price of the partner's share has to be at the market price or at the agreed rate at the date of buying; it cannot be at the face value (IFSB 2005a).

FIDUCIARY RISK

Fiduciary risk is defined by the IFSB as "the risk arising from IIFSs' failure to perform in accordance with explicit and implicit standards applicable to their fiduciary responsibilities." AAOIFI defines it as being legally liable for a breach of the investment contract either for noncompliance with shari'ah rules or for mismanagement of investors' funds. As a result of losses in investment, IIFS may become insolvent and therefore unable to either meet the demands of current account holders for repayment of their funds or safeguard the interests of their IAH. IIFS may fail to act with due care when managing investments, which results in the risk of possible loss of profits to IAH (IFSB 2005b; AAOIFI 1999).

Fiduciary risk is directly related to the unique relationship between IIFS and the Investment Account Holders, which is based on a profit-and-loss-sharing concept. The risk may arise when investing current account funds in a high-risk activity or mismanagement of those funds. In case of heavy losses on the investments financed by these funds, depositors may decide to go for legal cases. Also, if the IIFS allocates unjustified expenses to IAH due to misconduct or misuse of management expenses and is considered a violation of the code of conduct to act in a transparent manner. Insufficient due diligence, inadequate screening and monitoring, and lack of control while entering and managing partnership in musharakah and mudarabah contracts are further causes of this risk.

Fiduciary risk can be the major cause for (1) withdrawal risk in case depositors decide to withdraw funds due to loss of confidence in the IIFS; (2) legal risk in case of negligence, misuse, or misconduct of Investment Account Holders funds; (3) reputation risk in case the bank breaches the code of conduct, which may lead to panic withdrawal of funds by the depositors;

(4) insolvency risk if the bank fails to meet the customers' demands, as well as those of the current account and investment holders; (5) imposition of limitations and constraints on the bank's accessibility to and ability to acquire funds at a reasonable cost; and (6) it can have an adverse effect on the market price of the shareholder's equity (Iqbal and Mirakhor 2007; Greuning and Iqbal 2008).

There are some fundamental techniques to mitigate the fiduciary risk that must be used by IIFS. First, it is essential to establish a clear and formal set of policies that manages and governs the investment activities, the allocation of assets and profit between the IIFS and the investors, and the basis of allocating and utilizing of reserves, particularly the PER and IRR. Second, adequate procedure and control must be in place to ensure the quality of information. Third, it is necessary to disclose information in an adequate and timely manner to the IAH and the market to enable them to assess the risk profile and the investment performance.

The IIFS, under pillar three of the capital adequacy requirements, are required to disclose two sets of information pertaining to two critical areas, both qualitative and quantitative: (1) operational risk and (2) shari'ah governance.

- Qualitative disclosure for operational risk includes three sets of policies: (1) those related to incorporating operational risk measures into the management framework such as budgeting, target setting, performance review, and compliance; (2) those related to polices on processes such as tracking and reporting mechanisms for loss events, revision of such reports by both risk management and line management; and (3) those related to loss mitigation processes.
- Quantitative disclosure for operational risk includes risk-weighted assets equivalent for operational risk, as well as indicators of operational risk exposure such as gross income and amount of shari'ah noncompliance income.
- Qualitative disclosure for shari'ah governance includes: (1) the measures that are employed to ensure adherence to shari'ah with comparison to the international standards and the international standards of corporate governance and how it is applied; (2) explanations of how shari'ah noncompliance activities or transactions occurred, the treatment of income that is generated from such transactions, and to what extent shari'ah rulings are mandatory.
- Quantitative disclosure for shari'ah governance includes the volume of violations of shari'ah principles that occurred during the year, annual *zakat* contributions by the IIFS, and the annual remuneration of the shari'ah board members.

LEGAL RISK

Islamic banks face far more legal risk than conventional banks due to the nature and premature stage of Islamic commercial, which is derived from the Islamic law (shari'ah). Therefore, it is important to understand the origin, history and development of Islamic commercial law, its role and importance, how it affects and is affected by Islamic finance and Islamic banking in particular, and the major concerns regarding Islamic commercial law.

This section is dedicated to shedding some light on the history and development of Islamic commercial law, as well as to revealing the major concerns of Islamic banking with respect to legal risk.

History and Development

Shari'ah, the term literally meaning the path to a watering hole, is the law that governs every aspect of a Muslim's life. It includes not only the religious aspects of the Muslim life, which include prayer, fasting, the pilgrimage (*haj*), and the payment of *zakat*, but it also includes all aspects of daily life such as manners, codes of conduct, morality, and the basis of relationships with others. Shari'ah also covers and governs issues related to crime, marriage, divorce, international relationship and inheritance.

Fiqh is the Arabic term that means deep understanding or full comprehension. It is defined as "the knowledge of the rights and duties whereby human beings are enabled to observe right conduct in this life and to prepare themselves for the world to come" (Mideast & N. Africa Encyclopedia). Fiqh is the study and interpretation of shari'ah. Scholars (*Ulama*) are responsible for the interpretation of the divine law of God in relation to specific matters, by first revealing the primary source, which is the *Qua'ran* and the *Sunnah*. If they cannot reach a decision then they depend on the secondary source which is the *Ijm'a* (consensus), and *Qiyas* (analogical reasoning). There are four branches (the Arabic word is *furu*) in fiqh: (1) worship (*ibadat*), (2) contractual law (*mu'amalat*), (3) criminal law (*hudud*) and (4) family and personal law (*ahwal shakhsiya*).The methods used in fiqh are based on a methodology called "the roots of the law" (*Usulal Fiqh*) (Venardos 2007).

There are two primary sources for Islamic law: (1) the Quran and (2) the *sunnah*.

Quran, the first of the primary sources, is believed by Muslims to be the immutable and final revelation of God to human beings. Quran contains verses that have both general and explicit rules and guidelines. The *ayat al-ahkam* are the verses of the Quran that have specific rules and guidelines. There are three explicit rules that are specific to the commercial law aspect:

(1) forbiddance of *riba*, (2) forbiddance of taking the wealth of people by cheating, and (3) the importance of contracts in commercial dealings (Thomas 2005).

The sunnah, the second of the primary source, encompasses the sayings (*a hadith*), actions, and practices of the Prophet Mohammed (*pbuh*). Othman Bin Afan, the third of the Rashidun caliphate, initiated a process to write the Quran and to record the *hadith* more than one hundred years after the death of the Prophet Mohammed. During the Abbasid era, it was clearly evident to scholars that many of the *hadith* are forged or invented for political or theological purposes.

Therefore, they have developed methods to investigate the authenticity of the *hadith*, which adhere to two main principles:

1. The investigation of the chain of narrators going back to the original narrator. The process involves the moral character, truthfulness, and the power of memory of the transmitter. This process is called the *isnad*.
2. The acceptability of the subject of the *hadith*. The subject must have basis in the Quran or the sunnah, or in the established principles of human nature. This implies that *hadith* can either be an explanation of a principle found in these sources or an emerging branch of the principle. In addition, it should not contradict the Quran, the sunnah, or the established principles of human nature. This implies that it must conform to the entire framework of Islam.

The second source of Islamic law is the: *Ijm'a* (consensus), and *Qiyas* (analogical reasoning).

Ijm'a is the consensus and broad agreement of the scholars (Ulama) on issues that are applicable to Muslims in their daily life. Ijm'a is defined as the agreement of all Muslim scholars at the level of juristic reasoning in one age on a legal ruling. The scope of Ijm'a is limited to issues that are clearly not in conflict with the Quran and the sunnah. The rule that is agreed upon becomes part of the permanent body of Islamic law. The Islamic Schools of Law in the Sunni Islam accept Ijm'a on different basis. The *Hanafi* School accepts it on the basis of equity and they accept the opinion of the jurists of any age. The *Maliki* School accepts it on the basis of consideration of public interest and they are guided by the Ijm'a of the Scholars of Madina. The Shafi School is based on the Qiyas, which is the process of analogical reasoning. The *Hanbali* School accepts Ijm'a that is based only on the sunnah and by the companion of the Prophet (Weeramantry 1988).

Qiyas, in the Sunni Islamic jurisprudence, is the process of analogical reasoning in order to make an analogy with known injunction to a new injunction and is considered as the fourth source of Islamic law. It is considered an extension of the spirit and values of shari'ah to the modern Muslim's life.

There are some other common methodologies, such as *Istislah* which is related to the public interest and considers whatever brings about the greatest happiness for the greatest number of people to be good. *Urf* refers to the customs and practices of a given society. According to some sources, urf holds as much authority as *ijma*, and more than *qiyas*.

Ijtihad (individual struggle for understanding) is the process of making a legal decision by independent interpretation of the legal sources namely the Quran and the sunnah. Ijtihad involves problems that emerged and were not covered in the Quran, sunnah, and Ijm'a. Ijtihad is practiced by scholars who are called in Arabic *mujtahid*, who must meet the following qualifications: (1) be fully knowledgeable about the sources of Islamic law and Arabic language, (2) be an upright person who practices what he preaches, and (3) have the intellectual capacity to originate independent judgments and opinion (Kamali 2006). The opposite of ijtihad is *Taqlid*, which means imitation.

There are two opposite views in the Islamic legal literature with regard to ijtihad:

The first view is largely adopted by Western scholars and accepts the infamous notion, "The gate of ijtihad was closed," or in Arabic, "*insidad bab al-ijtihad.*" They argue that ijtihad, according to the Sunni Islamic jurisprudence, was last practiced in the tenth century when the four schools of Islamic laws were established, and that it is, therefore, outdated. Instead, they place a large emphasis on taqlid.

Joseph Schacht (1964) described the process as follows:

> By the beginning of the fourth century of the hijra (about 900 A.D.), however, the point had been reached when the scholars of all schools felt that all essential questions had been thoroughly discussed and finally settled, and a consensus gradually established itself to the effect that from that time onwards no one might be deemed to have the necessary qualifications or independent reasoning in law, and that all future activity would have to be confined to the explanation, application, and, at the most, interpretation of the doctrine as it had been laid down once and for all.

Claude Salhani (2006) mentioned that:

> Fearing too much change would weaken their political clout, the gates of ijtihad were closed to Sunni Muslims by religious scholars about 500 years ago. From then on, scholars and jurists were to

rely only on the original meaning and earlier interpretations of the Qur'an and the Hadith. However, there is now a growing movement among scholars and intellectuals to revive the practice of ijtihad.

The second view argues that the gates for ijtihad were never closed. One of the thinkers who adopted this view is Wael Hallaq (1984), who mentioned in his study about the closing of the gates of ijtihad that: A systematic and chronological study of the original legal sources reveals that these views on the history of ijtihad after the eighth century are entirely baseless and inaccurate. The gate of ijtihad was not closed in theory nor in practice. The study concluded that during the first five centuries of Islam, ijtihad was the cornerstone of the Sunni school of law. This is evident because Sunni has excluded all groups that rejected ijtihad. Secondly, ijtihad and mujtahids were necessary particularly in the higher ranks of government. From the sixth to twelfth centuries and onward, there is evidence of support for the conclusion that Muslims adopted the practice of appointing at least one mujtahid at the end of each century. There is consensus among both Hanbali school and the Shafi on the existence of mujtahid at all times.

Another thinker who adopted the same view is Mohammed Kamali (2006), who stated the following:

> *Until about 1500 CE, Muslim scholars were able to use the afore-mentioned processes of* ijtihad *to continually adapt in the face of changing conditions and new advances in knowledge. Unfortu-nately, about four centuries ago, as Muslim civilization began to weaken in the face of Western advances, Muslims adopted a more conservative stance and became defensive of prevailing values. Inno-vation and renewal were discouraged and* ijtihad *declined as result.*

Whether the gates of ijtihad were closed or not, it is clear that its use had declined tremendously during the last five centuries. This is why it is of utmost importance for today's scholars to find ways to revive this ijtihad process in order to ensure that Islam is up to date in the face of the challenges and innovations facing Muslim societies today and in the future.

The Islamic Schools of Law in the Sunni Islam, or *madh'hab*, are known as *Hanafi*, *Maliki*, *Hanbali*, and *Shafi*. The roots of the four schools go back to the third century of Islam at the time of the Abbasids' ruling, when there were almost 20 different schools. A madh'hab is a particular way of inter-preting fiqh; it reflects the different opinions on some laws and obligations of the shari'ah. The four schools share many of their rulings. The major differences between them are mainly in the importance and weight they give to the different sources of Islamic law.

The Hanafi school was the earliest established in the eighth century under the jurist Imam Abu Hanifa Al Numan, who was born and taught in Iraq. It dominates approximately one-third of the Muslim world, which makes it the most far-reaching school among the four. It uses reason, analogy, logic, and opinion in establishing laws. It was favored by various Muslim governments, most notably by the Ottoman Empire, because it was the most flexible and broad minded in its interpretation and judgments among all other schools. It is said to be the first school to establish contract rules for business transactions that involve resale for profit and payment for future delivery (Oxford 2007).

The Maliki school was established in the eighth century by Imam Malik ibn Anas Al-Asbahie, who was born and received his education in Medina. Imam Malik devoted himself to the study of fiqh, and he wrote one of the earliest books on hadith and fiqh. The major characteristic of this school is its consideration of the practice of the companions in Medina as a source of law (Oxford 2007). It rejects rational interpretation of the Quran, and it uses reasoning and analogy in formulating laws as long as they do not contradict the public good.

The Hanbali school was established in the ninth century by Imam Ahmad ibn Hanbal, who was born in Baghdad. It is considered to be the most strict and conservative of the Sunni law schools. The school uses reasoning and analogy only in very extreme cases and is said to be the most liberal with regard to commercial issues (Oxford 2007).

The Shafi school was established in the eighth century by Imam Muhammad ibn idris ash-Shafi, who was a student of Imam Malik. He received his education in Iraq and Egypt. In formulating laws, he places great emphasis on the sunnah and hadith as sources of shari'ah.

Islamic commercial law goes back to the early days of Islam. Up until the 1970s, the part of shari'ah that governs the commercial aspect was indeed neglected. Due to the rise of Islamic banking in the 1970s, the topic of Islamic commercial law began to rise. The history and development of Islamic commercial law, to some extent, matches the history and development of Islamic banks and can be divided into three periods:

The first is the early days of Islam until the late 1960s, where Islamic commercial law was not in focus due to the fact that there were no Islamic banks and that all commercial and corporate activities were performed as per the conventional banking system.

The second is the period starting from the 1970s until the late 1980s, which witnessed the rise of Islamic banks and the demand for shari'ah-compliant products and services, and subsequently, the need for Islamic commercial law to govern those activities. This period, from the 1970s to 1980s, also witnessed a very small number of Islamic banks and few shari'ah scholars possessing financial and practical experience and background. Also, the major focus of most Islamic banks was on the deposit mobilization function and not the utilization part. Another feature of this period is that most Islamic banking dialogues and literature were in the Arabic language.

The third period is from 1990 until the present, which has witnessed a large focus on and interest in developing Islamic commercial law to meet the large development and increasing demand for Islamic banking. This period is characterized by the large number of Islamic banks and Islamic windows operating through local and multinational conventional banks. Also, this period witnessed an increase in the number and complexity of shari'ah-compliant products and a large increase in the number of shari'ah scholars with a solid background and practical experience in Islamic finance. As opposed to the previous period and as a result of the large spread of Islamic banks across the globe, there has been a growing need to use the English language as a common language among banks instead of the Arabic language. Another major characteristic of this period is the broad acceptance of contracts as the main pillar for Islamic finance—specifically, those that are structured in a flexible fashion to meet the objectives of the concerned parties, provided they are compliant with *shari'ah* and at least one body of secular law (Delorenzo and McMillen 2007).

MAJOR CONCERNS WITH LEGAL RISK

For Islamic banks, the major concerns with regard to legal risk is the issue of enforceability. Whether shari'ah-based financial contracts are legally enforced in case of legal dispute is a matter of concern. The main two elements that have an effect on and raise the issue of enforceability of shari'ah-based contracts are (1) the documentation involved in the transaction and the terms and conditions of the contract, and (2) the globalization and ambiguous relationship between Islamic banks and the Western-style banking system and legal infrastructure. In terms of documentation, the Western-style banking as we mentioned earlier has a well-matured system that was established over three centuries ago. Therefore, the interpretation of terms and conditions stipulated in the documents are to a large extent transparent and predictable. In contrast, the documentation part in the shari'ah-based transactions and contracts are still in premature stages. The nonstandardization of practices among Islamic banks in different jurisdictions and the fact that the documentation is not well developed and articulated makes the interpretation to the terms and conditions not so transparent and predictability become difficult. In terms of globalization there are too many questions raised on how shari'ah rules can be enforced in the interest based economies and legal infrastructure, particularly in Western Europe and America (details in this issue in Delorenzo and McMillen 2007).

SUMMARY

Islamic banks are exposed significantly to operational risk due to the nature of its operations and the specific contractual features of their mode of finance. There are mainly three types of operational risk that are unique or significant in Islamic banks.

The first is the risk related to noncompliance with shari'ah rules and principles, which is unique and significant, being the core objective of Islamic banks. Failure to comply with shari'ah rules and principles will expose IIFS, in extreme cases, to reputation and insolvency risk as customers lose confidence and trust consequently will withdraw their funds and cancel their contracts with the bank. The IIFS, in addition, will lose any income that is generated from transactions or contracts that are done in a noncompliant manner as it is considered illegitimate. Shari'ah noncompliance risk is defined as "the risk that[that] arises from IIFS' failure to comply with the *Shari'ah* rules and principles determined by the *Shari'ah* Board of the IIFS or the relevant body in the jurisdiction in which the IIFS operates" (IFSB2005b). The IFSB, in its risk management principles for operational risk, has requested IIFS to: (1) maintain an adequate system and control, which includes the assigning of a shari'ah supervisory board; (2) all contract documentation, including all terms and conditions that govern the relationship between the bank and the customer be fully in compliance with shari'ah rules and principles; (3) a shari'ah compliance review be conducted independently by an adequate third party on an annual basis.

The second is the risk associated with the IIFS' fiduciary responsibilities toward all fund providers. Fiduciary risk is directly related to the unique relationship between IIFS and the Investment Account Holders. The IIFS is legally liable for a breach of the investment contract either for noncompliance with shari'ah rules and principles or for mismanagement of the investments that are funded by IAH and other depositors. As a result of losses in investment, IIFS may face insolvency and may not be able to either meet the demands of current account holders for repayment of their funds or safeguard the interests of their IAH.

The third is the legal risk, which is significant because of the premature stage of both the Islamic banking system and the Islamic commercial law that is derived from the Islamic law (shari'ah). Shari'ah is the law that governs every aspect of a Muslim's life, including religious and all aspects of daily life such as manners, codes of conduct, morality, and the basis of relationships with others. It also governs issues related to crime, marriage, divorce, international relationships, and inheritance. Fiqh is the human interpretation of the divine law by a methodology called "the roots of the law" (*Usulal Fiqh*). There are two sources of Islamic law: the primary source, which is the Quran and the sunnah; and the secondary source, which is the *Ijm'a* (consensus) and *Qiyas* (analogical reasoning).The fourth source is ijtihad (individual struggle for understanding). There are two opposite views with regard to ijtihad. On the one hand Western scholars believe that starting from the tenth century Muslims closed the gate of ijtihad and instead they adopted the methodology of imitation (*taqlid*). On the other hand, Muslim scholars argue that the gates for ijtihad were never closed. Between the two opposite views there are large consensus that ijtihad has tremendously declined after the tenth century. The development of the Islamic commercial law can be classified in three main periods, each of which had its one fuel and specific characteristics. The three periods are (1) the early days of Islam until the late 1960s, where commercial and financial transaction aspect of Muslims were not in focus, (2) 1970s until the late 1980s, which witnessed the rise of Islamic banks and the demand for shari'ah-compliant products and services, and (3) 1990 until the present, which has witnessed a large focus on and interest in developing Islamic commercial law to meet the large development and increasing demand for Islamic banking. Enforceability is the major concern to Islamic banks with regards to legal risk. The premature stage of Islamic banking makes it difficult to confidently state that shari'ah-based financial contracts are legally enforced, in many jurisdictions, in case of dispute. The main two issues that affect the enforceability of shari'ah-based contracts are (1) the documentation involved in the shari'ah-based transaction is not well developed and the interpretation of terms and conditions of the contract is not transparent, and (2) the ambiguous relationship between Islamic banks and the Western financial and legal infrastructure.

CHAPTER 6

The Islamic Capital Market

Any financial system has three core components: (1) a capital market, (2) a banking system, and (3) an insurance sector. Unfortunately, the capital market component in the Islamic financial system has not developed as fast as its banking system. This is mainly attributed to the lack of shari'ah-compliant tools used in both utilization and mobilization of funds in the long term, the lack of clear shari'ah guidance in this area, and ambiguous legal framework with regard to shari'ah transactions.

Until recent times, banks were mainly focusing on deposits as their major source of fund mobilization, and subsequently, they were mostly utilizing funds in short-term finance instruments, namely trade finance. As a result of the increasing demand for shari'ah-compliant finance, the Islamic capital market emerged as the major way to secure shari'ah-compliant, long-term finance for large government development projects and investments, and capital for investors to expand their business. It is also important to better manage and diversify the risk in the Islamic Financial System.

In this chapter, we review the Islamic capital market in terms of its definition, role, and importance; Islamic bonds (*sukuk*); and challenges to the market's development.

DEFINITION, ROLE, AND IMPORTANCE

Capital market is defined as a market in which people, entities, and governments who have excess funds, provide funding for the people, entities, and governments who need it. In simple terms, it is a place where you can raise capital for long-term periods. In doing this, capital market gives a great boost to the economy as a whole by channeling the savings into investments. Capital market can be primary market or secondary market. Primary market is where new issues of bonds or stocks are sold. This happens when a corporation or a government need funds; they issue securities to be sold to the public through a process called underwriting. In this process, banks guarantee a minimum price for business securities. Secondary market is where existing securities are bought and sold among investors and traders. Secondary market plays a very important role in providing liquidity in the market. There are also two types of capital market in the conventional system: (1) the debt market, which is the bond market, and (2) the equity market, which is the securities market.

The Islamic capital market plays a very important role in mobilizing funds and directing them to productive economic activities, providing stable long-tem funds for large investment projects and business expansion, ensuring financial stability through efficient and balanced allocation of both financial and economic resources within the economy, and allowing the Islamic Financial System to better diversify risk. The Islamic capital market consists mainly of bond market (sukuk), equity fund, and commodity fund.

THE ISLAMIC BOND MARKET (SUKUK)

Sukuk (plural of *sakk*, which is the Arabic word for *certificate*) is defined as certificates representing a proportional and undivided ownership right in tangible assets, a pool of predominantly tangible assets, or a business venture. These assets must be in a specific project or in investment activities that comply with shari'ah rules and principles. Sukuk is the Islamic equivalent of securities or bonds in the conventional system.

The major differences between the two can be summarized as follows:

- Bonds are certificates of debt owed by the issuer, whereas sukuk are instruments that represent a proportionate and undivided ownership right over the asset in which the funds are being invested.
- Sukuk can only be issued for specific shari'ah-compliant purposes and shari'ah-compliant assets, whereas bonds can be issued for general unspecified purposes.
- Sukuk are based on the real underlying asset; therefore, the income must be related to the purpose for which the funding is used.
- In the case of sukuk, investors have ownership claims on the specific assets or the underlying business venture, whereas in bonds they have general creditors' claim on the issuer.
- The fact that shari'ah requires all finance to be routed to productive purposes rather than speculative activities ensures that it has real economic values to reduce the risk of uncertainty.
- Sukuk cannot be traded in the secondary market unless the underlying assets represented by the certificate comprise the majority of real assets and financial rights.

The proportion of liquid to nonliquid assets is a debatable issue and according to Usmani, there are three views:

1. The first view, held by some scholars, is that the ratio of nonliquid assets should not fall below 51 percent because this means that the majority is nonliquid.
2. The second view argues that even up to 33 percent, it can be treated as a nonliquid asset.
3. The third view is based on the Hanafi jurisprudence, which argues that the asset can be traded irrespective of the proportion of the liquid part subject to two conditions: (1) the nonliquid portion should be in a considerable quantity, and (2) the total price should be more than the price of the liquid portion (which is purely theoretical).

SUKUK STRUCTURE AND TYPES

Sukuk structure, according to the IFSB new standard for capital adequacy requirements, can exist in three types: (1) asset-backed, (2) asset-based with a repurchase undertaking (binding promise) by the originator, and (3) pass-through asset-based (IFSB 2009a).

Asset-backed structure: Involves the physical ownership rights in the underlying assets or in the form of usufruct of such assets. This structure needs to meet the requirements set by a recognized external credit assessment institution (ECAI) for being an asset-backed structure. This structure exposes the sukuk holders to losses in case of the impairment of the assets.

Asset-based structure: According to this structure, the issuer purchases the assets and then leases them on behalf of the investors, using the funds received from the issued sukuk notes. In most cases, this structure takes the form of a sale-lease to the originator and backed by the issuer, with a binding purchase undertaking from the originator on the asset at maturity. The credit risk in this structure lies within the originator subject to any shari'ah-compliant credit enhancement by the issuer. The payment schedule of the repurchase undertaking and the capability of the originator to make the schedule payment to the issuer has weight in determining the credit rating by the ECSI. In case of default, in this type of structure, the sukuk holders need to have a right of recourse to the originator because the ownership rights over the underlying asset may not reliably result in an effective right of possession. Because the income of the asset is paid through the issuer to the investors, this type of structure is in some cases referred to as *pay-through*.

Pass-through asset-based sukuk structure: In this structure, a separate issuing entity purchases the underlying assets from the originator and packages them into a pool and acts as the issuer of the sukuk. This issuer requires the originator to provide recourse for the asset to the sukuk holder. In case of default by the originator, the issuer guarantees repayment by providing shari'ah-compliant credit enhancement.

There are many different types of sukuk. The Accounting and Auditing Organization of Islamic Financial Institutions (AAOIFI) has identified nine types of certificates: (1) *ijarah*, (2) *usufruct*, (3) *salam*, (4) *istisna*, (5) *murabaha*, (6) *musharaka*, (7) *muzara'a*, (8) *musaqa*, and (9) *mugharasa*.

> **Certificate of ownership in leased asset or *ijarah*:** In this type of certificate, the owner of a leased asset or a tangible asset, to be leased by promise, issues—on his own or through a financial intermediary acting on his behalf—certificates of equal value for the purpose of selling the asset, and receives its value through subscription. The certificate holder becomes the owner of the asset through undivided ownership and shares the profits and losses. Certificates that represent ownership of existing leased assets or assets to be leased on promise are tradable upon issuance and up to the date of maturity, provided the ownership of the assets is transferred to the holders of the certificates.
>
> **Certificate of ownership of *usufruct*:** These are certificates of equal value that are issued for specific purposes by the owner or through a financial intermediary. There are four categories of certificates under this group.
>
> 1. The certificate of ownership of usufruct of existing assets. This category has two types: (1) those issued for the purpose of leasing the asset and (2) those issued for the purpose of subleasing the asset. In both types, the issuer receives the rental from the revenue of the subscription and the holders of the certificates become joint owners of the usufruct. These certificates are tradable prior to entering into subleasing of the assets. The certificates represent rent receivable once subleasing takes place, and subsequently, they will be considered as debt owed by the second lessor and subject to the rules and regulations for disposal of debt.
>
> 2. The certificate of ownership of usufruct of described future assets, which is related to the usufruct of an asset that will be made in the future. These certificates can be tradable only upon the existence of the assets.
>
> 3. The certificate of ownership of services of a specified party, which are issued for the purpose of providing services through a

specified provider and receiving service charges in the form of subscription income. In this case, the holders of the certificate then become the owners of the services. These certificates are tradable prior to entering into subleasing of the services. The certificates represent rent receivable once subleasing takes place, and subsequently, they will be considered as debt owed by the second lessor and subject to the rules and regulations for disposal of debt.

4. The certificate of ownership of described future services. These certificates can be tradable only upon the identification of the source from which the services would be provided.

Salam **certificates:** These are certificates of equal value issued for the purpose of raising salam capital. In this type of certificate, the issuer is the seller of the goods of salam, the subscribers are the buyers of the goods, and the purchase price is the raised capital. The holders of the certificates are the owners of the goods and are entitled to the sale price of the certificate or the sale price of the salam goods sold in the case of parallel salam. In general, the commodity financed by such contracts tends to be for a short-term tenor. Salam was first introduced by the Bahrain Monetary Agency (BMA) in 2001 to be used as a liquidity tool for Islamic banks. Salam certificates are not tradable.

Istisna **certificates:** These are certificates of equal value issued for the purpose of raising funds for manufacturing. In this type of certificate, the issuer is the manufacturer (supplier/seller), the subscribers are the buyers of the manufactured product, and the funds raised from the subscription are the cost of production. The holders of the certificates are the owners of the product and are entitled to the sale price of the certificate or the sale price of the product sold in the case of parallel istisna. The certificates can be traded or redeemed if the funds are converted into real assets owned by the holders during the lifetime of the certificate. If the funds are used immediately as a price in parallel istisna or the manufactured product is delivered to the end purchaser, the certificate can only be traded according to the rules of disposal of debts.

Murabaha **certificates:** These are certificates of equal value issued for the purpose of financing the purchase of goods. This is the most common instrument in Islamic finance. The issuer of the certificate is the seller of the commodity, the subscribers are the buyer, and the funds raised are the purchase cost of the commodity. The holders of the certificate own the commodity and are entitled to its sale price. These certificates are tradable after closing of subscription, allotment, and commencement of activity.

Musharaka **certificates:** These are certificates of equal values based on participation contracts. Such certificates are issued for the purpose of raising funds for establishing new projects, developing an existing project, or financing business activities. The holders of the certificates become the owner of the project of the activity. There are three forms of certificates for managing for musharaka certificates depending on the form of management: (1) participation certificate, where the management of the project or activity is appointed to one of the partners; (2) mudaraba certificate, where the management is assigned to the mudarib; and (3) investment agency, where the management is appointed to an agent. These certificates are tradable after closing of subscription, allotment, and commencement of activity.

Muzara'a, musaqa, **and** *mugharasa* **certificates:** These are certificates of equal values used for the purpose of raising funds for (1) sharecropping in the case of muzara'a, (2) irrigation in case of musaqa, and (3) agriculture in the case of mugharasa. The holders of the certificates become entitled to a share in the crop or plantation as per the terms and conditions. Muzara'a and musaqa certificates are tradable after closing of subscription, allotment, and commencement of activity, provided that the holders of the certificate are the owners of the land. Mugharasa certificates are tradable after closing of subscription, allotment, and commencement of activity, regardless of the ownership of the land.

To summarize, there are nine different types of sukuk that are identified by the AAOIFI. All of them fall under three main structures, which are (1) the asset-backed structure, (2) the asset-based with a repurchase undertaking structure, and (3) the binding promise by the originator structure and the pass-through asset-based structure.

CHALLENGES FACING THE DEVELOPMENT OF THE MARKET

The Islamic capital market has many challenges and obstacles to overcome. These may be classified into three major groups: (1) shari'ah-related legal and regulatory framework in which the capital market operates, (2) the development of capital market instruments, and (3) the introduction of innovative and new tools. The Islamic capital market, while being in a primitive and premature stage, can benefit tremendously from the mature and well established and advanced conventional capital market counterpart.

Shari'ah Related Group (Shari'ah Experts and Shari'ah Interpretations)

The major two concerns in this group are (1) the shari'ah expertise and (2) the interpretation of shari'ah principles. It is important to have shari'ah experts who have a solid understanding of the nature and mechanism of sukuk as well as practical experience in dealing with the different types. It is also very important to unify shari'ah decisions and disclose them in a transparent manner. The variation in shari'ah interpretation negatively affects the credibility of the Islamic Financial Market. Therefore, it's crucial to establish one shari'ah supervisory board for the whole Islamic Financial System in the country. It is also important to ensure global harmonization among the different supervisory authorities and the conventional regulatory bodies in order to benefit from their long experience and to gain international recognition.

Legal and Regulatory Framework

There is a great need for effective legal infrastructure that complies with shari'ah principles. Most capital markets operate within legal systems that are designed for conventional operations and in most cases do not comply with shari'ah principles. One of the major concerns is the enforceability of contracts, to which the legal framework must ensure adherence. On the regulatory front, one must emphasize the importance of enforcing the rules. While much has been done by the regulatory authorities, such as IFSB and AAOIFI, in terms of issuing standards to regulate the Islamic Financial System, there is a need to ensure the harmonization of these standards and practices with the internationally accepted conventional standards and practices in order to gain international acceptance and creditability.

Development of Capital Market Instruments

Development of capital market instruments and the introduction of innovative new tools are instrumental in developing the Islamic capital market. Due to the nature of Islamic finance being mostly asset-backed, there is a need to transfer the ownership of the underlying assets. Transferring ownership is associated with the additional cost of tax that is imposed by most jurisdictions, which results in an increase in the cost of products (JCR-VIS 2005). The development of a secondary market is key to the development of capital market. This is important so as to provide investors with flexibility to enable them to effectively manage their liquidity. Also, the development of sukuk with different maturities is important in order to enable IIFS to manage funds in a more effective way.

SUMMARY

Capital market in the Islamic Financial System has developed at a slower pace compared to the overall banking system. There are three main reasons for this:

1. The limited scope of the functions of Islamic banks until recent times. Islamic banks were heavily dependent on deposits in their fund mobilization and on short-term finance in their fund utilization functions.
2. The lack of clear shari'ah guidance in this area and the lack of shari'ah scholars with a strong and solid financial background.
3. The ambiguous legal framework with relation to shari'ah transactions.

With the large expansion and enlarged scope of Islamic banks across the globe, the Islamic capital market emerged as a major player in the Islamic Financial System. Capital market played a significant role in providing shari'ah-compliant long-term financing for large government development projects and investments, and capital for investors to expand their business. It has also provided banks with liquidity and tools to better manage and diversify the risk in their portfolios.

The Islamic capital market consists mainly of bond market or sukuk, equity fund. Sukuk is the Islamic equivalent to securities or bonds in the conventional system. There are many differences between sukuk and conventional bonds, as explained earlier in this chapter, which are related to the core differences between the two. Whereas sukuk are instruments that represent a proportionate and undivided ownership right over the asset in which the funds are being invested, bonds are a certificate of debt owed by the issuer. There are three main structures under which the many types of sukuk can be classified: (1) the asset-backed structure, (2) the asset-based with a repurchase undertaking structure and the binding promise by the originator, and (3) the pass-through asset-based structure.

There are many challenges and obstacles facing the development of the Islamic capital market, which fall under three main categories:

1. Shari'ah: This includes the lack of shari'ah experts with a solid understanding of and practical experience in capital markets. The variation in shari'ah interpretation adversely affects the credibility of the Islamic Financial Market and makes harmonization among the different supervisory authorities and conventional regulatory bodies difficult.
2. Legal and regulatory: These issues arise from the fact that the Islamic capital market operates within a legal framework designed for conventional activities.
3. Development of capital market instruments: This includes the need for more innovative instruments and to develop a more effective secondary market.

PART

Three

Capital Adequacy

CHAPTER 7

The Importance and Role of Capital-Literature Review

There are two major approaches in the literature of bank capital: (1) the definition, constituents, and functions of capital; and (2) the need for supervisory regulations and adequacy of bank capital in particular.

The definition of capital and its constituents was a debatable issue for a long time. There is consensus, however, that capital is divided into two tiers or categories: (1) the core or primary capital and (2) the supplementary or secondary capital. The debate, however, was on the constituent of capital and what role debt instruments should play in the capital base. The reason for the debate lies in the permanence of the capital elements. Permanence means that there is no maturity. Primary capital has no maturity, whereas secondary capital elements have maturity. The Basel Committee on Banking Supervision has, to a large extent, narrowed this debate through the Basel Capital Adequacy Accord (1988), by determining the role and constituents of capital. Basel II has not changed the part concerning the definition, role, and constituents of capital in the agreement. This gives a strong signal that there is a high level of comfort with the definition, role, and constituents set by the committee.

The second approach, which involves capital adequacy and the need for supervisory regulations, is a debatable topic and has two opposite views. On the one hand, those who are proregulation argue that supervisory regulations are needed to determine the level of capital needed and to protect depositors. On the other hand, the proderegulation argument is that bankers are more aware of the level of capital that needs to be maintained, financial markets are equipped to evaluate the sufficient level of capital needed, and institutions with too little capital will not be able to attract funds from uninsured depositors. Moreover, they argue that shareholders will put pressure on managers if they take excessive risk.

Capital and its constituents in Islamic banking have a different role than in conventional banking because of the different nature of Islamic financial assets and the associated risk. The Basel Capital Adequacy Accord I and II did not differentiate between conventional and Islamic banking. The Islamic Financial Services Board (IFSB) has set the Capital Adequacy Standard for Islamic Financial Institutions based mainly on the work of Basel II, with the unique characteristics of Islamic finance in mind.

DEFINITION, FUNCTIONS, AND IMPORTANCE OF CAPITAL

In this section, we review the literature of bank capital in general, as it is mainly applicable for both conventional as well as Islamic banking. In the last part of this section, we will highlight the differences with regard to Islamic financial institutions.

Reed et al. (1984) mentioned that capital interpretation has been a debatable issue and that the reason for the debate arises from the nature of the elements of the capital base, equity, and debts. Where equity is permanent in the sense that it has no maturity, debt has maturity, and once the instrument matures, the capital is reduced. In 1982, the Federal Financial Institutions Examination Council defined bank capital as follows:

- **Primary capital:** common stock, perpetual preferred stock, capital surplus, undivided profits, contingency reserves, other capital reserves, and reserves for loan losses.
- **Secondary capital:** limited-life preferred stock and subordinated notes and debentures. Secondary capital cannot amount for more than 50 percent of the primary capital.

The financing instruments in the secondary capital are set as a percentage that is based on its maturity and must be phased out of the bank's capital as they approach maturity. There are three main functions of bank capital:

1. **Protective:** the primary function that provides protection for depositors in case of liquidation and maintains bank solvency by providing a cushion against losses so that the bank could continue operations.
2. **Operational:** includes the provision of funds for the purchase of land, building machinery and equipment, and providing a buffer to absorb occasional operating losses.
3. **Regulatory:** aims to provide confidence to both depositors and the supervisory authorities. A strong capital base would assure and impose confidence to depositors.

Roussakis (1984) also divided the capital available to banks into equity capital and debt capital. He showed that debt capital was first introduced during the Great Depression, when issuing additional common stock was not possible. During the 1950s and 1960s, banks were not in favor of raising funds in these forms, as it was associated with troubled banks. In December 1962, the comptroller of the currency issued a ruling that permitted banks to issue capital notes and debentures as part of their ordinary raising of capital. These instruments provide some advantages to banks, namely that they do not require reserve backing or Federal Deposit Insurance Corporation (FDIC) insurance assessments; they minimize the need for liquidity reserves against them enabling the bank to place most of the sales proceeds in long-term, higher-yielding assets; and the administrative cost associated with them is much lower than acquiring larger deposits from the money market.

Gardner and Mills (1988) explained that as capital has several functions with different relative importance among customers, managers, owners, and regulators, consensus on the definition of capital is lacking. As such, capital can be classified into two broad categories:

The first category is the net worth, which is the amount by which the value of the institution's assets exceeds the value of its liabilities, whether short or long term, insured or uninsured. It consists of common equity and preferred stock. Everyone agrees on the common equity as a capital component because it fulfills all purposes of capital (long-term source of funds, provides the initial funding to begin operations, promotes confidence, supports growth, and reduces moral hazard). The case of preferred stock, however, is not as clear-cut as common equity because of the fact that some are issued with maturity dates and others are not, and some are convertible and others are not. Moreover, it has a claim on income and assets subordinate to the claims of depositors and other creditors. The sum of common equity and preferred stocks is the firm's total equity capital.

The second category is the long-term debt, which has to meet three conditions to qualify as capital:

1. It must have an original maturity of seven years or more.
2. It must be clearly identified at the time of issuance as subordinate to deposits.
3. It must be uninsured.

Greuning and Bratanovic (1999) emphasized the fact that bank capital directly and indirectly influences every aspect of banking activities. Capital is a key factor that contributes to the safety and soundness of the banking system. It provides confidence to depositors because of its ability to absorb losses. It also determines the banks' lending capacity because banks cannot expand their balance sheets beyond the level determined by its capital adequacy ratio.

Three factors that bank capital should have are as follows:

1. It must be permanent.
2. It must not impose mandatory fixed charges against earnings.
3. It must allow for legal subordination to the rights of depositors and other creditors.

Nasser (2001) mentioned that there are two main sources of funds available to the bank: its own sources and outside sources, which mainly consist of customer deposits. The first source contains three elements: (1) paid-up capital, (2) reserves and unpaid profits, and (3) provisions.

According to Nasser, bank capital has three main functions:

1. The establishment and operational function that includes the provision of funds for the purchase of land, building machinery and equipment, and providing a buffer to absorb occasional operating losses.
2. The financing function, which may be needed at the early days of the establishment, whereby a bank has to finance some transactions to give confidence in the market until deposits start to flow in.
3. The protection function, which is the primary function that provides protection for depositors in case of liquidation, and maintains bank solvency by providing a cushion against losses so that the bank could continue operations.

Goodman and Becker (2003) and Tarbert (2000) mentioned that the importance of bank capital arises from the fact that a bank's role as a financial intermediary involves many risks, the most important of which is credit risk. The availability of bank capital for business risks is a key concern for the well-being of the banking system. The capital of a bank acts as a buffer against credit and operative losses of a bank as well as potential liquidity shortfalls. Also, capital as a financial cushion protects depositors and deposit insurance agents by absorbing a bank's losses.

The Basel Committee on Banking Supervision (1988) stated that capital is a firm's cushion against adversity. It protects the firm from insolvency in case of losses, and banks can go up to 100 percent of their capital while meeting their obligations and continuing to operate. The Basel Capital Accord identified two types of capital: tier one and tier two.

Tier one is the core capital and consists of two elements:

1. Paid-up share capital/common stock.
2. Disclosed reserves that include retained earnings and capital surplus (paid-up capital in excess of par value).

It is important to note that goodwill is deducted from tier one.
Tier two is the supplementary capital and consists of five elements:

1. Undisclosed reserves.
2. Asset revaluation reserves.
3. General provisions/general loan loss reserves.
4. Hybrid (debt/equity) capital instruments.
5. Subordinated term debt.

The main function of bank capital is its ability to absorb losses. Based on that fact, the constituents of capital were determined. The classification of capital as regulatory capital is based less on the instrument's residual interest in the assets and more on its maturity dates. The fact that nonequity capital has maturity does not represent risk of current redemption. Therefore, nonequity instruments can serve as both regulatory capital in building the financial cushion that absorbs a bank's losses and thus, protects depositors (BCOBS 1988).

Grais and Kulathunga (2007) noted that for Islamic financial institutions (IIFS), tier one capital is the same as defined in Basel II except for the elements of the reserves. The reserves included in tier one are the shareholders' portion of the profit-equalization reserve, which is included in the disclosed reserves; ordinary paid-up share capital/common stocks; disclosed reserves from post-tax retained earnings; and noncumulative perpetual preferred stock (goodwill to be deducted). Tier two capital (supplementary capital) will not include any hybrid capital instruments or subordinated debts, as these would carry interest and contravene shari'ah principles. Also, the AAOIFI committee on capital adequacy concluded that Profit-Sharing Investment Accounts (PSIA) should not be included in the capital base in tier two.

There are mainly two differences in capital between conventional and Islamic banks: (1) in conventional banks, paid-up capital can take the form of normal shares and preferential shares; (2) in Islamic banks, it can only take the form of normal shares. Reserves and unpaid profit in Islamic banks are part of the shareholder's equity; therefore, they should be deducted from the net profit of the shareholders only and not from the net profit of the whole organization.

According to the Islamic Financial and Services Board, Islamic bank capital is classified into two tiers: (1) tier one consists of the core capital and reserves, and (2) tier two is a mix of money from both shareholders and depositors (Khasawna 2008). Unlike conventional banks, each tier in the capital has a different risk to cover. There are two types of risk: (1) operational risk, which is covered by the shareholders' part of the capital, and (2) credit and market risk, which is covered by both the shareholders and depositors. The numerator of the capital adequacy ratio in Islamic banks consists of two tiers also: (1) the paid-up capital, and (2) reserves + investment reserves + revaluation reserves. Tier one covers the operational risk only, and tier two covers the credit and market risk (IFSB 2008).

HISTORY OF CAPITAL ADEQUACY REGULATIONS

The history of capital adequacy measurement and regulations goes back to the second decade of the twentieth century. The capital funds to total deposits was the longest used ratio to determine capital adequacy. In 1914, the comptroller of the currency (OCC), one of the three federal regulatory agencies having responsibility for commercial banks—the other two are the Federal Reserve System (Fed) and Federal Deposit Insurance Corporation (FDIC)—stated that by law, all national banks are to maintain at least $1 in capital funds for each $10 of deposits. It was not until after the Great Depression of the 1930s that it was realized that this ratio is only serving the purpose of measuring the liquidity, whereas the focus should be measuring solvency of banks. This was the beginning of using the capital to asset ratio to measure the bank's capital adequacy. During World War II, banks directed most of their investments to low-risk and low-yield assets, namely U.S. government bonds. In order to encourage banks to continue this trend, the Federal Reserve in its new ratio of capital to risk assets has excluded the U.S. government securities from the risk assets when calculating the capital adequacy.

After World War II, it was clear that capital adequacy should be associated with items in the balance sheet that are subject to losses. In 1948, the comptroller of the currency sized the capital-to-deposit ratio and started to use risk-asset ratio, which is the ratio of capital funds to loans and investments other than U.S. government securities. Originally, the ratio was 1 to 5 then later increased to 1 to 6 (capital funds were equal to at least 16.67 percent of risk assets).

In 1952, an adjusted risk asset approach, issued by the Federal Reserve, was in place. The adjusted approach assigned separate capital requirements to each category of assets according to the risk associated with it. The approach was further revised in 1956 to provide additional protection to banks from reduction in liabilities, as well as protection from the loss in investments, by introducing a liquidity test. The revised approach assigned different capital requirement to the different categories of both assets and liabilities.

The period from the 1960s through the end of the 1970s witnessed divided opinions on the definition of capital and the methodology used to measure capital adequacy. The three regulatory agencies failed to develop a solid and unified definition of capital and a method to measure capital adequacy.

In late 1981, a new framework for capital adequacy was developed by the three federal regulatory agencies. The framework included a definition of capital and guidelines for capital adequacy measurement. The new framework divided capital into primary capital, which consists of items that are permanent in nature, and secondary capital, which includes items that are nonpermanent in nature. The framework classified financial institutions into three categories according to their adequacy of capital, in addition to setting the minimum level of primary capital in the total capital.

There were two major criticisms to the use of the capital-to-asset ratio: (1) it encourages banks to move into investing in a higher risk asset, as it has the same capital required for lower risk assets and subsequently there is an increased risk in the banking system as a whole; and (2) it encourages banks to expand their off balance sheet activities as they not subject to capital requirements.

Starting in 1996, there was an increasing trend in the United States and Europe to work jointly, seeking international cooperation and agreement. In January 1987, a proposal for a revised risk-based capital framework for banks and bank holding companies, developed jointly by the United States and the Bank of England, was announced. At the same time, there was another framework for risk-based capital under process initiated by 11 large industrial countries (Belgium, Canada, France, Germany, Italy, Japan, Netherlands, Sweden, United Kingdom, United States, Switzerland, and Luxembourg). And, in late 1988, the final guideline was adopted (Alfriend 1988; Reed et al 1984; and Omar 1995).

THE NEED FOR BANKING REGULATIONS AND SUPERVISION

Gardner and Mills (1988) raised the issue of who should decide on capital adequacy. They demonstrated two opposite views. Advocates to deregulation argue that the financial market is sufficient to provide a mechanism by which institutions that have low capital would not be able to attract funds through uninsured depositors. Moreover, shareholders will protect their interest and impose pressure on managers if they take excessive risk. Opponents of this view argue that many institutions are not exposed to market discipline. Moreover, more public disclosure of bank activities is required.

Tarbert (2000) demonstrated two opposite points of view regarding the importance and need for governments to regulate capital adequacy. The argument against government regulations was based on the logic that if the government sets a Capital Adequacy Standard (CAS), only three outcomes are possible:

1. The CAS determined by the regulator will match the CAS determined by the bank.
2. The government standards will be lower than what banks deems sufficient. Banks will either ignore government regulations and maintain a higher level of capital or obey the regulations at their peril. The later situation may cause a moral hazard, since banks could justify imprudent management by arguing that they met the minimal standards required by law.
3. The requirement would be higher than the optimal amount of capital needed for efficient banking operations. In this case, banks' profitability will be reduced, and interest rates on loans may go up.

Those who are pro-government regulations argued that there are at least four specific reasons provided by regulators mandating minimal bank capital, which are:

1. Capital represents a cushion that protects banks against run by depositors.
2. It reduces the risk of systemic bank failure, since banks are linked together through a payment system, and the collapse of one bank may affect the whole banking system.
3. Capital cushion protects taxpayers in countries that have a deposit insurance regime.
4. International capital adequacy standards would prevent a "race to the bottom" situation, which arises from competition to over-leverage assets.

Stevens (2000) gave two reasons for the need for banking regulations and supervision:

1. To redress a moral hazard, since banks in most countries are protected by government safety nets, including a lender of last resort and/or deposit insurance. Safety nets give banks incentives to take excessive risk.
2. A reserve bank carries on a banking business, requiring careful attention to its own counterparty risk exposures.

He also mentioned that a bank's capital typically includes the amount paid by shareholders and its retained earnings, as well as certain liabilities that have lowest priority when paying off the creditors of a failed bank. Minimum capital requirements are among the earliest forms of government banking regulations.

Schuler (1992), in an overview of the world history of free banking, defined free banking as a banking system with a competitive note issue, low legal barriers to entry, and no central control of reserves. He criticized the argument, claiming that depositors and shareholders cannot adequately discipline commercial banks' credit expansion by themselves because they lack the necessary information. Therefore, a central bank can regulate commercial banks to prevent them from ever-expanding credit or help them in a crisis by being a lender of last resort. He argued that free banking systems were, on the whole, more stable than central banking systems during times of peace and no less stable than central banking systems during war time. He mentioned that banks within a free banking system were concerned with guarding their own reserves. Moreover, free banking systems were able to provide themselves with liquidity during a crisis through the local inter-bank lending market or through other banks that were willing to rescue a troubled bank for a high interest rate on a loan or for acquisition of the bank. He concluded that free banking systems did not encourage the development of lender of last resort and that regulations were the reasons for countries to adopt central banking systems.

Sharing the same view, Dowd (1999) concluded that there is no economic justification for capital adequacy regulations. He added that no one yet has provided a convincing case for it on grounds of market failure and that no one has yet been able to prove that capital adequacy regulations can provide a better solution to laissez-faire banking. He further criticized the main traditional argument supporting capital adequacy regulations noting three main points: (1) no clear justification provided by the advocates of this argument to support their argument, (2) the moral hazard problem is due to the government failure and not market failure, and (3) protecting the small depositors on the expense of the taxpayers particularly the small ones cannot be justified.

Dowd also defended the experience of free banking, concluding that the historical record gives little support to the claim that free competition tends to destabilize the banking system. Free banking systems were rarely subject to major banking crises, and there is evidence that the crises that did occur were usually caused by major external factors, such as a crisis in a regulated banking system nearby or by government intervention of some sort.

The IFSB states the objectives of the standard as follows: (1) To address the specific structure and contents of shari'ah-compliant products and services offered by the Islamic Financial Services (IIFS) that are not specifically tackled by the currently adopted and proposed international Capital Adequacy Standard and shari'ah-compliant mitigation; (2) To standardize the approach in identifying and measuring risk in shari'ah-compliant products and services. And in assigning risk weights thereto, which creates a level playing field amongst the IIFS in adopting and developing risk identification and measurement practices that meet internationally acceptable prudential standard. The standard is targeted at noninsurance institutions offering only Islamic financial services, and the supervisory authority may, at its own discretion, extend calculation of the minimum capital adequacy requirements to Islamic window operations that are self-contained or other IISF operations that fall within their jurisdiction. In addition, the risk weighting methodology set out in the standard may be applied to shari'ah-compliant assets held by Islamic windows that are not self-contained or by other institutions holding such assets. Also, any IIFS operation falls within the scope on a fully consolidated basis at the holding company level within a group or subgroup of IIFS. The standards are not to be applied at the consolidated level to a group or subgroup that consists of entities other than IIFS, as defined in the standard (IFSB 2005a).

According to Archer and Abdel Karim (2007), the need for capital adequacy for Islamic financial institutions stems from the fact that Islamic banks are not immune from systemic risk that may result from large volumes of panic withdrawals of Profit Sharing Investment Accounts (PSIA) and current account depositors. They describe it primarily as liquidity risk. Also, in the environment in which Islamic banks operate, there may be a more general lack of market discipline. They have concluded that the rationales for capital adequacy regulations for conventional banks are applicable to Islamic banks. There are two main differences, which are technical rather than conceptual in the identification, measurement, and mitigation of credit and market risk. The first is in the case of assets, the differences are more of a conceptual nature, as they are not normally found in the conventional bankbooks, and if they do, they receive very high risk weighting under Basel II. Other major conceptual differences are the economic characteristics on unrestricted PSIA, which vary from one country to the other. In some countries, they are regarded as virtual deposits, not loss bearing, and entitled to a fairly predictable return. In other countries, they are seen as a form of limited-term equity investment, which is in line with the nature of shari'ah principles.

Iqbal and Mirakhor (2007) attributed the need for banking regulations, supervision, and capital adequacy requirements to the growth of Islamic financial industry worldwide. The Basel II framework represents the basis for Islamic capital adequacy requirements. It was argued that the nature of intermediation by Islamic banks is different from conventional banks; therefore, there may be a difference in the capital adequacy requirements. They highlighted two main features of Islamic banks: (1) the nature of intermediation and (2) the risk weights of assets held by Islamic banks. (See Table 7.1.)

SUMMARY

Understanding capital is a crucial prerequisite to understanding the rationality and importance of capital adequacy regulations. The definition, role, and what constitutes capital is a long-debated issue. The Basel Committee on Banking Supervision in the first accord 1988 has set the definition, role, and constituent of capital. The revised framework, Basel II has kept the same unaltered which gave a strong signal that there is large consensus on the definition, role, and constituent of capital.

Capital is the firm's cushion against adversity. It protects the firm from insolvency in case of losses; banks can go up to 100 percent of their capital while meeting their obligations and continuing to operate. Capital has two components: (1) core capital and (2) supplementary capital. The major difference is that core capital is permanent while supplementary capital has maturity.

Capital in Islamic banks, to a large extent, has a similar definition and role. The two major differences in capital between conventional and Islamic banks are: (1) paid-up capital can take the form of normal shares and preferential shares in conventional and can only be in the form of normal shares in the Islamic banks; and (2) in tier two, Islamic banks can not include hybrid capital instruments or subordinated debts because these instruments involve interest, which is in contradiction to shari'ah principles.

The need for capital adequacy regulation was felt from the early years of the twentieth century. The history of capital adequacy measurements and

TABLE 7.1 Bank Capital Definition Matrix: Conventional and Islamic

Author	Primary/Core Capital	Secondary/Supplementary Capital
Conventional Reed and others (1984)	Primary capital, as defined by the Federal Financial Institutions Examination Council, consists of common stock, perpetual preferred stock, capital surplus, undivided profits, contingency reserves, other capital reserves, mandatory convertible instruments, and reserve for loan losses. The difference between primary and secondary capital hinges on the permanence of capital. Primary capital is permanent in the sense that it has no maturity.	Secondary capital consists of limited-life preferred stock and subordinated notes and debentures. Secondary capital cannot amount to more than 50 percent of the amount of primary capital, and the financing instruments in the secondary capital must be phased out of the bank's capital as they approach maturity.
Gardner and Mills (1988)	Net worth is the amount by which the value of the institution's assets exceeds the value of its liabilities. It consists of common equity and preferred stocks.	Debt capital is a long-term debt instrument, such as subordinated notes and debentures. They will qualify as capital under three conditions: (1) must have an original maturity of seven years or more, (2) must be clearly identified at the time of issuance as subordinate to deposits, and (3) must be uninsured.
Roussakis (1984)	Equity capital identifies the value of the stockholders' investment in the business. Equity capital consists of common stock, surplus, undivided profits, and contingency reserves.	Debt capital consists of capital notes and debentures. They are fixed-claim, interest-bearing obligations that enable banks to raise capital. They are unsecured and subordinate to the claims of depositors and other creditors.
Basel Capital Adequacy Accord (2004)	Core capital (tier one) consists of two elements: (1) paid-up share capital/common stock and (2) disclosed reserves that include retained earnings and capital surplus (paid-up capital in excess of par value).	Supplementary capital (tier two) consists of five elements: (1) undisclosed reserves, (2) asset revaluation reserves, (3) general provisions/general loan loss reserves, (4) hybrid capital instruments, and (5) subordinated term debt. The total of tier two elements is limited to 100 percent of the total tier one elements. Subordinated term debt not to exceed 50 percent of tier two elements.

Islamic IFSB 2005	Tier one capital will be the same as defined in Basel II except for the reserves. These reserves would include the shareholders' portion of the profit-equalization reserve, which is included in the disclosed reserves, ordinary paid-up share capital/common stocks, disclosed reserves from post-tax retained earnings, and noncumulative perpetual preferred stock (goodwill to be deducted).

Unlike conventional banking:

1. Paid-up capital can only take the form of normal shares.
2. Reserves and unpaid profit are part of the shareholder's equity; therefore, they should be deducted from the net profit of the shareholders only and not from the net profit of the whole organization.
3. Tier one covers the operational risk only. | Tier three: consists of short-term subordinated debt that meet the following conditions: (1) unsecured, subordinated, and fully paid up, (2) original maturity of at least two years, and (3) not repayable before the agreed repayment date unless the supervisory authority agrees.

Tier two capital (supplementary capital) will not include any hybrid capital instruments or subordinated debts, as these would carry interest and contravene shari'ah principles. Also, the AAOIFI committee on capital adequacy concluded that Profit-Sharing Investment Accounts (PSIA) should not be included in tier two. Unlike conventional banking, tier two covers the credit and marketing risk.

Tier three: consists of short-term subordinated debt that meets the following conditions: (1) unsecured, subordinated, and fully paid up, (2) original maturity of at least two years, and (3) not repayable before the agreed repayment date unless the supervisory authority agrees. |

regulations reveals that there were two major conceptual views to this issue. During the period 1914 to 1930, the capital adequacy ratio was set as capital fund to deposits, which actually means that this ratio was only serving the purpose of measuring liquidity and not solvency. Starting in 1930, after the Great Depression, it was clear that capital adequacy should be related to the items in the asset side of the balance sheet that are subject to losses.

The capital adequacy standards for Islamic banks set by the IFSB are mainly drawn from the work of Basel II. Therefore, I found it important to dedicate the next chapter to understanding Basel I (1988) and Basel II (2004).

CHAPTER 8

The Regulatory Framework of the Conventional Banking System: Basel I and II

T he regulatory framework for Islamic financial institutions and the work of the Islamic Financial Service Board (IFSB) are mainly drawn upon the work and regulatory framework of Basel capital adequacy accord. Therefore, this chapter is dedicated to providing a detailed background and overview of the regulatory framework and the regulatory bodies that govern the conventional banking system.

THE REGULATORY BODIES

In this section, we will discuss two regulatory bodies: (1) the Bank for International Settlement (BIS) and (2) the Basel Committee on Banking Supervision. The BIS is the oldest international financial institution and the principal center for international central bank cooperation. Among many other things, the BIS plays an important role in promoting transparency of the monetary policies across its members. The Basel Committee on Banking Supervision is the major regulatory agency that deals with regulatory issues related to international active banks across member countries.

The Bank for International Settlements (BIS)

The Bank for International Settlements (BIS) in Basel, Switzerland, was established in 1930 by the efforts of the governor of the Bank of England and the German finance minister for the purpose of facilitating the money transfers required for settling the reparation payments imposed on Germany under the Treaty of Versailles, following World War I. After World War II, the BIS was accused of helping the Germans during the War in looting assets from the occupied territories. Also, it was accused of receiving large quantities of gold stolen by Germany from central banks in Belgium and the Netherlands as wartime payments. Subsequently, the Bretton Woods agreement of 1944 called for the liquidation of the BIS. There were two opposite views, one headed by the United States, who recommended the dissolution of the BIS; and the other headed by England, who opposed the recommendation. Finally, in April 1945, it was decided to stop the resolution to dissolve the BIS. Despite being an international organization, the BIS was originally owned by both government and private shareholders. Presently, however, and after forcefully buying its shares from private owners, it has become fully government owned by its 57 central bank members.

BIS is the world's oldest international financial institution and remains to this day the principal center for international central bank cooperation. The main focus of the bank's activities is the cooperation among central banks, and increasingly, other agencies in pursuit of monetary and financial stability. The bank's main tasks, as they have developed over the past 80 years, can be summarized as follows:

- To provide a forum for central bank cooperation. The BIS acts as the prime forum for information exchange and cooperation among central banks worldwide.
- Within the framework of international cooperation, the BIS conducts research contributing to monetary and financial stability, collects and publishes statistical material on international finance, and—through committees of national experts—formulates recommendations to the financial community aimed at strengthening the international financial system.
- To perform traditional banking functions, such as reserve management and gold transactions, for the account of central bank customers and international organizations. In addition, the BIS has performed trustee and agency functions. Thus, the BIS was the agent for the European Payments Union (EPU, 1950–1958), helping the European currencies restore convertibility after World War II. The BIS has also acted as the agent for various European exchange rate arrangements, including the European Monetary System (EMS, 1979–1994), which preceded the move to a single currency.
- Finally, to provide and organize emergency financing to support the international monetary system when needed (Bank for International Settlements 2003).

BIS plays an important role in enhancing the predictability and transparency of the monetary policies among its members. The two most important elements of an effective monetary policy, which receive serious attention from the BIS, are (1) the capital adequacy regulations and (2) the reserve requirement transparency. BIS, in its role in setting the capital adequacy requirements, seeks to prevent economic crises that may result from speculative lending that is not supported by adequate capital. In addition, the BIS encourages banks to establish and keep reserves at acceptable levels to enhance the safety and soundness of the banking systems and to make them transparent in order to provide confidence and comfort to customers and depositors in the banking system.

The Basel Committee on Banking Supervision

The committee was established at the end of 1974 by the Central Bank Governors of the Group of Ten (G-10) countries as a direct result of the failure of two major international banks, namely, Herstatt Bank and Franklin National Bank (Heffernan 1996). Herstatt was a private West German bank with large foreign exchange activity. The bank collapsed in June 1974 when the German regulators withdrew its license, forcing the troubled bank to liquidate. The collapse of the bank had severely impacted the global payment and settlement system. This is because the German regulators shutdown the bank in the middle of the day after releasing the payment of Deutsche Marks by depositors and other banks to Herstatt in exchange for U.S. Dollars, which were to be delivered to their accounts in New York. Because of the time difference, however, the U.S. correspondent banks suspended all payments and the counterparty did not receive their payments. Franklin National Bank was at this time the 20th largest bank in the United States. The bank was involved in money laundering operations and other illegal transactions. In October 1974, the bank was declared insolvent due to mismanagement and fraud and was considered the largest bank failure in the United States. The collapse of the two banks in 1974 caused a confidence crisis in the financial system and called for the setting of global standard regulations. The committee was also established as a result of the deterioration of the Third World debts; the increase of the doubtful loans that were granted by international banks, particularly U.S. banks; and the severe competition initiated by Japanese banks with Western banks, as Japanese banks used to operate at a very low level of capital, which resulted in higher profit than Western banks.

Committee members come from the G-10 countries (actually, there are 11 countries: Belgium, Canada, France, Germany, Italy, Japan, the Netherlands, Sweden, Switzerland, United Kingdom, and the United States), plus Argentina, Australia, Brazil, China, Hong Kong, India, Indonesia, Korea, Luxembourg, Mexico, Russia, Saudi Arabia, Singapore, South Africa,

Spain, and Turkey. The main purpose of the Basel Committee is to consider regulatory issues related to activities of international banks in member countries. The primary objective of the committee's work has been to close gaps in international supervisory coverage in pursuit of two basic principles:

1. No foreign banking establishment should escape supervision.
2. Supervision should be adequate.

Working toward these objectives, the committee has reached several concordats and agreements. The first agreement was the 1975 Basel concordat, which defined the roles and responsibilities of the authorities in the parent and host countries regarding the supervision of foreign branches or subsidiaries of banks. The supervision of liquidity would be the primary responsibility of the host country. Solvency of bank branches would be the responsibility of the parent country, and solvency of foreign subsidiaries was the responsibility of the host country. The concordat was revised in 1983 as a result of the supervisory gaps that were revealed after the scandal and the collapse of the Banco Ambrosiano in 1982. The bank was established in Milan, Italy, in 1896, mainly to serve religious purposes. From 1960 onward, the bank extended largely through a network of overseas banks and companies and started illegal transactions of transferring money out of Italy. In 1982, the bank collapsed and was taken over by the Bank of Italy. The revised concordat assigned the responsibility for solvency problems arising from subsidiaries and liquidity problems arising from either a subsidiary or branch jointly to host and parent countries. The solvency problem arising from a branch was the responsibility of the central bank of the parent country because a branch has no legal independence and is considered to be an integral part of the parent company.

Two major issues were not addressed in both concordats: (1) lender of the last resort and (2) the extension of deposit insurance to all deposit liabilities (Heffernan 1996). In December 1987, after years of work to secure international convergence of supervisory regulations governing the capital adequacy of international banks, the committee published the proposals for the new regulations, followed by a consultative process in all G-10 countries. The proposals were also circulated to supervisory authorities worldwide. In 1988, the committee introduced the Basel Accord that established a single set of capital adequacy standards. In 1995, an amendment to the accord was in place and introduced market risk. A revised framework for Basel II was formulated and announced in 2004 (Basel Committee on Banking Supervision 2004).

The committee does not possess any formal supranational supervisory authority, and its conclusions do not, and were never intended to, have legal force. Rather, it formulates broad supervisory standards and guidelines and recommends statements of best practice in the expectation that individual authorities will take steps to implement them through detailed arrangements that are best to their own national systems. The committee reports to the Central Bank Governors of the G-10 countries and seeks the governors' endorsement for its major initiatives. In addition, however, since the committee contains representatives from institutions that are not central banks, the decisions it takes carry the commitment of many national authorities outside the central banking fraternity. The committee's secretarial unit is provided by the Bank for International Settlements in Basel. The 12-person secretarial unit is mainly staffed by professional supervisors on a temporary basis from member institutions. In addition to undertaking the secretarial work for the committee and its many expert subcommittees, it stands ready to give advice to supervisory authorities in all countries (Bank for International Settlements 2003). The committee is neither a national organization of any country nor an official international regulatory agency, like the United Nations committee, or one created by a treaty. Therefore, legal scholars classify it as an International Financial Regulatory Organization (IFRO) (Tarbert 2000).

BASEL CAPITAL ACCORD I: 1988

In July 1988, the Basel agreement on risk-based capital was signed at the Bank for International Settlements in Basel, Switzerland, by Central Bank representatives from the G-10 countries. The agreement came into effect with two fundamental objectives: (1) to strengthen the soundness and stability of the international banking system and (2) to have a fair framework and high degree of consistency in its application to banks in different countries, with the aim of diminishing an existing source of competitive inequality among international banks. The document of the agreement is divided into four sections. The first two describe the framework: the constituents of capital and the risk weighting system. The second two deal with the target standard ratio, as well as the transitional and implementation arrangements (BCOBS 1988).

The Constituent of Capital

Capital is a firm's cushion against adversity. It protects the firm from insolvency in case of losses, which can go up to 100 percent of its capital while meeting its obligations and continuing its operations. Absorption of losses, particularly the unexpected ones that arise from a bank's asset portfolio or off-balance sheet activities, is considered the major role of capital. Bank capital is divided into two tiers: (1) core capital and (2) supplementary capital.

Tier one is the core capital and consists of two elements:

1. Paid-up share capital/common stock.
2. Disclosed reserves, including retained earnings and capital surplus (paid-up capital in excess of par value). One adjustment is to be made: goodwill is to be deducted from tier one.

Tier two is the supplementary capital and consists of five elements:

1. Undisclosed reserves.
2. Asset revaluation reserves.
3. General provisions/general loan loss reserves.
4. Hybrid (debt/equity) capital instruments.
5. Subordinated term debt.

The following limitations are to be followed. First, the total of tier two elements will be limited to 100 percent of total tier one elements. Second, subordinated term debt is not to exceed 50 percent of tier one elements (BCOBS 1988).

Risk Weights and the Target Ratio

The framework is set in a simple five weights: 0, 10, 20, 50, and 100 percent. Each group of assets and off-balance sheet exposure is weighted according to one of the five weights in relation to its relative risk. The central focus of this framework is the credit risk, which is defined as the possibility of losses due to borrowers' defaults or decreased ability to repay their debts. Moreover, the country's risk was considered, as the agreement differentiated between two groups of countries:

1. Countries that are full members of the Organization of Economic Cooperation and Development (OECD) or countries that have special lending arrangements with the International Monetary Fund. These countries are considered to have low risk and subsequently, may be assigned low risk weights.
2. Non-OECD countries, which include the remaining countries of the world. These countries are considered to be of higher risk and do not enjoy reduction in the risk weights similar to the first group.

The standard ratio of capital-to-weighted risk assets is set at 8 percent, of which the core capital element will be at least 4 percent. This common ratio was expected to be observed by international banks in member countries by the end of 1992. This allows a four-and-a-half year transitional period for banks to make any necessary adjustments. The transitional period was from the date of the agreement (July 1988) to the end of 1992. After that, all banks were expected to meet the standards in full. The implementation was to take place at the national level by the supervisory authorities in light of their different legal structures and existing supervisory arrangements.

Amendments to the Accord

In December 1995, the committee approved two amendments to the accord, which were to be in effect by 1997, at the latest.

The first was the adoption of a new set of capital requirements to support market risk exposure arising from interest rates and foreign exchange exposures as well as bank trading accounts (accounts that contain assets held for short-term trading purposes).

In addition, the committee introduced a third tier to the capital base in the form of subordinated debt with a minimum original maturity of two years. In order for short-term subordinated debt to be eligible as tier three capital, it needs to have the following characteristics:

- Unsecured, subordinated, and fully paid up.
- Original maturity of minimum two years and no premature repayment without the approval of the supervisory authorities.
- Neither interest nor principal amounts can be paid, even at maturity, if capital will fall or remain below the minimum capital requirements.

Tier three capital would only be used, at the discretion of the supervisory authority, to meet market risk and be limited to 250 percent of the bank tier one capital that is required to support market risk.

Market Risk

Market risk is defined as the risk of losses in on- and off-balance sheet positions arising from movements in market prices. Market risk was first introduced in January 1996, as an amendment to Basel accord I. It required banks to measure and apply capital charges in respect to their market risks in addition to their credit risks. In November 2005 it was again amended. There are two types of risks that are subject to capital requirements:

1. The risk related to interest rate as per the instruments and equities in the trading books, which applies to the current market value of items in the banks' trading books. As per the new definition that came into

effect in November 2005, trading books consists of positions in financial instruments and commodities held for the purpose of trading or hedging other elements of the trading books.

2. The foreign exchange risk and commodities risk, which applies to the total currency and commodity positions of the bank. This is subject to discretion to deduct structural foreign exchange positions.

There are two methods to measure market risk: (1) the standardized measurement method, which separately calculates the specific risk and the general market risk arising from debt and equity positions, and (2) the internal model, which is a Value-at-Risk (VAR) model, and is advanced and designed to estimate the probability of losses in the net open position based on statistical analysis. VAR is best used in banks that deal with large transactions and carry out material trading activities in multiple jurisdictions. The capital charge under the Standardized Approach is the summation of the risk calculated for each of the four categories of risk addressed by the amendment: (1) interest rate, (2) equity position, (3) foreign exchange, and (4) commodities risk, plus the price risk of options.

In order to use the internal model approach, banks need to meet the following criteria set by the supervisory authority:

- A sound risk management system.
- Sufficient numbers of skilled staff who are capable of using sophisticated models in the areas of trading, control, audit, and back office.
- A sound track record of risk measurement.
- Continuous implementations of stress tests.

The cooperation between the home and the host supervisory authorities is crucial to ensure efficient approval process.

As per the amendment, the minimum capital requirement for the bank is the credit risk requirements plus the capital charge for market risk. The credit risk requirements include the credit counterparty risk on all over-the-counter derivatives in the trading or the banking books, and exclude the debt and equity securities in the trading books and all positions in commodities. The market can be calculated by either of the two methods or can be a mix of both.

Criticism and the Need for Change

After seven years of implementation and adoption by more than 100 nations, the Capital Adequacy Standard came to a point where a change had to be made. It was accused of setting inaccurate capital ratios that led to regulatory arbitrage and the international credit crunch. It was also accused of encouraging banks to move into higher risk assets and subsequently increasing the overall risk in the banking system. The major criticisms around the accord were as follows:

- It encouraged banks to engage in regulatory arbitrage. Since capital adequacy regulations require a certain amount of capital to be held as a cushion against each loan, there is a possibility that two loans of equal risk were to be assessed at different risk levels and thus placed in two different categories. In addition, if the risk weight assigned to one loan is far below its inherent risk, the bank places this asset with a higher yielding loan requiring the same or less regulatory capital. This may have actually provided an incentive for banks to take more risk.
- The minimum capital requirement is a crude measure of bank risk; it could lead banks to shift their portfolio toward lower quality claims within a risk bucket. Since the minimum capital requirement applies for all claims within a certain category, regardless of the quality and rating of the corporation, blue-chip multinationals are placed in the same risk category as a local restaurant.
- There is no ground for the 8 percent capital ratio in any financial model of capital adequacy. In addition, many countries have made special provisions to raise the 8 percent ratio either in specific cases or on a universal basis.
- The presumption that equity serves as a better cushion than debt is, to some extent, academic, because debt holders have more incentive than equity owners to ensure that banks act more prudently in their capacity as risk takers.
- The impossibility of leveling the playing fields because of the immense variance of regulations and market structure among nations.
- The existing framework does not take into consideration the operational risk that emerges from increasing electronic transactions and the emergence of new products.
- In the country risk, this calibration distinguished only between OECD and non-OECD countries, which is considered unjustifiably discriminatory (Mohamed 2002; Shaker 2002; Tarbert 2000; Benink and Wihlborg 2001; Davis 1999; Lopez 1999).

BASEL CAPITAL ACCORD II: 2004

In June 1999, the committee published the first consultative Basel II paper and received numerous substantial criticisms from the national regulators and the banking industry. The major criticisms to the revised accord were in regard to its complexity in terms of mathematical-statistical modeling, data warehousing, and organizational consequences. With the support of national regulators and the banking industry, the second consultative paper completed three qualitative impact studies. In January 2001, the committee issued a proposal for a new Basel capital accord, Consultative Document 2001, which once finalized, would replace the then-current 1988 capital accord. In April 2001, the committee initiated a Quantitative Impact Study (QIS) of banks to gather the data necessary to allow the committee to gauge the impact of the proposal for capital requirements. In June 2001, the committee released an update on its progress and highlighted several important ways in which it had agreed to modify parts of its earlier proposal—based, in part, on industry comments. In December 2001, the committee announced a revised approach to finalizing the new accord and the establishment of an accord implementation group. The committee received more than 250 comments on its January 2001 proposal. In November 2001, another study (QIS 2.5) was undertaken to gain industry feedback about potential modifications to the committee's proposals. In April 2003, the committee conducted three quantitative impact studies related to its proposal, which resulted in many valuable improvements to the original proposal (BCOBS 2001).

The fundamental objective of the committee's work to revise the 1988 accord has been to develop a framework that would further strengthen the soundness and stability of the international banking system, while maintaining sufficient consistency that ensured capital adequacy regulations would not be a significant source of competitive inequality among internationally active banks. It also aimed to promote the adoption of stronger risk management practices by the banking industry, and this is viewed as one of its major benefits. In developing the revised framework, the committee sought to arrive at the following:

- Significantly more risk-sensitive capital requirements that are conceptually sound and at the same time pay due regard to particular features of the present supervisory and accounting systems in individual member countries.
- Make greater use of assessments of risk provided by banks' internal systems as inputs to capital calculations.
- Provide a range of options for determining capital requirements for credit risk and operational risk to allow banks and supervisors to select approaches that are most appropriate for their operations and financial infrastructure.
- Adopt a more advanced approach to capital adequacy supervision that has the capacity to evolve with time in order to keep pace with market developments and advances in risk management practices.

- Review and monitor the definition of eligible capital.
- Continue to engage the banking industry in a discussion of prevailing risk management practices, including those practices aiming to produce quantified measures of risk and economic capital.

To achieve these goals, the committee set the new proposal to consist of three mutually reinforcing pillars, which together are expected to contribute to enhancing the safety and soundness of the financial system. The three pillars are (1) minimum capital requirements, (2) supervisory review processes, and (3) market discipline. The three pillars are a package; therefore, the revised accord cannot be considered fully implemented unless all three are in place. However, if in certain jurisdictions it is not possible to implement all three pillars fully, the committee recommends considering more intensive use of the other pillars. For example, supervisors can use the supervisory review process to encourage improvement in transparency in instances where supervisors do not have the authority to require certain disclosure. Such an arrangement, however, should be a temporary measure because a balanced implementation of all three pillars is the permanent solution.

The revised framework introduced important changes to the present accord. First, the OECD status approach that determines the risk charge for sovereigns and banks would be replaced by another approach based on external rating assessments. Moreover, there would be recognition that blue-chip multinationals may, subject to a prime rating, have a risk weight closer to that of investment grade banks (Davis 1999). Finally, though market risk would not change, the framework would enhance the treatment of credit risk and introduce capital charges for operational risk (Tiner and Kingsley 2001).

In June 2004, the new framework and the standards it contained were endorsed by the Central Bank Governors and heads of banking supervision of the G-10 countries. It set out the details of the agreed framework for measuring capital adequacy and the minimum standards to be achieved, which the national supervisory authorities represented in the committee would propose for adoption in their respective countries.

THE REVISED FRAMEWORK

The revised framework known as Basel II consists of four parts:

1. Part one, scope of application, details how capital requirements are to be applied within a banking group.
2. Part two is the first pillar, which details the calculation of the minimum capital requirements for credit risk, market risk, and operational risk.

3. Part three is the second pillar, which outlines expectations concerning the supervisory review process.
4. Part four is the third pillar, which outlines expectations concerning market discipline.

Scope of Application

As stated in the document, the framework will be applied on a consolidated basis to internationally active banks. This is the best means to preserve the integrity of capital in banks with subsidiaries by eliminating double gearing, which occurs when one entity holds regulatory capital issued by another entity within the same group, and the issuer is also allowed to count the capital in its balance sheet. The framework will include, on a fully consolidated basis, any holding company that is a parent entity within a banking group to ensure that it captures the risk of the whole banking group. A banking group is one that engages predominantly in banking activities, and in some countries, a banking group may be registered as a bank. The framework will also apply to all internationally active banks at every tier within a banking group—on a fully consolidated basis. In addition, as one of the principal objectives of supervision is the protection of depositors, it is essential to ensure that capital recognized in capital adequacy measures is readily available for those depositors. Accordingly, supervisors should test that individual banks are adequately capitalized on a stand-alone basis. To the greatest extent possible, all banking and other relevant financial activities conducted within a group containing an internationally active bank will be captured through consolidation. Significant minority investments, securities, and other financial entities, where control does not exist, will be excluded from the banking group's capital by deduction of the equity and other regulatory investments. Also, a bank that owns an insurance subsidiary bears the full entrepreneurial risks of the subsidiary and should recognize on a group-wide basis the risks in the whole group. Significant minority or majority investments in commercial entities that exceed certain materiality levels will be deducted from the bank's capital. Materiality level will be determined by national accounting standards and/or regulatory practice. The materiality level that will be applied in commercial entities for individual significant investments is 15 and 60 percent of the bank's capital for the aggregate of such investments (BCOBS 2004).

The Minimum Capital Requirements

The first pillar again establishes the requirements for the minimum capital to be held by banks, which are intended to serve as a baseline capital buffer against losses realized from the actualization of credit and accompanying risks. The new accord framework maintains the minimum requirement of 8 percent of capital-to-risk weighted assets, as set out in the 1988 accord. Under the new accord, the denominator of the minimum total capital ratio will consist of three parts: (1) the sum of all risk-weighted assets for credit risk, (2) the sum plus 12.5 times the sum of the capital charges for market risk, and (3) operational risk. For example, for a bank with $875 of risk-weighted assets, a market risk capital charge of $10, and an operational risk capital charge of $20, the denominator of the total capital ratio would equal:

$$\$875 + [(\$10 + \$20) \times 12.5)] = \$1,250$$

Capital adequacy ratio will be measured according to the following formula:

$$\text{Capital Ratio} = \frac{\text{Total Capital}}{\text{Credit Risk} + \text{Market Risk} + \text{Operational Risk}}$$

The numerator, which is the qualifying capital, will remain the same. The change will be in the denominator, which consists of the total weighted risk assets.

Pillar 1 covers regulatory capital requirements for market, credit, and operational risk. For credit and operational risk, there are ranges of options. Interest-rate risk is treated in Pillar 2.

Measuring Credit Risk   There are two approaches set to measure credit risk: (1) the standardized approach and (2) the Internal Rating-Based (IRB) approach.

The Standardized Approach   The standardized approach is conceptually the same as that used in the Basel I, but is more risk-sensitive. Under the standardized approach, the bank allocates a risk weight to each of its assets and off-balance sheet positions and produces a sum of risk-weighted asset values, while Basel I provides only one risk weighted category of 100 percent for corporate lending. Basel II provides four categories: 20, 50, 100, and 150 percent. The weights on banks' assets will depend on the external credit rating provided by commercial rating agencies, such as Moody's and Standard & Poor's. Highly rated corporate claims would receive a 20 percent weight, while low-rated corporate claims would receive 150 percent weight. Unrated claims would receive 100 percent, residential mortgage

50 percent, and customer loans 100 percent weight (Lopez 1999; Paglia and Phlegar 2001; Stevens 2000).

The Internal Rating-Based Approach (IRB) The Internal Rating-Based (IRB) approach is suitable for large, sophisticated banks that already use internal systems for evaluating the risk of individual credit exposure. Unlike the standardized approach, the IRB approach requires a bank to estimate each borrower's credit worthiness. For each exposure class (similar treatment for corporate, bank, and sovereign exposure, and a separate framework for retail, project, and equity exposure), the treatment is based on three main elements (1) risk components, (2) risk weight function, and (3) minimum requirements.

1. Risk components, where a bank may use either its own or standard supervisory estimates. The risk component is made up of (a) the Probability of Default (PD) associated with borrowers in each of the internal grades as per the bank's internal measures of credit risk, (b) Loss-Given Default (LGD), which is the amount per unit of exposure that bank expect to recover from the borrowers, (c) Exposure at Default (EAD), which is the bank exposure to the borrower at the time of default, and (d) Effective Maturity(M), which measures the effective maturity for each facility. There are two approaches for the estimation of LGD: (a) the foundation approach, and (b) the advanced approach. According to the foundation approach, the LGD value is set by supervisory rules. The rating must be based on mathematical-statistical methods and should predict the default probability of each debtor or transaction. Banks are allowed to adjust the risk weightings to less than 100 percent if the PD qualifies for such capital reduction. The standard weight of the remaining risk components is determined by the regulatory agencies. The advanced approach requires a detailed analysis of the facility-level risk factors such as collateral, covenants, and loan terms. Banks are to use the methods of the foundation approach to determine the PD. For the LGD and EAD risk components, however, banks are allowed to estimate based on individual data histories (Goodman and Becker 2003).

2. A risk-weight function that converts the risk component into risk weight to be used by banks in calculating risk-weight assets. IRB risk weight is expressed as a single continuous function of the PD, LGD, and in some cases, M of an exposure. This function provides a mechanism by which the risk components are converted into regulatory risk weights. It also allows for greater risk differentiation and accommodates the different rating grade structure of banking institutions.

3. A set of minimum requirements that a bank must meet to be eligible for IRB treatment. Banks must meet a full set of minimum requirements to be eligible for the IRB. The minimum requirements for the foundation approach address the following:
   - Meaningful differentiation of credit risk.
   - Completeness and integrity of rating assignment.
   - Criteria of rating system.
   - Estimation of PD.
   - Data collection and IT system.
   - Internal validation and disclosure.

For the advanced approach, banks must meet all the minimum requirements of the foundation approach, as well as additional minimum requirements for the relevant risk component that they are estimating. The committee has stated that its long-term aim is to develop a flexible framework that more accurately reflects the risk to which banks are exposed. The IRB approach is, therefore, the next logical step after the standardized approach.

Operational Risk   The framework defines operational risk as the risk of loss resulting from inadequate or failed internal processes, people and systems, or external events. This definition includes legal risk, but excludes strategic and reputation risk. Capital allocation against operational risk is one of the most debatable topics between regulators and bankers. There are three major problems with operational risk:

1. The definition of what it means is an issue, as it is difficult to explain where it begins and where it ends.
2. There is no wholly satisfactory methodology to assess operational risk. There are areas that need close managerial attention and understanding of the factors that appear to increase operational risk, such as unclear reporting lines, poor management information, geographical distance from the head office, and insufficient management strength.
3. There is the concern of double counting with elements of credit risk. For example, items such as losses resulting from poor credit documentation may be defined as operational risk (Stewart 2001).

The Supervisory Review Process

The Supervisory Review Process requires supervisors to ensure that each bank has sound internal systems in place to assess the adequacy of its capital based on a thorough evaluation of its risks. The framework stresses the importance of developing an internal capital assessment system and setting targets for capital that are commensurate with a bank's particular risk profile and control environment. This internal process would then be subject to supervisory review and intervention, where appropriate. In this regard, the committee has made it very clear that the framework is in no way intended to replace the judgment and expertise of bank management or to shift the responsibility of maintaining capital adequacy to supervisors. On the contrary, management has the most complete understanding of the risks its institution faces, and it has the ultimate responsibility for managing those risks. Moreover, capital should not be regarded as a substitute for addressing fundamental lack of control or inadequate risk management processes. There are three main areas that are treated under Pillar 2:

1. Risk considered under Pillar 1 but not fully captured, such as credit concentration risk and interest-rate risk in banking books.
2. The assessment of compliance with the minimum standards and disclosure requirements of the more advanced methods in Pillar 1.
3. Factors external to the bank, such as business cycle effects.

There are also four core principles for effective banking supervision:

1. Banks should have a process for assessing their overall capital adequacy in relation to their risk profile, as well as a strategy for maintaining their capital levels at an acceptable level. In order to have solid processes, each bank should have a board of directors and senior management oversight, sound capital assessment, comprehensive assessment of risks, monitoring and reporting, and internal control review.
2. Supervisors should review and evaluate banks' internal capital adequacy assessments and strategies, as well as their ability to monitor and ensure their compliance with regulatory capital ratios. Supervisors should take appropriate supervisory action if they are not satisfied with the results of this process. The periodical review needs to involve on-site examinations or inspections, off-site review, discussions with bank management, review of work done by external auditors, and periodic reporting.
3. Supervisors should expect banks to operate above the minimum regulatory capital ratios and should have the ability to require banks to hold capital in excess of the minimum.
4. Supervisors should seek to intervene at an early stage to prevent capital from falling below the minimum level required to support the risk characteristics of a particular bank and should require rapid remedial action if capital is not maintained or restored (BCOBS 2004).

Market Discipline

The purpose of Pillar 3 is to complement the Minimum Capital Requirements (Pillar 1) and the Supervisory Review Process (Pillar 2). The third pillar aims to strengthen market discipline through enhanced disclosure by banks. Effective disclosure is essential to ensure that market participants can better understand banks' risk profiles and the adequacy of their capital positions.

There are general considerations set by the committee, the first of which is achieving appropriate disclosure. Supervisors have the authority to require banks to provide information in the form of regulatory reports and to make all or part of it public. Also, in some cases, the disclosure is a qualifying criteria under Pillar 1 to obtain lower risk weightings and/or to apply a specific methodology.

The second consideration is that the disclosure framework should not conflict with requirements under accounting standards that are broader in scope.

Third, based on the materiality concept, each bank should decide which disclosure is relevant for its purposes. Information would be regarded as material if its omission or misstatement could change or influence the assessment or decision of a user relying on that information for the purpose of making an economic decision. This definition is consistent with the International Accounting Standards and with many national accounting frameworks.

Fourth, the disclosure set out in Pillar 3 should be made on a semi-annual basis, except for qualitative information providing a summary of the bank's risk management objectives and policies, which can be done annually, and information about the capital and tier one, which can be done on a quarterly basis.

Fifth, in a limited situation, where disclosure of information would undermine a bank's competitive advantage, banks may not need to disclose information (BCOBS 2004).

THREE METHODS FOR CALCULATING OPERATIONAL RISK

The framework presents three methods for calculating operational risk: (1) the basic Indicator Approach, (2) the Standardized Approach, and (3) the Advanced Measurement Approach. All banks are encouraged to use more sophisticated approaches to match their risk profiles. A bank will not be permitted to revert to a simpler approach once it has been approved for a more advanced approach unless supervisors determine that it is no longer required.

Basic Indicator Approach

According to this approach, banks must hold capital for operational risk equal to the average over the previous three years of a fixed percentage (donated alpha) of positive annual gross income. A figure for any year in which annual gross income is zero or negative should be excluded from both the numerator and denominator when calculating the average. Gross income is defined as net interest income plus net noninterest income. The charge may be expressed as follows:

$$K_{BIA} = \frac{[\Sigma(GI_{1...n} \times \alpha)]}{n}$$

where K_{BIA} = the capital charge under the Basic Indicator Approach

GI = annual gross income, where positive, over the previous three years

n = number of the previous three years for which gross income is positive

α = 15 percent, which is set by the committee, relating the industry wide level of required capital to the industry wide level of the indicator

The Standardized Approach

According to this approach, banks' activities are divided into eight business lines: (1) corporate finance, (2) trading and sales, (3) retail banking, (4) commercial banking, (5) payment and settlement, (6) agency services, (7) asset management, and (8) retail brokerage.

The capital charge for each business line is calculated by multiplying gross income by a factor (denoted beta) assigned to the business line. Beta serves as proxy for the industry-wide relationship between the operational risk loss experience for a given business line and the aggregate level of gross income for that business line. The total capital charge is calculated as the three-year average of the simple summation of the regulatory capital charge across each of the business lines in every year. The total capital charge may be expressed as follows:

$$K_{TSA} = \frac{\{\Sigma_{years\,1\text{-}3}\,\max[\Sigma(GI_{1\text{-}8} \times \beta_{1\text{-}8})o]\}}{3}$$

where K_{TSA} = the capital charge under the Basic Indicator Approach

$GI_{1\text{-}8}$ = annual gross income in a given year, as defined above in the Basic Indicator Approach, for each of the eight business lines

TABLE 8.1 Business Line and Beta Factor

Business Line	Beta Factor (%)
Corporate finance (β_1)	18
Trading and sales (β_2)	18
Retail banking (β^3)	12
Commercial banking (β_4)	15
Payment and settlement (β_5)	18
Agency services (β_6)	15
Asset management (β_7)	12
Retail brokerage (β_8)	12

Source: Basel Committee on Banking Supervision (2004).

$\beta_{1-8} =$ a fixed percentage, set by the committee, relating the level of required capital to the level of the gross income for each of the eight business lines

The values of the beta factors are detailed in Table 8.1.

The Advanced Measurement Approach (AMA)

In order to qualify for use of the Advanced Measurement Approach (AMA), a bank must assure its supervisors that at a minimum:

- Its board of directors and senior management are actively involved in the oversight of the operational risk-management framework.
- It has an operational risk-management system that is conceptually sound and is implemented with integrity.
- It has sufficient resources in the use of the approach in the major business lines as well as the control and audit areas.

A bank applying the AMA will be subject to a period of initial monitoring by its supervisors in order to determine whether the approach is credible and appropriate. The internal measurement system in the bank must reasonably estimate unexpected losses based on the combined use of internal and relevant external loss data, scenario analysis, bank-specific business environment, and internal control factors. The bank's measurement system must also be capable of supporting an allocation of economic capital for operational risk across business lines in a manner that creates incentives to improve business line operational risk management.

There are both qualitative and quantitative standards and risk mitigation for operational risk that need to be in place before it is permitted to use AMA. Qualitative standards include:

- An independent operational risk management function that is responsible for the design and implementation of the bank's operational risk-management framework.
- Close integration of the bank's internal operational risk management system into the day-to-day risk-management process of the bank.
- Regular reporting of operational risk exposure and loss experience to management in the business unit, senior management, and the board of directors.
- Good documentation of the bank's operational risk-management system.
- Regular reviews of the operational risk-management processes and measurement systems by internal and/or external auditors.
- Validation of the operational risk-measurement system by external auditors and/or the supervisory authority to verify that the internal validation processes are operating in a satisfactory manner, and the assurance that data flows and processes associated with the risk-measurement system are transparent and accessible.

Quantitative standards include:

- AMA soundness standard.
- Detailed criteria describing a series of quantitative standards that will apply to internally generated operational risk, as defined by the committee.
- Banks tracking internal loss data according to the criteria set out by the committee.
- Use of relevant external data by the bank's operational risk-management system, especially when there is reason to believe that the bank is exposed to infrequent, yet potentially severe losses.
- Bank's use of scenario analysis of experts in conjunction with external data to evaluate its exposure to high-severity events.
- A bank's firm-wide risk assessment methodology must capture key business environment and internal control factors that can change its operational risk profile (BCOBS 2004).

Under AMA, banks are allowed to recognize the risk-mitigating impact of insurance in the measures of operational risk used for regulatory minimum capital requirements. The recognition of insurance mitigation will be limited to 20 percent of the total operational risk capital charge calculated under

AMA. Partial use of the AMA is permitted for some of the bank's operations with the following conditions: First, all operational risk of the bank's global, consolidated operations must be captured. Second, all the bank's operations that are covered by AMA should meet the qualitative criteria for using AMA, while those parts of its operations that are using one of the simpler approaches should meet the qualifying criteria for that approach. Third, to provide the supervisor with a plan specifying the timetable to which it intends to roll out the AMA across all its operations.

SUMMARY

The Basel Committee on Banking Supervision was established by the Central Banks of the Group of Ten (G-10) countries as a result of the failure of two major international banks. The major objective of the committee was to close the gap in international supervisory coverage that was revealed as a result of these two incidents. In July 1988, the Basel agreement on risk-based capital was signed and came into effect with two main objectives: (1) to strengthen the soundness and stability of the international banking system and (2) to have a fair framework and high degree of consistency in its application to banks in different countries, with the aim of diminishing an existing source of competitive inequality among international banks. In 1996, the committee introduced market risk as an amendment to the accord. Accordingly, banks were required to measure and apply capital charges with respect to their market risks in addition to their credit risk. Market risk was again amended in November 2005.

The major two criticisms of the accord were that (1) it provided banks with incentive to take more risk because the same amount of regulatory capital is assigned to all different asset categories regardless of the level of risk associated with each asset category, and (2) operational risk was not included in the accord.

The revised framework (referred to as Basel II) came into effect in 2004, after extensive work that started in June 1999. The major objectives were to further strengthen the soundness and stability of the international banking system, while maintaining sufficient consistency among internationally active banks that capital adequacy regulations would not be a significant source of competitive inequality. It also aimed to promote the adoption of stronger risk management practices by the banking industry, and this is viewed as one of its major benefits. The revised framework introduced three pillars: (1) the minimum capital requirement, (2) the supervisory review process, and (3) market discipline. It has also introduced operational risk, along with the credit and market risk in the denominator of the CAR formula.

CHAPTER 9

The Regulatory Framework of Islamic Banks

The capital adequacy framework for Islamic financial institutions consists of three pillars similar to Basel II: (1) the minimum capital requirement, (2) the supervisory review process, and (3) market discipline. Unlike Basel II, where the three pillars are laid down in one document, the Islamic Financial Services Board (IFSB) released the three pillars in three separate standards. The first pillar, representing the minimum capital requirement, was issued in December 2005 in a document called Capital Adequacy Standard, which is our discussion in this chapter. The second and third pillars, representing the supervisory review process and market discipline, were both released in December 2007, and they will be discussed in Chapters 10 and 11, respectively.

This chapter first sheds some light on the background of the capital adequacy framework for Islamic financial institutions. The framework for the Capital Adequacy Standard, which represents Pillar 1 and is issued by the Islamic Financial Services Board, is presented first. We then examine the definition and role of capital in Islamic banking, as well as the differences between Islamic and conventional banks. Finally, the chapter looks closely at the calculation of capital adequacy ratio and the requirements for each of the Islamic instruments.

BACKGROUND

The Islamic Financial Services Board (IFSB), which is based in Kuala Lumpur, was officially inaugurated on November 3, 2002, and started operations on March 10, 2003. It serves as an international standard-setting body of regulatory and supervisory agencies that have vested interest in ensuring the soundness and stability of the Islamic financial services industry, which includes banking, capital market, and insurance. The IFSB promotes the development of a prudent and transparent Islamic financial services industry through introducing new and adopting existent international standards consistent with Islamic shari'ah principles and recommending them to be put into practice. The work of the IFSB complements that of the Basel Committee on Banking Supervision, the International Organization of Securities Commissions, and the International Association of Insurance Supervisors. The IFSB has 164 members, out of which 14 are regulatory and supervisory authorities, and that is in addition to the International Monetary Fund, World Bank, Bank for International Settlements, Islamic Development Bank, Asian Development Bank, Islamic Corporation for the Development of the Private Sector, and 117 market players and professional firms operating in 33 jurisdictions. Malaysia, the host country of the IFSB, enacted the Islamic Financial Services Board Act of 2002, which gives the IFSB the immunities and privileges that are usually granted to international organizations and diplomatic missions (IFSB www.ifsb.org).

Thus far, the IFSB has issued seven standards, principles, and technical notes for the Islamic financial services industry, focusing on risk management, capital adequacy, corporate governance, the supervisory review process, transparency and market discipline, recognition of ratings on shari'ah-compliant financial instruments, the shari'ah governance system, as well as the development of Islamic money markets. The IFSB is also working on four new standards and guidelines, namely (1) special issues on capital adequacy, (2) governance of investment funds, (3) corporate governance in *takaful* operations, and (4) conduct of business. The standards prepared by the IFSB follow a lengthy due process as outlined in its Guidelines and Procedures for the Preparation of Standards/Guidelines, which involves, among other things, the issuance of exposure draft, and where necessary, the holding of a public hearing. The IFSB is also involved in the promotion of awareness of issues that are relevant to or have an impact on the regulation and supervision of the Islamic financial services industry through international conferences, seminars, workshops, training sessions, meetings, and dialogue staged in many countries (IFSB www.ifsb.org).

THE CAPITAL ADEQUACY STANDARD (CAS)

The Islamic Financial Services Board has issued the Capital Adequacy Standard (CAS; or The Standard) for institutions (other than insurance institutions) offering only Islamic financial services (IIFS). The term IIFS refers to financial institutions that mobilize funds as deposits and investment accounts in accordance with shari'ah rules and principles, as well as invest them in accordance with shari'ah-compliant investment and financing instruments. The objective of the standard, as stated in the IFSB document, are (1) to address the specific structure and contents of the shari'ah-compliant products and services offered by the IIFS that are not specifically addressed by the currently adopted and proposed international Capital Adequacy Standard and shari'ah-compliant mitigation, and (2) to standardize the approach indemnifying and measuring risk weight (RW), thereby creating a level playing field amongst the IIFS in adopting and developing risk identification and measurement practices that meet internationally acceptable prudential standards.

The CAS is mainly based on the documents of the Basel Committee on Banking Supervision: "International Convergence of Capital Measurements and Capital Standards: A Revised Framework, June 2004 (Basel II)," and "Amendment to the Capital Accord to Incorporate Market Risk, January 1996," with the necessary modifications and adaptations to cater for the specificities and characteristics of the shari'ah-compliant products and services offered by the IIFS. The Standard covers minimum capital adequacy requirements based on the Standardized Approach with respect to credit risk and the Basic Indicator Approach for operational risk of the IIFS, regarding Pillar 1 of Basel II and the various applicable measurement methods for market risk set out in the 1996 market risk amendment. It does not address the requirements covered by Pillar 2, the supervisory review process, and Pillar 3, market discipline, of Basel II, as these issues are covered by separate standards (IFSB 2005a).

The Standard has been endorsed by the Shari'ah Advisory Committee of the Islamic Development Bank and co-opted by shari'ah scholars representing central banks and monetary agencies, which were members of the IIFS in December 2005. The shari'ah rules and principles set in The Standard do not represent an exhaustive list of diverse practices among the various IIFS, and compliance with the principles stated does not imply the IFSB consented that the products and services they offer are in accordance with shari'ah principles. The IIFS need to adopt the requirements set by their supervisory authorities and shari'ah boards to ensure that their activities are in compliance with shari'ah rules and principles.

Scope of Application

The Standard will be applied to (1) institutions offering only Islamic financial services excluding insurance institutions, (2) Islamic "window" operations that are self-contained or other institutions offering Islamic financial services that fall within their jurisdiction at the description of the supervisory authority, (3) the risk weighting methodology may be extended to shari'ah-compliant financing assets held by Islamic window operations that are not self-contained, or by other institutions holding such assets, and (4) any IIFS on a consolidated basis at the holding company level within a group or subgroup of IIFS or on an individual basis subject to the approval of the supervisory authorities. The Standard will not be applied at the consolidated level to a group or subgroup that consists of entities other than IIFS (IFSB 2005a).

Specificities of Islamic Financial Instruments

Islamic financial instruments are asset-based (murabahah, salam, and istisna, which are based on the sale or purchase of an asset, and ijarah, which is based on selling the benefits of such assets), profit-sharing (musharakah and mudarabah), or sukok (securities) and investment portfolios and funds, which may be based on the above assets. The IIFS gross return refers to the spread between the cost of the asset and the amount that can be recovered from selling or leasing it. Such instruments may involve exposure to market (price) risk with respect to the asset, as well as credit risk with respect to the amount due from the counterparty. In the case of profit-sharing instruments, the exposure is of the nature of an equity position held for trading and is similar to an equity position in the banking books as described in Basel II. It is dealt with under credit risk, except in the case of investment in assets for trading purposes, which is dealt with under market risk.

A Matrix Structure

The capital adequacy requirements are based on the principle that the level of the bank's capital should be related to the bank's specific risk profile. The determination of the capital adequacy requirements is based on the component of risk, namely credit, market, and operational risk. The Islamic banks' characteristic of mobilizing funds in the form of risk-sharing investment accounts, together with the materiality of financing transactions, impacts the overall risk of the balance sheet and, subsequently, assessment of the capital requirements.

The CAS is structured in a matrix format so that the minimum capital adequacy requirements regarding both the credit and market risk exposures arising from a given type of financial instrument are dealt with under the heading of that instrument. It is divided into seven sections, C1 to C7, where the minimum capital adequacy requirements for both credit and market risks are set for each of the shari'ah-compliant financing and investment instruments.

C1: *Murabahah* and *Murabahah* for the Purchase Orderer

C2: *Salam* and Parallel *Salam*

C3: *Istisna* and Parallel *Istisna*

C4: *Ijarah* and *Ijarah Muntahia Bittamleek*

C5: *Musharakah* and Diminishing *Musharakah*

C6: *Mudarabah*

C7: *Sukuk* held as investment

The provisions for operational risk and the treatment of Profit Sharing Investment Accounts are set separately.

THE DEFINITION AND ROLE OF CAPITAL

The definition of what constitutes capital has long been an issue of debate. There is wide acceptance, however, of the capital structure that has been set by the Basel Committee, where capital is segregated into three tiers:

Tier one: Core capital consists of (1) ordinary paid-up share capital/ common stock, (2) disclosed reserves from post-tax retained earnings, and (3) noncumulative perpetual preferred stock (goodwill is to be deducted).

Tier two: Supplementary capital consists of (1) undisclosed reserves, (2) asset revaluation reserves, (3) general provisions/general loan-loss provisions, (4) hybrid debt/equity capital instruments, and (5) subordinated term debts.

Tier three: consists of short-term subordinated debt that meets the following criteria (1) unsecured, subordinated and fully paid up, (2) an original maturity of at least two years and not to be repayable before the agreed repayment date unless the supervisory authority agrees, and (3) a lock-in clause stipulating that neither interest nor principal amounts can be paid, even at maturity, if capital will fall or remain below the minimum capital requirements.

It should be noted that eligible tier two should not exceed total tier one capital, and subordinated debt should not exceed 50 percent of tier one

TABLE 9.1 Classification of Capital in Islamic Banking for Capital Adequacy Calculation

Classification	Content
Tier One, Core Capital	Ordinary paid-up share capital/common stocks, disclosed reserves from post-tax retained earnings, shareholders' portion of the Profit Equalization Reserve (PER), which is included in the disclosed reserves
Tier Two, Supplementary Capital	Undisclosed reserves, asset revaluation reserves, general provisions/general loan-loss provisions
Tier Three	Short-term debt conditioned to unsecured, subordinated and fully paid up, with an original maturity of at least two years and not to be repayable before the agreed repayment date unless the supervisory authority agrees including a lock-in clause

capital. Also, tier three will be limited to 250 percent of the bank's tier one capital, which is required to support market risks (IFSB 2005a).

The definition of capital in Islamic banks (as shown in Table 9.1) is similar to that in Basel II except for the following factors:

Tier one: The reserves include the shareholders' portion of the Profit Equalization Reserve (PER), which is included in the disclosed reserves. The share of the investment account holder in the PER and the whole of the Investment Risk Reserve (IRR) (none of which is attributed to the shareholders) are excluded from capital. They are taken in the measurement of the amount of risk-weighted assets attributed to the investment account holders.

Tier two: There are no hybrid capital instruments or subordinated debts, as these would bear interest and contradict shari'ah principles. Also, the AAOIFI committee on capital adequacy concluded that PSIA are not to be included in tier two (IFSB2005).

The IFSB has set the minimum capital adequacy requirement for IIFS at a rate not lower than 8 percent of the total capital.

DETERMINATION OF RISK WEIGHTS

The nature of risk in Islamic banks differs from conventional banks because of the different nature of assets between the two. Whereas the assets in conventional banks are based on debts, the assets in Islamic banks range from trade finance to equity partnership. Therefore, some of the Islamic banks' instruments carry additional risks that are not a factor in conventional banks.

Subsequently, according to Greuning and Iqbal (2008), the calculation of risk weights is different for Islamic banks than for conventional banks because:

- Assets based on trade are not truly financial assets and carry risks other than credit and market risk.
- Nonfinancial assets such as real estate, commodities, and ijarah and istisna contracts have special risk characteristics.
- Islamic banks carry partnership and profit and loss-sharing assets that have a higher risk profile.
- Islamic banks do not have well-defined instruments to mitigate and hedge risk, such as derivatives, which raises the overall risk of assets.

There are two formulas applied for the calculation of the capital adequacy requirements. The Standard Formula, where eligible capital is divided by total risk-weighted assets (credit and market risk) plus operational risk excluding the risk-weighted assets funded by PSIA (credit and market risk). The risk-weighted assets are determined for credit risk and adjusted for operational and market risk by multiplying by 12.5. The Supervisory Discretion Formula is modified to accommodate the existence of reserves maintained by Islamic banks to minimize displaced commercial, withdrawal, and systemic risks. In this formula, the risk-weighted assets funded by unrestricted PSIA and the risk-weighted assets funded by PER and IRR of unrestricted PSIA are excluded.

In countries where Islamic banks maintain Profit Equalization Reserve (PER) and Investment Risk Reserve (IRR), the supervisory authority has the discretion to apply three options. The first is to adjust the denominator of the Capital Adequacy Requirements (CAR) formula as it deems appropriate. The second is to include a specified percentage of assets financed by the investment account holders in the denominator of the CAR. And the third is to deduct a certain fraction of the weighted assets financed by PER and IRR from the denominator, as these reserves reduce the displaced commercial risk.

The IFSB Standard Formula is:

$$\frac{\text{Eligible Capital}}{[\text{Total Risk-Weighted Assets (Credit and Market Risks)} + \text{Operational Risks}] - \text{Total Risk-Weighted Assets funded by PSIA}}$$

Notes:

Risk weighting includes those financed by restricted and unrestricted PSIA.

Profit-sharing investment account balances include PER and IRR.

Credit and market risks apply to on-and off-balance sheet exposure.

The IFSB Supervisory Discretion Formula is:

$$\frac{\text{Eligible Capital}}{\begin{array}{c}[\text{Total Risk-Weighted Assets (Credit + Market Risks) + Operational} \\ \text{Risks}] - [\text{Risk-weighted assets funded by Restricted PSIA (credit and} \\ \text{market risk)} + (1\text{-\&}) \text{ risk-weighted assets funded by unrestricted} \\ \text{PSIA (credit \& market risk)} + \text{\& Risk-weighted assets funded by} \\ \text{PER and IRR of unrestricted PSIA (credit and market risk)}]\end{array}}$$

Notes:

Risk weighting includes those financed by restricted and unrestricted PSIA.

Profit-sharing investment account balances include PER and IRR.

Credit and market risks apply to on-and off-balance sheet exposure and refers to the portion assets funded by unrestricted PSIA, which is to be determined by the supervisory authority.

CREDIT RISK

Credit risk exposure in Islamic financing arises in connection with accounts receivable in murabahah contracts, counterparty risk in salam contracts, accounts receivable and counterparty risk in istisna contracts, lease payments receivable in ijarah contracts, and sukok held to maturity in the banking books. Credit risk is measured according to the standardized approach of Basel II except for exposure arising from investments by means of musharakah or mudarabah contracts in assets in the banking book. Such contracts are exposed to credit risk in the form of capital impairment risk, and risk weights are assigned using the methods proposed by Basel II for equity exposure in the banking book or at the supervisor's discretion using the slotting criteria for specialized financing. The assignment of risk weights takes the following into consideration:

- The credit risk rating of a debtor, counterparty, or other obligor or a security based on external credit assessments. The supervisory authority

will assign External Credit Assessment Institutions (ECAI) to be used in assigning credit ratings for the purpose of calculating credit risk weights.
- The credit risk mitigation techniques used by the IIFS.
- The types of underlying assets that are sold/collateralized or leased by the IIFS.
- Amount of specific provisions made for the overdue portion of accounts receivable or lease payments receivable.

Credit Risk Mitigation (CRM)

The exposure in respect of a debtor, counterparty, or obligor can be adjusted or reduced by taking into account the credit risk mitigation techniques that are used by the IIFS. The most common techniques are:

- *Hamish Jiddiyyah* (HJ), a refundable security deposit taken by the IIFS prior to establishing the contract. It carries a limited recourse to the extent of damages incurred by the IIFS when the purchase orderer fails to honor a binding Promise to Purchase (PP) or Promise to Lease (PL). The IIFS have recourse to the clients in the PP/PL if the HJ is insufficient to cover the damages. In the case of nonbinding PP/PL, the HJ will be refunded to the client and will, therefore, not be considered as CRM.
- *Urboun* is earned money held after a contract is established as collateral to guarantee contract performance. It is for the benefit of the IIFS if the purchaser or lessee breaches the contract within the agreed terms.
- Guarantee from a third party, which can be for a fixed period and for a limited amount, without any consideration being received by the guarantor.
- Pledge of assets as collateral, which should be a shari'ah-compliant asset of monetary value that can be lawfully owned and is saleable, specifiable, deliverable, and free of encumbrance. The pledge must be legally enforceable.
- Leased assets under ijarah or IMB contracts fulfill a function similar to that of collateral that may be repossessed by the lessor in case of default by the lessee (IFSB 2005a).

Market Risk

Market risk is defined as the risk of losses in on-and-off balance sheet positions arising from movements in market prices. There are three types of risks in IIFS that are subject to market risk capital requirements:

The first type is the equity position risk in the trading book and market risk on trading positions in sukok. The capital charge for securities in the

IIFS trading book consists of two elements that are calculated separately for the following types of risk:

- Specific risk, which is 8 percent on all long-equity positions and must be calculated on a market-by-market basis. The capital charge can be reduced to 4 percent for a liquid and well-diversified portfolio subject to meeting the supervisory authority requirements.
- General market risk, which is 8 percent on all long-equity positions and must be calculated on a market-to-market basis.
- Specific risk in case of sukok in the trading book and will depend on the RW of the issue and the term to maturity of the sukok.

The second type of risk in IIFS that is subject to market risk capital requirements is the foreign exchange risk, where the capital charge to cover the risk of holding or taking long positions in foreign currencies and gold and silver is calculated in two steps: (1) measuring the exposure in a single currency position, and (2) measuring the risk inherent in an IIFS portfolio mix of long and short positions in different currencies.

The third type of risk in IIFS that is subject to market risk capital requirements is the commodities and inventory risk, which can be measured using the Maturity Ladder Approach or the Simplified Approach for the purpose of calculating the capital charge. In both approaches, each commodity position is expressed in terms of the standard unit of quantitative measurement of weight or volume. The net position in each commodity will then be converted at current spot rates into the reporting currency (IFSB 2005a).

Operational Risk

Operational risk as defined in The Standard is the risk of losses resulting from inadequate or failed internal processes, people, and systems or from external events, which include but are not limited to, legal risk and shari'ah-compliance risk. This definition does not include strategic and reputation risk. The measurement of capital to cater for operational risk in the IIFS may be based on either: (1) the Basic Indicator Approach set out in Basel II, where a fixed percentage of 15 percent of the annual average gross income over the previous three years is set aside, or (2) the Standardized Approach set out in Basel II, where the percentage varies according to the line of business from 12 to 18 percent, being 18 percent for corporate finance, trading and sales, and payment and settlement; 15 percent for commercial banking and agency services; and 12 percent for retail banking, asset management, and retail brokerage. Gross income is defined as: (1) net income from financing activities, which is gross of any provisions and operating expenses and of depreciation of ijarah assets, (2) net income from investment activities, and (3) fee income less than investment account holders' share of income. Shari'ah-compliance risk is a type of operational risk facing the IIFS that may lead to non-recognition of income. Following are some of the shari'ah requirements to be complied with by the IIFS with respect to financing contracts (IFSB 2005a).

Murabahah and ijarah contracts:

- The asset is in existence at the time of sale or lease, or the lease contract is preceded by acquisition of the usufruct of that asset in case of ijarah.
- The asset is legally owned by the IIFS when it is offered for sale.
- The asset is to be used by the buyer/lessee for activities or business permissible by shari'ah.
- There is no late payment, penalty fee, or increase in price in exchange for extending or rescheduling the date of payment of accounts receivable or lease receivable, irrespective of whether the debtor is solvent or insolvent.

Salam and istisna contracts:

- The sale and purchase contracts cannot be interdependent or inter-conditional on each other.
- There is no penalty clause for a delay in the delivery of a commodity that is purchased under salam; however, it is allowed in istisna and parallel istisna.
- The subject of an istisna contract may not physically exist upon entering into the contract.

Musharakah and mudarabah contracts:

- The capital of the IIFS is to be invested in shari'ah-compliant investments or business activities.
- A partner in musharakah cannot guarantee the capital of another partner, or a mudarib guarantee the capital of the mudarabah.
- The purchase price of another partner's share in a musharakah with a binding promise to purchase can only be set as per the market value or as per the agreement at the date of buying. It is not permissible to stipulate that the share be acquired at its face value.

The IIFS are not required to set aside an additional amount over and above the 15 percent; as such, risk cannot be ascertained owing to lack of data. The supervisory authority, however, has the discretion to impose a higher percentage as it deems necessary (IFSB 2005a).

Profit Sharing Investment Accounts (PSIA)

Profit Sharing Investment Accounts (PSIA) are a pool of investment funds with the IIFS on the basis of mudarabah, where they are managed under the *Wakalah* contract. Those contracts are based on the profit sharing and loss bearing arrangements. There are two PSIA categories: (1) unrestricted, where the IIFS have the full discretion to make the investment decision, and (2) restricted, where the investment is subject to specific criteria specified in the contract or agreed upon between the Investment Account Holder (IAH) and the IIFS. The capital amount of the PSIA is not guaranteed by the IIFS, and any losses arising from the investment or asset financed by the PSIA funds are to be borne by the IAH, except for cases where there is negligence or misconduct. Subsequently, such assets do not carry risk for IIFS' own capital and, therefore, would not require regulatory capital. This means that assets funded by either restricted or unrestricted PSIA would be excluded from the calculation of the denominator of the capital ratio. The operational risk implied in such contracts, however, will be taken care of in the calculation of operational risk. The PSIA carries a unique risk called *displaced commercial risk*.

This risk arises when the IIFS tend to increase the rate of return to investment account holders as an incentive to keep their funds in the institution on the expense of its share of profit as mudarib. The rate of return to the client is smoothed at the expense of profit attributable to the shareholders. This occurs when a bank underperforms during a period and is unable to generate adequate profit for distribution to the account holders. There are two types of reserves to minimize the adverse impact of income:

1. The Profit Equalization Reserve (PER), which is funded by setting aside a portion of gross income before deducting the bank's own share as agent. The reserve provides a cushion to ensure smooth future returns and to increase the owner's equity for bearing future shocks.
2. The Investment Risk Reserve (IRR), which comes out of the income of the investors-depositors after allocating the bank's share to offset the risk of future investment losses. Of course, the basis of computing such reserves should be predefined and fully disclosed.

MINIMUM CAPITAL REQUIREMENTS FOR ISLAMIC FINANCING ASSETS

This section discusses the foundations and rules set by the IFSB to determine the minimum capital adequacy requirements for Islamic financing assets to cover credit and market risk. The instruments we will discuss are murabaha and murabahah for the purchase orderer, salam and parallel salam, istisna and parallel istisna, ijarah and ijarah muntahia bittamleek, musharakah and diminishing musharakah, mudarabah and sukok.

Murabahah and Murabahah for the Purchase Orderer (MPO)

The IFSB defined a murabahah contract to be an agreement whereby the IIFS sell to a customer at acquisition cost (purchase price plus other direct costs), in addition to an agreed profit margin—a specified kind of asset that is already in their possession. Murabahah for the Purchase Orderer (MPO) is a contract that refers to an agreement whereby the IIFS sell to a customer at cost, plus an agreed profit margin—a specified kind of asset that has been purchased and acquired by the IIFS based on a Promise to Purchase (PP) by the customer. This promise can be a binding or nonbinding PP (IFSB 2005a).

Murabahah and Non-Binding MPO   The credit exposure will be measured based on the accounts receivable, which is recorded at their cash equivalent value. The accounts receivable will be assigned risk weight (RW) based on the credit standing to the obligor (purchaser or guarantor) as rated by an ECAI, which is approved by the supervisory authority. In case the obligor is not rated, then 100 RW will be assigned.

As for the market risk, the asset will be treated as inventory and will be applicable to a 15 percent capital charge (15 percent of the amount of the position).

Binding MPO   In the case of binding MPO, the IIFS are exposed to default on the purchase orderer's obligation to purchase the commodity in their possession. In this case, the IIFS will recourse the HJ paid by the customer and will dispose the asset to a third party. If the IIFS has the legal right to recoup from the orderer any loss on disposing of the asset after taking the HJ, then the claim receivable will be exposed to credit risk, which will be measured as the amount of the asset's total acquisition cost minus the market value of the asset and minus the amount of HJ. If the IIFS have no right, then they will be exposed to market risk, which is mitigated by the HJ (IFSB 2005a). In this case, the IIFS is only exposed to credit risk and no market risk.

Salam and Parallel Salam

The IFSB defined a salam contract to be an agreement to purchase at a predetermined price a specified kind of commodity that is to be delivered on a specified future date in a specified quantity and quality. As the buyer, the IIFS make full payment of the purchase price upon execution of a salam contract or within a period not exceeding two or three days as deemed permissible by the Shari'ah Supervisory Board (SSB).

Parallel salam occurs when the IIFS enter into a back-to-back contract to sell a commodity with the same specification as a purchased commodity under a salam contract to a party other than the original seller. In this case, the IIFS are protected from having to take delivery of the commodity and warehousing, and they also hedge the price risk of the original salam contract. The two contracts, salam and parallel salam, are not interconditional or interdependent, which means that there is no legal basis for offsetting credit exposure between the two contracts.

The credit risk weight will be assigned based on the credit standing of a seller or counterparty, as rated by an ECAI to the receivable amount generated from the purchase of a commodity based on a salam contract. The RW is to be applied from the date of the contract made between both parties until the maturity of the salam contract, which is upon receipt of the purchased commodity. The capital requirement is to be calculated on the receivable net of specific provisions of any amount that is secured by eligible collateral or any amount that is past due by more than 90 days.

The market risk or price risk on the commodity exposure in salam can be measured by either the Maturity Ladder Approach or the Simplified Approach, where there is a capital charge of 15 percent of the net position in each commodity, plus an additional 3 percent toward the potential losses in parallel salam if the seller in the original salam fails to deliver and IIFS have to purchase an appropriate commodity in the spot market.

Istisna and Parallel Istisna

The IFSB defined an istisna contract to be an agreement to sell or buy from a customer a nonexistent asset, which is to be manufactured or built according to the ultimate buyer's specifications and is to be delivered on a specified future date at a predetermined selling price. As the seller, the IIFS have the option to manufacture or build the asset on their own or to engage the services of a party other than the ultimate buyer by entering into a parallel istisna contract. There are two main categories of istisna:

1. Full-recourse istisna, where the receipt of the selling price by the IIFS depends on the financial strength or the payment capability of the customer. The source of repayment is derived from various other customer activities and does not depend solely on the cash flows from the underlying asset.

2. Limited and nonrecourse istisna, where the receipt of the selling price by the IIFS depends partially or primarily on the revenue generated by the subject asset. In this case, the IIFS face revenue risk arising from the asset's ability to generate cash flow, instead of the credit worthiness of the customer. The two contracts, istisna and parallel istisna, are not interconditional or interdependent, which means that there is no legal basis for offsetting credit exposure between the two contracts.

Credit risk weight will be assigned according to the category of the contract. In the full-recourse istisna, the receivable amount generated from the selling of an asset will be assigned RW based on the credit standing of the customer as rated by the ECAI that is approved by the supervisory authority. In the limited and nonrecourse istisna: If the project is rated by the ECAI, then the RW will be based on the rating of the buyer. If not, then the RW will be based on the supervisory slotting criteria approach for project finance. The capital requirement is to be calculated on the receivable net of specific provisions of any amount that is secured by eligible collateral or any amount that is past due by more than 90 days.

There is no capital charge for market risk in the case of istisna and parallel istisna with full-recourse istisna. As for istisna without parallel istisna, there will be a capital charge of 1.6 percent, which is equivalent to 20 percent RW on the balance of unbilled Work-in-Process (WIP) inventory.

Ijarah and Ijarah Muntahia Bittamleek (IMB)

An ijarah contract refers to an agreement made by the IIFS to lease to a customer an asset specified by the customer for an agreed period against specified installments of lease rental. It commences with a promise to lease that is binding on the part of the potential lessee prior to entering the contract. An ijarah muntahia bittamleek or ijarah wa iqtina is a form of lease contract that offers the lessee the option to own the asset at the end of the lease period either by purchase of the asset through a token consideration or payment of the market value, or by means of a gift contract. The IIFS as a lessor in an ijarah contract, both operating and IMB, maintain their ownership in the leased asset while transferring the right to use or usufruct to an enterprise as the lessee for an agreed period at agreed terms and conditions. All liabilities and risks pertaining to the leased asset are to be borne by the IIFS, including obligations to restore any impairment and damage to the leased asset, which is not due to the misconduct or negligence of the lessee.

In both contracts, ijarah and ijarah muntahia bittamleek, the IIFS are exposed to credit risk regarding the estimated value of the lease payments with respect to the remaining period of the ijarah. This exposure is mitigated by the market value of the leased asset, which may be repossessed. The net credit risk exposure will be assigned RW based on the credit standing of the lessee or counterparty as rated by an ECAI. The capital requirement is to be calculated on the receivable net of specific provisions of any amount that is secured by eligible collateral or any amount that is past due by more than 90 days. The supervisory authority has the discretion to apply preferential RW for certain types of leased assets, such as real estate, as they deem appropriate (IFSB 2005a).

The capital charge to cater for market risk with respect to the leased asset from the acquisition date until the disposal can be categorized as nonbinding PL or binding PL. With nonbinding PL, assets are considered as inventory and the capital charge will be 155 of the amount of the asset's market value as per the Simplified Approach. In the case of binding PL, the IIFS are exposed to default on the lessee orderer obligation to lease the asset in their possession. In this case, the IIFS will recourse the HJ paid by the customer and will dispose the asset to a third party. If the IIFS have the legal right to recoup from the orderer any loss on disposing of the asset after taking the HJ, then the claim receivable will be exposed to credit risk, which will be measured as the amount of the asset total acquisition cost minus the market value of the asset and minus the amount of HJ. If IIFS have no right, then they will be exposed to market risk, which is mitigated by the HJ (IFSB 2005a).

Musharakah and Diminishing Musharakah

The IFSB defined a musharakah contract to be an agreement between the IIFS and a customer to contribute capital in various proportions to an enterprise, whether existing or new, or to ownership of a real estate or moveable asset either in a permanent basis or on a diminishing basis, where the customer progressively buys out the share of the IIFS (diminishing musharakah). Profit generated by that enterprise or real estate/asset is shared in accordance with the terms of the musharakah agreement, while losses are shared in proportion to the respective contributor's share capital. The IIFS are exposed either to capital impairment risk or to credit risk, depending on the structure and purpose of the musharakah and the type of asset in which the funds are invested.

In order to determine the minimum capital adequacy requirements, the IFSB has divided musharakah into three main categories:

First is the private commercial enterprise to undertake trading activities in foreign exchange, shares, and commodities. This type exposes the IIFS to foreign exchange, equities, or commodity risk. The investment in foreign exchange will require an 8 percent capital charge on the greater of either net-long or net-short position and an 8 percent capital charge on the net position of gold/silver. The investment in quoted shares will require a total capital charge of 16 percent, which can be reduced to 12 percent for a well-diversified portfolio and subject to meet the criteria determined by the supervisory authority. Investment in commodities will be measured by the Maturity Ladder Approach or the Simplified Approach.

Second is the private commercial enterprise to undertake a business venture other than that stated in the first type. This type of musharakah exposes the IIFS to the risk as an equity holder, which is similar to the risk assumed by a partner in venture capital, but not to market risk. The IIFS, as equity investors, serve as the first loss position, and their rights and entitlements are subordinated to the claims of secured and unsecured creditors. There are two methods to calculate the equity exposure:

1. **Simple Risk Weight Method:** The RW will apply to the exposure net of specific provisions based on equity exposures in the banking books.
2. **Slotting Method:** The IIFS are required to map their RW into four supervisory authorities and to assign RW accordingly.

The third is the joint ownership of real estate or movable assets, which is divided into two subcategories:

1. Musharakah with ijarah subcontract, where rental income is generated through the lessee of the asset to a third party by means of an ijarah contract. In this case, the IIFS are exposed to credit risk, which is mitigated by the collateral represented by the leased assets. In case the lessee is the IIFS partner, then there is exposure to credit risk with respect to the partner's obligation to service the rent. RW will be based on the credit standing of the counterparty or lessee, as rated by the ECAI.
2. Musharakah with murabahah subcontract, where the IIFS are entitled to their share of revenue from selling the assets to a third party. In this case, the IIFS will be exposed to credit risk in respect of the murabahah receivable from the buyer or counterparty. RW will be based on the credit standing of the counterparty or lessee as rated by the ECAI (IFSB 2005a).

Mudarabah

The IFSB defines mudarabah as an agreement between the IIFS and a customer, whereby the IIFS would contribute capital to an enterprise or activity that is to be managed by the customer as the mudarib. Profit generated by the enterprise or activity is shared in accordance with the terms of mudarabah agreement, while losses are to be borne solely by the IIFS unless the losses are due to the mudarib's misconduct, negligence, or breach of contractual terms. Mudarabah financing can be either restricted, where the IIFS as capital providers allow the mudarib to make investments according to specific restrictions, or unrestricted, where the IIFS allow the mudarib to invest freely based on his skills and experience (IFSB 2005a).

In order to determine the minimum capital adequacy requirements, the IFSB has divided mudarabah into three main categories:

The first category is private commercial enterprise to undertake trading activities in foreign exchange, shares, and commodities. This type exposes the IIFS to foreign exchange, equities, or commodity risk. The investment in foreign exchange will require an 8 percent capital charge on the greater of either net-long or net-short position and an 8 percent capital charge on the net position of gold/silver. The investment in quoted shares will require a total capital charge of 16 percent, which can be reduced to 12 percent for a well-diversified portfolio and subject to meet the criteria determined by the supervisory authority. Investment in commodities will be measured by the Maturity Ladder Approach or the Simplified Approach.

The second category is private commercial enterprise to undertake a business venture other than that stated in the first type. This type of mudarabah exposes the IIFS to the risk as an equity holder, but not to market risk. There are two methods to calculate the equity exposure: (1) Simple Risk Weight Method, where the RW will apply to the exposure net of specific provisions based on equity exposure in the banking books, and (2) Slotting Method, where IIFS are required to map their RW into four supervisory authorities and to assign RW accordingly.

The third category is mudarabah investments in project finance, where the IIFS advance funds to a customer who acts as mudarib in a construction contract for a third-party customer, who is the ultimate customer. The ultimate customer will make progress payment to the mudarib, who in turn makes payments to the IIFS. The essential role of the IIFS in this structure is to provide bridging finance to the mudarib pending their receipt of the progress payments. In this structure, the IIFS have no direct or contractual relationship with the ultimate customer. The IIFS are exposed to both credit risks, where the mudarib or the ultimate customer fails to pay, and to capital impairment risk in case the project results in a loss. The overall credit exposure in this case can be divided into three parts:

1. The amount receivable by the IIFS from the mudarib with respect to progress payments due from the ultimate customer, whereby the amount will be paid directly to the repayment account with the IIFS.

The RW will reflect the credit standing of the ultimate customer. In case there is no such arrangement, then it would reflect the credit standing of the mudarib.

2. The amount held in the repayment account with the IIFS will have zero RW.

3. Any remaining balance of the funds advanced by the IIFS to the mudarib would have an RW of 400 percent. Unless otherwise rated, the treatment will be by using either of the two methods that apply in the second category (IFSB 2005a).

Sukuk

Sukuk is divided into two broad categories:

1. **Asset-based sukuk:** Underlying assets offer fairly predictable returns to the sukuk holders, such as in the case of salam, istisna, and ijarah.

2. **Equity-based sukuk:** Returns are determined on the sharing of profit and loss in the underlying investment, which does not offer fairly predictable returns (IFSB 2005a).

In this section, we examine the different types of sukuk and the basis for measuring the capital requirement.

Salam Sukuk   This represents fractional ownership of the capital of a salam transaction, where the capital is constituted by an advance payment to counterparty as the supplier of a commodity to be delivered at a future date. This type of sukuk is nontradable, and the gross return to the holders consists of the margin or spread between the purchase price of the asset and its selling price. The credit and market risk in salam. Sukuk is similar to that of the salam contract, where the RW for credit risk is based on the counterparty, and market risk can be measured either by the Simplified Approach or Maturity Ladder Approach.

Istisna Sukuk   This represents a fractional share in the project financing of an undertaking to manufacture or construct an asset for a customer at a price to be paid in future installments, the total of which equals the total face value of the sukuk, in addition to mark up. The sukuk can be in the form of serial notes or certificates with different maturity dates that match the progress schedule of installments as agreed between the customer of the asset and the IIFS, and it is tradable. The IIFS are exposed to credit risk from the time the manufacture or construction work commences by the IIFS until the whole amount or all the installments are paid by the purchaser. The RW is based on the counterparty or customer. If there is a third party providing guarantee, then its RW will be applicable if it is lower than the counterparty. In addition, RW of 20 percent will be added to cater for the price risk.

Ijarah Sukuk   This represents the holder's proportionate ownership in a leased asset, where the sukuk holders will collectively assume the rights and obligations of the lessor. The sukuk holder will enjoy a share of the lease rental proportionate to the ownership share in the leased asset and will assume a proportionate share of any loss if the leased asset is destroyed, or will bear the cost of meeting the obligation to provide an alternative asset. The ijarah sukuk is tradable from the issuance date, as the subject matter is a nonfinancial asset owned by the sukuk holder. The risk measurement is similar to that of the ijarah and ijarah muntahia bittamleek (IFSB 2005a).

Musharakah Sukuk   This represents the direct pro rata ownership of the holder in the assets of a private commercial enterprise or a project, where the subscription money is normally employed in purchasing nonliquid assets, real estate, or movable assets. A musharakah sukuk is a profit and loss-sharing instrument, where the exposure is of the nature of an equity position in the banking book, except in the case of investment in assets for trading purposes. The certificate can be tradable provided that noncash and receivable assets are not less than 30 percent of the market capitalization. The treatment of risk is based on the intent of the underlying investments in musharakah (IFSB 2005a).

Mudarabah Sukuk   Sukuk holders subscribe to the certificate issued by a mudarib and share the profit and bear any losses arising from the mudarabah operations. The returns to the holders are dependent on the revenue generated by the underlying investment. The treatment of risk is based on the intent of the underlying investments in mudarabah.

RECOMMENDATIONS

The contractual agreement between Islamic banks and investment account holders is based on the concept of sharing profits sharing and losses bearing, which makes investment account holders a unique class of quasi-liability holders. Although they are not part of the bank's capital, they are expected to absorb all losses on investments made through their funds, unless there is evidence of negligence or misconduct on the part of the bank. The nature of intermediation and liabilities in Islamic banks has a great impact in the determination of adequate capital.

First, the mudarabah contracts in the liability side of the balance sheet are based on profit sharing and loss bearing arrangement. Any losses arising from the investment or asset financed by the PSIA funds are to be borne by the IAH, except for cases where there is negligence or misconduct. In this case, IIFS are not required to maintain regulatory capital to cater to the credit or market risk. Such assets are only considered for operational risk.

Second, investments funded by current accounts should be subject to adequate risk weights and capital allocation, as they carry commercial banking risk.

Third, the presence of displaced commercial risk and the practice of income smoothing have indirect implications for Islamic banks' capital adequacy, which a regulator takes into account.

Finally, Islamic banks can face a moral hazard issue. Since the bank as an agent is not liable for losses, but shares the profits with the investment account holder; it may have an incentive to maximize the investments funded by the account holder and attract more account holders than it has the capacity to handle. This can lead to investment decisions that are riskier than the investment account holder is willing to accept. Such incentive misalignment may lead to higher displaced commercial risk, which needs higher capital requirements.

The recommendation revolves around the need to protect the interest of PSIA, and the unrestricted PSIA in particular. Restricted PSIA usually involves high profiles that have the knowledge and experience in a particular line of business; therefore, when placing their funds they usually know the risk profile involved in that line of business. In contrast, the profiles of unrestricted PSIA are usually less knowledgeable of specific lines of business. Both restricted and unrestricted do not have any control over the investment operated by the financial institutions. Therefore, they are both in need of additional protection.

It is recommended to adjust the standard and supervisory discretion formulas as follows:

1. Standard formula to include in the denominator total risk-weighted assets (credit + market risks) plus operational risks less risk-weighted assets funded by restricted PSIA (credit + market risks) only.

This means that IFSB should allocate regulatory capital against the risk-weighted assets(credit and market risk) funded by the unrestricted PSIA.

2. Supervisory discretion formula to include in the denominator total risk-weighted assets (credit + market risks) plus operational risks. Less § [risk-weighted assets funded by PER and IRR of unrestricted PSIA (credit + market risks)] only.

This means that the supervisory authority has the description to request IIFS to allocate regulatory capital against PSIA both restricted and unrestricted.

This will aim to achieve the following:

- Strengthen the safety and soundness of the financial system by further strengthening the capital adequacy measurements.
- Provide a cushion against loss of the PSIA capital.
- Eliminate the moral hazard issue that arises as a result of the tendency of the IIFS management to take excessive risk, aiming for higher returns.
- Provide additional comfort and confidence to PSIA, particularly unrestricted PSIA to place their funds with the IIFS.

Corporate Governance

CHAPTER 10

The Supervisory Review Process and Issues

One of the main factors that contributes to the safety and soundness of a banking system is its supervisory system. In most countries, a supervisory system is mainly designed to protect individual consumers in banks and to set measures to eliminate or reduce systemic failure of the banking system. Inadequate capital is considered to be on top of the list of reasons for bank failure. This chapter discusses the following points:

- The supervisory review process.
- Supervisory issues related to Islamic banking.
- Islamic windows issues.
- The relationship between risk analysis and bank supervision.

THE SUPERVISORY REVIEW PROCESS

The Supervisory Review Process (SRP) constitutes Pillar 2 in Basel II and is a critical part of the capital adequacy framework. In 2007, the IFSB also issued guideline principles for the SRP, drawn mainly from Basel II. The guideline principles for Islamic banks cover the areas of capital adequacy, risk management, and internal control. They are designed to take into consideration the risk characteristics related to shari'ah compliance such as shari'ah scholars, the methodology of rate-of-return calculation and shari'ah audit scope. The Supervisory Review Process, in general, is designed to (1) ensure that banks have adequate capital to support all risks inherent in their business profile and business environment, and (2) encourage banks to develop and use better polices and internal processes for assessing and managing capital adequacy in relation with their risk profile, operations, and business strategy.

The supervisors play a crucial role in the process, as they need to review the bank's internal capital adequacy assessments and processes to ensure that capital position is consistent with the risk profile and strategy and to enable supervisory intervention if the bank's capital is not sufficient or consistent with the risk profile. Another important role of supervisors is to ensure compliance with the minimum standards and disclosure requirements.

There are four internationally agreed upon underpinning supervisory reviews measures in Basel II, which are equally applicable in a broader sense for Islamic banks:

1. Banks must have a process in place for assessing their overall capital adequacy that is consistent with their risk profiles and a strategy for maintaining their capital level at an acceptable level.
2. Supervisors should review and evaluate bank's internal capital adequacy assessments and strategies, as well as their ability to monitor and ensure compliance with regulatory capital ratio. Supervisors should take appropriate supervisory action if they are not satisfied with the result of this process.
3. Supervisors should expect banks to operate above the minimum regulatory capital ratios and should have the ability and power to require banks to hold capital in excess of the minimum requirement as deemed appropriate.
4. Supervisors should seek to intervene at an early stage to prevent capital from falling below the minimum level required to support the risk characteristics of a particular bank and should require rapid remedial action if capital is not maintained or restored (IFSB, 2007b).

There are six key elements in the SRP set by the IFSB:

First, the preconditions set out by the revised Basel II for effective banking supervision, which are relevant in a broad sense to Islamic banking. The supervisory authority should design the framework, taking into consideration the specific requirements of Islamic principles and at the same time meeting the international prudential standards and creating a level playing field for both IIFS and conventional banks. It is necessary to have a well-developed public infrastructure that includes among other things (1) a system of business laws, (2) an internationally acceptable accounting principles and rules, (3) a system of independent audit, (4) efficient and secure payment and clearing system to control counterparty risks, and (5) adequate supervision of and well articulated rules to govern the other financial and nonfinancial markets. The fact that IIFS has no access to funds from lender of last resort or discount window make it important for IIFS to have a contingency plan to obtain funds when needed.

Second, supervisors must ensure that banks meet the minimum capital adequacy requirements and that requirements are based on analysis of the asset portfolio and take into account rate-of-return risk and displaced commercial risk, which may arise as a result of the issue of IAH treatment. Also, banks should demonstrate that their capital is commensurate with the level of their overall risk exposure. The supervisory authority has the discretion to authorize the use of approaches to credit risk measurements other than the standardized approach, which is covered under the Standard. The supervisory authority has also the discretion to request IIFS to allocate additional capital charges for operational risk as needed.

The third element is related to risk management, corporate governance, and audit and compliance. With regard to risk management supervisory authorities need to ensure the adequacy of risk-management framework in place, including the IIFS systems of controls. Islamic banks, in their course of operations, must ensure compliance to shari'ah rules and principles, because failing to comply with shari'ah will lead to severe consequences. During their assessment of the internal control of the IIFS, supervisors must ensure adherence to the key elements set out in the IFSB guiding principles on risk management and corporate governance. The supervisory authority should assess the IIFS profile under the different risk categories, the concentration risk, and the risk mitigation techniques. With regard to corporate governance, the supervisory authority adopts a tailored-based approach to review the IIFS. This means that each IIFS is required to adopt corporate governance elements appropriate with its business. With respect to audit and compliance, the supervisory authority asses the adequacy of the control and compliance functions through discussions with the IIFS compliance and internal audits and also with the external audits.

Fourth, the supervisory authority must ensure the proper treatment of the related party transactions. A related party is defined by the IFSB as a member of the board of directors or senior management, a shari'ah advisor, or an external auditor of the institution. These tend to be major shareholders or other similarly vested parties, with whom the institution has business transactions that may be for the benefit of that party rather than the institution's shareholders and IAH. This may be done through auditing or on-site inspections.

Fifth is related to the transparency and market discipline, regarding which it is crucial for the supervisory authority to reinforce discipline and fiduciary duties toward various stakeholders, particularly the IAH with regard to IIFS's compliance with shari'ah rules and principles. It is important to ensure that financial reporting available to IAH, being the party that carries the risk, includes information about the performance of the investments. The accuracy, reliability, and timeliness of the information helps to protect the IAH interest and enhance system safety. Supervisory authority also must ensure adequate and timely disclosure of information on risk and returns in order to provide early warning signals.

Finally, the sixth element is regarding consolidated and home-host supervision. Consolidated supervision is defined as "a comprehensive approach to banking supervision which endeavors to evaluate the strength of an entire group, taking into account all the risks which may affect a bank or individual regulated firms within the group, regardless of whether these risks are carried in the books of the bank or of related entities. This group-wide approach to supervision, whereby all the risks of a banking group are taken into account, wherever they are booked, goes beyond accounting consolidation"(ASBA). Supervisory authorities should design a framework for the purpose of effective sharing of information and coordination for enhancing the prudential supervision and the management of crisis management. The framework should have standard formats for confidentiality requirements, reciprocal undertaking in relation to information sharing, right contacts, and competent people, and should help with language and interpretation of terms. For cross-sector supervision where the range of activities of the IIFS cross the supervisory authorities, there is a need for close coordination and dialogue between the different authorities to clearly assign the roles and responsibilities and to clearly establish the central point of contacts. Cross-sector occurs, for example, when the IIFS has a separate line of business that is supervised by separate supervisory authority such as *Takaful*. In case of unregulated subsidiaries to the IIFS, the supervisory authority needs to assess the risk exposure and whether its transferred to the regulated entities and vice versa in order to take necessary measurements (IFSB 2007b). Eventually the objective of consolidated supervision are to ensure that there is no supervisory gaps and that no foreign bank escape supervision, to prevent capital double leveraging, and to ensure that banks assess their risk on a global base (BCOBS 2000). For the home-host relationship, the supervisory authority, while providing a regulatory environment for IIFS to operate smoothly across jurisdiction, should manage crisis on a national basis. In addition supervisors, while assessing the potential and appetite of IIFS in taking risk, should keep an eye on whether the IAH funds are protected and to what extend through deposit insurance schemes.

SUPERVISORY ISSUES OF ISLAMIC BANKING

The supervisory implications of regulating both Islamic and conventional banks raise two main questions: (1) Can both Islamic and conventional banks be regulated by one single regulator? and (2) Is one single regulatory approach or regime possible for both conventional and Islamic banks?

A regulatory framework in general revolves around the possible response to financial failures. The way the regulator copes in order to survive financial crises depends to a large extent on the depth and maturity of the system: the more mature the system, the more substantial its ability to survive. The fact that Islamic banking is an evolving industry raises several issues. First, there is a need for a clear and robust set of regulatory measurements in order to provide enough clarity for Islamic banks to operate. Second, it is difficult for regulators to set such regulatory measurements based on shari'ah interpretations and rulings, as those lack consistency. In order to create the most appropriate regulatory environment, regulators should draw upon the experience of the conventional counterparty; however, they should bear in mind the unique characteristics of Islamic finance. The third issue revolves around the role and responsibilities of the shari'ah board, which is an integral part of the Islamic finance system. The shari'ah board ensures that all products and services offered and all operations and activities of Islamic banks comply with the shari'ah rules and principles. The fact that there are so many shari'ah boards in one banking system leads to inconsistency and nonstandard practices within this one system.

There are three major concerns in this aspect that adversely affects the supervisory review process in Islamic banks:

1. The limited number of shari'ah scholars who are experienced in both shari'ah and finance results in a high concentration pool of scholars for different Islamic banks. This causes problems such as conflict of interest, slow growth of the industry compared to the conventional financial market, and the delay of launching products due to the lengthy process of obtaining shari'ah approvals.
2. The role and responsibilities of the shari'ah board and their decisions and interpretations being inconsistent across firms and markets. Despite the fact that The Accounting and Auditing Organization for Islamic Financial Institutions have provided guidance on the composition and role of the shari'ah committee, there is no mandatory implementation of such standards across the industry.
3. The ambiguousness regarding what action should be taken by regulators if the shari'ah board does not conduct the necessary review (Bhambra, 2007).

ISSUES SPECIFIC TO ISLAMIC WINDOWS

The IFSB, in its guideline principles for the SRP, has set guidelines and principles that need to be fulfilled by the institutions in order to overcome the following concerns regarding the operation of Islamic windows.

First, the institutions should have an effective system in place to separate Islamic assets and funds from conventional ones, and the system must be transparent. Second, the supervisory authority must ensure that the institutions offering Islamic financial services through Islamic windows have effective internal systems, procedures, and controls in place to provide reasonable assurance that the transactions and dealings are shari'ah-compliant and that appropriate risk-management policies and practices are in place and are being followed. Third, Islamic windows are expected to provide evidence that they have appointed a competent shari'ah board or scholars. Fourth, the supervisory authority, while assessing the capital adequacy requirement of the parent conventional bank, needs to take into consideration the shari'ah-compliant assets of the window, as well as the risk-bearing nature of the shari'ah-compliant funds that are invested in these assets. Finally, the source of funds that is used to manage liquidity shortage for Islamic windows needs to be transparent and disclosed to the supervisory authorities (IFSB 2007).

THE RELATIONSHIP BETWEEN BANKING SUPERVISION AND BANK RISK MANAGEMENT

Banking supervision is one of the key factors in a stable and sound banking system, and it is an integral part of the whole process. The responsibilities of banking supervision include:

- Issuance and withdrawal of banking licenses on an exclusive basis.
- Issuance and enforcement of prudential regulations and standards.
- Prescribing and obtaining periodic reports to perform off-site surveillance and on-site examination.
- Assessment of fines and penalties and the initiation of emergency actions.
- Closure and liquidation of banks.

An effective supervisory system will consist of off-site surveillance, which is based on the analysis of financial data provided by banks and works as an early warning device, and on-site examination, which enables supervisors to examine the future viability of banks. On-site examination builds on and supplements the off-site surveillance. The scope and objectives of the supervision are determined mainly by identifying whether they look only to safeguard the stability of the banking system or if they wish to extend it to protect the interests of depositors (Greuning and Iqbal 2008). The Basel Committee on Banking Supervision has set certain standards for effective supervision, which are largely applicable for Islamic banking.

First, the supervisory authority must have a clear, achievable, and consistent framework of responsibilities and objectives, as well as the ability to achieve them. Second, in case of more than one supervisory authority, they all must operate within a coordinated framework to avoid regulatory or supervisory arbitrage. Third, the supervisory authority must have adequate resources, including the staffing, funding, and technology needed to meet the set objectives. Fourth, supervisors must be protected from personal and institutional liability for actions taken in good faith while performing their duties. Fifth, supervisory agencies should be obliged to cooperate and share relevant information both domestically and abroad. In their course of business, banks face risk, namely financial, operational, business, and event risk, which should be identified, monitored, and controlled. In each type of risk, the supervisory authority sets prudential guidelines to which the banks must adhere. The effectiveness of bank risk management with regard to identifying, measuring, monitoring, managing, and controlling all types of risk, as well as complying with the prudential guidelines set by the banking supervision, is a key element in an effective supervisory process (BCOBS 2004).

SUMMARY

The supervisory system is one of the main factors that contribute to the safety of a banking system. The system is designed to reduce the systemic failure by ensuring that banks have adequate capital to support all risks inherent in their business profile and business environment, and encouraging banks to develop and use better polices for assessing and managing capital adequacy in relation to their risk profile. After all, business strategy with regard to the inadequacy of capital is one of the main reasons for bank failure.

The supervisors play a crucial role in the process, as they need to review the bank's internal capital adequacy assessments and processes to ensure that capital position is consistent with the risk profile and strategy and to enable supervisory intervention if the bank's capital is not sufficient with the risk profile. They must also ensure compliance with the minimum standards and disclosure requirements.

There are four supervisory reviews measures in Basel II that are equally applicable in a broader sense for Islamic banks:

1. Banks must have a process in place for assessing their overall capital adequacy, which is consistent with their risk profiles, as well as a strategy to maintain this process at an acceptable level.
2. Supervisors should review and evaluate bank's internal capital adequacy assessments, as well as their ability to ensure compliance with regulatory

capital ratio. They should also take appropriate action if they are not satisfied with the result of this process.

3. Supervisors should expect banks to operate above the minimum regulatory capital ratios, and they should have the ability to require banks to hold capital in excess of the minimum requirement.

4. Supervisors should seek to intervene at an early stage to prevent capital from falling below the minimum level required to support the risk characteristics of a particular bank.

The IFSB has issued guideline principles for the SRP, drawn mainly from Basel II, which take into consideration the specific requirements of Islamic principles and at the same time meet the international prudential standards. There are many major concerns with the supervisory review for Islamic banks. Some of these concerns are the need for a clear and robust set of regulatory measurements in order to provide enough clarity for Islamic banks to operate. Also, the lack of consistency in shari'ah interpretations makes it difficult for regulators to set such regulatory measurements, which leads to inconsistency and nonstandard practices within the one system.

The major concerns related to the operations of Islamic windows are the separation of the Islamic assets and funds from conventional ones. The supervisory authority must ensure that the institutions offering Islamic financial services through Islamic windows have effective internal systems and controls in place to ensure that the operations and transactions comply with shari'ah principles and rules. In addition, supervisors must take into consideration the risk associated with the shari'ah-compliant assets of the window while assessing the capital adequacy requirement. Liquidity management for Islamic windows is another area of concern that needs to be transparent and disclosed to the supervisory authorities.

CHAPTER 11

Corporate Governance
in Islamic Banking

In the last few years, most countries across the globe have witnessed great difficulties in their banking systems due to the collapse of major banks in the United States and Western Europe. The year 2008 witnessed the collapse of Lehman Brothers, the largest investment bank in the United States. Then, 2009 witnessed the shutdown of 130 banks in the United States alone. Some other major banks were bailed out by their governments to save them from falling down. In some other countries like the United Arab Emirates, central banks had to step in to alleviate depositors' fears by issuing laws to guarantee all individual deposits for three years. Subsequently, the banking crisis was reflected in the global economy, and it was one of the primary contributors to the international economic crisis we are now experiencing. The fact that all these problems arose, despite the implementation of global standards and regulations by the banking systems in these countries, has raised the importance of the issue of corporate governance.

The major milestone in corporate governance started in 1998, when the Organisation for Economic Co-operation and Development (OECD) developed the principles of corporate governance upon the OECD Council meetings in 1998. The principles were agreed upon in 1999, and they were adopted by most countries across the world. They are considered, by the Financial Stability Forum, as one of the 12 Key Standards for Sound Financial Systems. A review of the principles was performed in 2002, upon a request from OECD Ministries, to evaluate the effectiveness of the principles. The review took into consideration both the economic and corporate governance challenges inside and outside the OECD countries. The revised principles were issued in 2004. Being aware of the fact that every country has it's unique, economic, social, legal, and cultural characteristics, the principles were set as guidelines that can be used by the individual governments in evaluating and developing their regulatory framework for corporate governance, as well as for any organization or corporation that aims to develop a sound and effective corporate governance system (OECD 2004).

According to Greuning and Iqbal (2008), the increasing attention to corporate governance in recent years is due to four factors:

1. The growth of institutional investments such as pension funds, insurance companies, and mutual funds, and their increasing role in the major industrial economies.
2. The increasing criticism regarding the effectiveness of controlling and monitoring publicly held corporations, particularly in the United Kingdom and the United States, which led to suboptimal economic and social development.
3. The rising trend to move into corporate governance models extended to a wider circle of stakeholders rather than focusing only on shareholders.
4. The impact of the increasing trend toward deregulation and liberalization of the institutional investors' activities.

Banks are extremely important to the development of the economy. In their role of collecting and utilizing funds, banks help in maintaining market stability and in providing low-cost capital, which stimulates growth in the economy. Corporate governance in such banks is a major element in this development. In addition, good corporate governance is considered an integral part of the institutional foundation of an economy as well as a way to minimize the systemic risk in the banking system (Yunis 2007).

Corporate governance issues in conventional banks are, in a broad sense, applicable to Islamic banks; therefore, the work of IFSB in corporate governance was mainly drawn upon the existing framework set by international bodies such as the Basel Committee on Banking Supervision and the OECD. Subsequently, I find it very important to give a brief history regarding corporate governance in conventional banks.

There are two major approaches to the issue of corporate governance.

The first approach focuses on the issue of whether there is a need for a separate analysis of corporate governance for banks. On the one hand, as argued by Levin (2003), banks are similar to any other organization where they have shareholders, debt holders, a board of directors, and competitors. Therefore, separate corporate governance of banks is not self-evident and needs justification. On the other hand, Caprio and Levine (2002) identify three characteristics that they claim necessary and sufficient to hold independent discussion of the corporate governance of banks:

1. Banks in general are more complex than other financial institutions and they have heavy interrelation with all economic aspects.

2. Banks are exposed to heavy regulations, and third, the widespread government ownership of banks raises specific governance issues.
3. In addition, Charkham (2003) added that the collapsing effect of banks exceeds by far other institutions, as it affects a wider circle of people and undermines the financial system itself, and subsequently, the whole economy.

Yunis (2007) argued that banks have an additional layer of specific characteristics that requires an additional layer of analysis. He identified three distinctive features:

1. Banks operate in a different manner from general corporations in the delivery of their business in the market. Therefore, it is important to create a degree of transparency to give confidence to customers as well as the market.
2. Banks are generally heavily regulated when compared to other corporations.
3. Banks have a wider definition of stakeholders.

The second major approach to the issue of corporate governance is whether corporate governance should focus mainly on protecting the interests of shareholders or should be enlarged to protect the interests of other stakeholders (Macy and O'Hara 2003). The main point in this debate is whether the directors of the organization give more care and loyalty to the shareholders of the organization or to the other stakeholders. This point leads to the different models of corporate governance.

DEFINITION OF CORPORATE GOVERNANCE

Corporate governance, in general, is defined by the OECD as being:

> *a set of relationships between a company's management, its board, its shareholders, and other stakeholders. Corporate governance also provides the structure through which the objectives of the company are set, and the means of attaining those objectives and monitoring performance are determined. Good corporate governance should provide a proper incentive for the board and management to pursue objectives that are in the interests of the company and its shareholders and should facilitate effective monitoring. The presence of*

effective corporate governance within an individual company and across an economy as a whole helps to provide a degree of confidence that is necessary for the proper functioning of a market economy. (OECD 2004)

Corporate governance can also be defined as

a set of organizational arrangements, whereby the actions of the management of a corporation are aligned as far as possible with the interests of its respective stakeholders. There are three kinds of stakeholders' rights which are control rights, cash flow rights, and information rights. Shareholders have control, cash flow, and information rights, where other stakeholders, such as creditors, may have cash flow and information rights. (Yunis 2007)

Furthermore, according to Greuning and Iqbal (2008), corporate governance is defined as

a set of relationships between the bank's management, its board, its shareholders, and other stakeholders. It relates to the manner in which the business of the bank is governed, including setting corporate objectives and the bank's risk profile, aligning corporate activities and behaviors with the expectation that management will operate in a safe and sound manner, and running day-to-day operations within an established risk profile while protecting the interests of depositors and other stakeholders.

There are five key elements to sound corporate governance:

1. A well-articulated strategy that can measure the overall success and contributions of individuals.
2. Robust financial risk management function, an adequate internal control system, and a functional process with the necessary checks and balances.
3. Adequate corporate values, code of conduct, and other standards of appropriate behavior and effective systems for ensuring compliance.
4. The assignment and enforcement of clear responsibilities, decision-making authority, and accountabilities that are appropriate for the bank's risk profile.
5. Financial and managerial incentives for the board, management, and employees to act in an appropriate manner.

CORPORATE GOVERNANCE MODELS

There are mainly two models that reflect the different aims and objectives of corporate governance: (1) the Anglo-American (also referred to as neo-liberal) model, and (2) the Continental European model.

The Anglo-American model to corporate governance adopts the view that the creation of value for shareholders should be given priority over the interests of other stakeholders. This position corresponds to the political and economic conditions and the development of the macroeconomies of the United States and the United Kingdom. This narrow view of stakeholders and their rights is clearly evident in the framework for financial reporting developed by the Financial Accounting Standards Board in the United States (Statement of Financial Accounting Concepts No. 1) and the International Accounting Standards Board (IASB Framework). In addition, this is also evident in the United Kingdom's Financial Reporting Council's (FRC) Code of Corporate Governance, which has been endorsed by the Financial Services Authority (FSA), the financial regulator for the United Kingdom. The FRC code reflects the following characteristics:

- The use of a voluntary code of good practice to be observed by corporations to promote good corporate governance over and above the basic requirements of company law.
- No specific focus on corporate social responsibility, but a strong focus on the rights of shareholders.
- Reliance on socially aware shareholders to enforce socially responsible behavior by management and market discipline, to be exercised by investors without reference to any other stakeholder groups (Yunis 2007).

The Continental European model to corporate governance is referred to as the neo-statist model in France and the neo-corporatist model in Germany. This model adopts the view of equal attention to be given to the interests of the other stakeholders in the organization, as well as to the interests of the shareholders (Archer and Karim 2007). The model provides equal consideration to other stakeholders, such as employees, and to other groups affected by the organization's activities. Such groups should have representation in the organization's organs of governance, such as the supervisory board. As there is a specific focus on the social role of such organizations, the public interest may be represented by supervisory board members with government affiliations. It is worth mentioning that while this model gives more weight to consensus behavior between leaders of the industry and representatives of labor with a proactive role of the government, this position gives less attention to market discipline and voluntary codes than the neo-liberal model.

THE OECD PRINCIPLES

The OECD principles represent the most effective and internationally accepted guidelines of corporate governance. The principles consist of six principles that address and set the guidelines for the following areas: (1) the effectiveness of the framework, (2) the shareholders' rights and the ownership's key functions, (3) the treatment of shareholders, (4) stakeholders and their roles, (5) transparency and disclosure, and (6) the board of directors' roles and responsibilities (OECD 2004).

Principle 1: The corporate governance framework should promote transparent and efficient markets be consistent with the rule of law and clearly articulate the division of responsibilities among different supervisory, regulatory, and enforcement authorities.

This principle sets the guidelines for developing an effective framework that:
- Impacts and promotes economic performance, market integrity, and transparency.
- Is consistent with the legal system and prevailing regulatory requirements.
- Ensures the protection of the public interest through a clearly articulated division of responsibilities across the jurisdiction.
- Gives complete and full power, authority, and resources to regulators, supervisors, and enforcement authorities to enable them to conduct their duties in a satisfactory and timely manner.

Principle 2: The corporate governance framework should protect and facilitate the exercise of shareholders' rights.

This principle sets the guidelines for shareholders' rights that need to be incorporated in the framework. This includes their right in the ownership and management, participation and information in decisions pertaining to fundamental changes or amendments, voting in general shareholders' meetings, the disclosure of the capital structure, and facilitation of the exercise of ownership right by all shareholders.

Principle 3: The corporate governance framework should ensure the equitable treatment of all shareholders, including minority and foreign shareholders. All shareholders should have the opportunity to obtain effective redress for violation of their rights.

This principle sets the rules and guidelines for the equality of treatment of all shareholders within any series of a class, the prohibition of insider trading, and the disclosure requirements of the members of the board regarding their involvement in the matters or transactions of the corporation.

Principle 4: The corporate governance framework should recognize the rights of stakeholders established by law or through mutual agreements and encourage active cooperation between corporations and stakeholders in creating wealth, jobs, and the sustainability of financially sound enterprises.

This principle sets the guidelines for protecting the interests and rights of the shareholders to access and have reliable information. Also, the employees' right to freely and safely communicate their concerns to the board is addressed.

Principle 5: The corporate governance framework should ensure that timely and accurate disclosure is made on all material matters regarding the corporation, including the financial situation, performance, ownership, and governance of the company.

It is important to have complete disclosure of both financial and nonfinancial information in a timely manner and according to high-quality standards. In addition to an annual independent audit that should be conducted, an external audit should be in place.

Principle 6: The corporate governance framework should ensure the strategic guidance of the company, the effective monitoring of management by the board, and the board's accountability to the company and the shareholders.

This principle sets the guidelines for the responsibilities of the board towards the company, the shareholders, and stakeholders. It also sets the requirements needed for the board to effectively make decisions and manage the company.

The guideline principles of the OECD are relevant, to a large extent, to Islamic banks. The IFSB principles on corporate governance are mainly drawn upon these principles with special catering for shari'ah rules and principles.

THE CORPORATE GOVERNANCE FRAMEWORK

The objective of corporate governance in Islamic banking is to set a rule-based incentive system that preserves social justice and order among all members of society. The governance processes and structures are necessary to protect the ethical standards and interests of the shareholders and stakeholders. Corporate governance should encompass:

(a) a set of organizational arrangements whereby the actions of the management of IIFS are aligned, as far as possible, with the interests of its stakeholders; (b) provision of proper incentives for the organs of governance such as the Board of Directors, Shari'ah Supervisory Board and management to pursue objectives that are in interests of the stakeholders and facilitate effective monitoring, thereby encouraging IIFS to use resources more efficiently; and (c) compliance with Islamic Shari'ah rules and principles. (IFSB 2006)

The IFSB has set the corporate governance framework based on the existing internationally accepted frameworks, codes, and best practices. There are currently seven guiding principles set by the IFSB to cater to the following four areas:

1. General governance approach.
2. The rights of Investment account holders.
3. Shari'ah compliance.
4. Transparency of financial reporting.

The main objectives of the guiding principles are:

- To support and assist IIFS to explore areas that need better corporate governance and processes.
- To support and provide stakeholders with the sufficient knowledge and awareness of corporate governance issues in IIFS to enable them to exercise monitory and advisory roles.
- To provide better understanding of corporate governance issues for IIFS—to enable them to enhance their existing practices—and to the supervisory authorities, in evaluating the effectiveness of the framework.

General Governance Approach

The framework needs to clearly define the strategic roles and functions as well as the accountability and responsibilities of all stakeholders of the board of directors and its committees, the executive management, the Shari'ah Supervisory Board, and the external auditors. The board of directors, being responsible for implementing the governance policy framework, will assign a governance committee and an audit committee.

TABLE 11.1 General Governance Approach of IIFS

Principle 1.1	IIFS shall establish a comprehensive governance policy framework which sets out the strategic roles and functions of each organ of governance and mechanisms for balancing the IIFS' accountabilities to various stakeholders.
Principle 1.2	IIFS shall ensure that the reporting of their financial and non-financial information meets the requirements of internationally recognized accounting standards which are in compliance with shari'ah rules and principles and are applicable to the Islamic financial services industry as recognized by the supervisory authorities of the country.

Source: Islamic Financial Services Board (2006).

The governance committee's primary objective is to protect all stakeholders apart from the shareholders. The committee is responsible for ensuring that governance polices are implemented by all organs of management, and for providing the board of directors with adequate information and recommendations in this regard.

The audit committee's primary objective is to ensure the integrity of the financial reporting controls and procedures adopted on behalf of the stakeholders. The audit committee will work closely with the internal and external auditors to monitor and review all the accounting policies applied and to provide the board of directors with adequate information and recommendations in this regard. Table 11.1 shows the IFSB's two principles related to the general governance approach.

The Rights of Investment Account Holders (IAH)

The relationship of IAH with the IIFS is one of the most complicated and critical issues in Islamic banking, and corporate governance in particular. There are two main concerns in this relationship: (1) the rights and the means of IAH to control and influence the management investment decisions, and (2) the alignment of strategies adopted by the IIFS with the risk and return expectations of the IAH. To account for those concerns, the IIFS is required to have in place adequate mechanisms to appoint qualified investment managers and to set investment policies that are appropriate with regard to the risk expectations of the IAH. In addition, IIFS need to disclose information in a timely and sufficient manner to IAH, both unrestricted and restricted. Table 11.2 shows the IFSB principles related to the rights of investment pertaining to IAH.

TABLE 11.2 Rights of Investment Account Holders (IAH)

Principle 2.1	IIFS shall acknowledge the rights of IAH to monitor the performance of their investments and the associated risks, and put into place adequate means to ensure that these rights are observes and exercised.
Principle 2.2	IIFS shall adopt a sound investment strategy which is appropriately aligned to the risk and return expectations of IAH (bearing in mind the distinction between restricted and unrestricted IAH), and be transparent in smoothing any returns.

Source: Islamic Financial Services Board (2006).

Compliance with Shari'ah Rules and Principles

Complying with the shari'ah rules and principles is the primary objective of IIFS. There are two issues that need to be fulfilled in order to meet this objective:

1. The enforcement of a proper system that is designed to ensure shari'ah compliance.
2. To promote awareness and enhance public confidence in the shari'ah scholars.

The board of directors, therefore, is required to set in place an efficient and adequate system for obtaining rulings from shari'ah scholars, applying *fatawa* and monitoring shari'ah compliance. In addition, rules and principles issued by the shari'ah scholars need to be available to the public. Table 11.3 shows the IFSB principles related to compliance with shari'ah rules and principles.

TABLE 11.3 Compliance with Shari'ah Rules and Principles

Principle 3.1:	IIFS shall have in place an appropriate mechanism for obtaining rulings from shari'ah scholars, applying Fatawa and monitoring shari'ah compliance in all aspects of their products, operations and activities.
Principle 3.2:	IIFS shall comply with the shari'ah rules and principles as expressed in the ruling of the IIFS's shari'ah scholars. The IIFS shall make these rulings available to the public

Source: Islamic Financial Services Board (2006).

TABLE 11.4 Transparency of Financial Reporting in Respect of Investment Accounts

Principle 4.0	IIFS shall make adequate and timely disclosure to IAH and the public of material and relevant information on the investment accounts that they manage.

Source: Islamic Financial Services Board (2006).

Transparency of Financial Reporting in Respect of Investment Accounts

Transparency and disclosure of financial information is crucial to streamline the relationship between IAH and IIFS. The IIFS is required to disclose information in an adequate and timely manner regarding: (1) the basis of profit calculation and asset allocation, (2) the basis of allocation and utilization of PER and IRR, and (3) any major or material changes in the policies and investment strategies, system of smoothing returns, and the basis of calculation of PER and IRR. Table 11.4 shows the IFSB principles related to the transparency of financial reporting in investment accounts.

MOBILIZATION AND USE OF FUNDS

The objective of corporate governance in Islamic banking is to set a rule-based incentive system that preserves social justice and order among all members of society. The governance processes and structures are necessary to protect the ethical standards and interests of the shareholders and stakeholders. In order to understand the specific corporate governance issues in Islamic banks, we must examine the bank's salient characteristics in both functions of mobilization and utilization of funds. There are two main sources of funds that are used by Islamic banks to mobilize funds:

1. Investment accounts, which are mainly based on a profit-sharing and loss-bearing mudarabah contract, where the funds are managed on behalf of the holders. Investment accounts are of limited duration, and holders have the right to withdraw their funds subject to certain terms and conditions.
2. Current accounts, which are capital guaranteed, sight deposits, can be withdrawn at any time, and are not entitled to any remuneration.

   In addition, Islamic banks raise funds by issuing equity shares.

On the utilization function, Islamic banks use various shari'ah-compliant products such as mudarabah, musharakah, ijarah, salam, and istisna to invest funds available from funds managed for investment account holders (IAH); the bank's own funds, which are the shareholders' funds; and funds from current accounts. There are two types of IAH funds: (1) unrestricted IAH funds, which are invested at the bank's discretion, normally in the same asset pool, where the current accounts and the bank's own funds are invested; and (2) restricted IAH funds, which involve a separate asset pool that is distinct from the bank's own funds.

The major corporate governance concern in Islamic banking arises from the nature of the relationship between the IAH as fund providers and the bank in its capacity as fund manager. One of the absolute requirements for a mudarabah contract, which regulates the relationship between the IAH and the bank, is the transfer of control over investment decisions, including all operating policies of the mudarabah from the IAH to the bank as a mudarib. This clear separation between the IAH and their invested capital, means that they have no right to intervene in these investments and policies, which is the sole prerogative of the mudarib. Also, the separation of capital ownership from management under the mudarabah contract does not provide any rights of governance or oversight to IAH in exchange for their funds.

In addition to the lack of governance rights of the IAH, they do not have the following:

- Benefit of a board of directors to monitor management on their behalf.
- Right to receive an annual report and to appoint external auditors.
- Right to take part and vote in an annual general meeting or other general assembly.
- Right to participate in appointing the SSB of the bank.

The major question that arises is: Why do unrestricted IAH deposit their funds with Islamic banks to manage theses funds on their behalf as equity investors, while they do not get any governance rights in exchange for their funds and the risk they bear, but only the hope that they will receive a return on those funds? The possible answer is that IAH depend on the monitoring of the shareholders, as they face the same risk and there is no major conflict of interest between them (Archer and Abdel Karim 2007).

On the one hand, the above hypothesis suggests that shareholders have the ability to exercise effective control over the management that would serve to safeguard IAH interests. On the other hand, and in situations where there is diffuse shareholders or concentrated ownership, this assumption will not be valid. In the case of diffuse shareholders, management will have significant discretion over the control of corporate assets. In general, diffused shareholders do not have enough experience or incentive to exercise sufficient control over management. In addition, diffuse shareholders and IAH get the minimum amount of disclosure of information about the actual return, how much the return is subject to smoothing, and the risk profile of the assets in which their funds are invested—all of which help in decision making. In the case of concentration of ownership, large investors act in accordance with their own interests, which may be at the expense of other investors. In addition, they usually get preferential treatment at the expense of other investors and stakeholders.

Further topics that raise serious governance concerns in Islamic banking are the Profit Equalization Reserve (PER) and the Investment Risk Reserve (IRR). A PER is funded by setting aside a portion of gross income before deducting the bank's own share as agent. The reserve provides a cushion to ensure smooth future returns and to increase the owners' equity for bearing future shocks. An IRR is set out of the income of the investors-depositors after allocating the bank's share to offset the risk of future investment losses.

Although the practice of maintaining reserves is becoming common, yet there are some critics. While this practice is in alignment with prudent risk management, it raises several governance issues that need to be discussed.

First, limited disclosure of such reserves makes IAH uncomfortable. For example, if a loss is absorbed by the IRR and was due to negligence or misconduct, it will be very difficult for the IAH to know because of the insufficient disclosure. In addition, the legal systems in countries where Islamic banks operate are not clear in both the IAH's rights for compensation in the case of such events and in the criteria to prove such negligence or misconduct. Second, investment account holders do not have the right to influence the use of such reserves and to verify the exposure of overall investment. Third, short-term investors may feel that they are subsidizing the returns for long-term investors. Fourth, some banks require IAH to waive their rights to these reserves. Islamic banks should standardize the practice, and the basis of computing such reserves should be predefined and fully disclosed. Also, the rights of IAH to these reserves should be clearly stated and explained to the depositors. Fifth, both PER and IRR will reduce the incentive of IAH and shareholders to monitor the performance of Islamic banks and the possibility of IAH to withdraw their funds, which would negatively affect market discipline. Sixth, it may increase the appetite of the management of Islamic banks to take more risk, which raises a moral hazard problem similar to conventional banks, where this is covered by a deposit-guarantee scheme. Finally, having a shari'ah board for every institution is not efficient. There needs to be only one set of shari'ah-compliant rules to ensure appropriate corporate governance. The suggestion is to have one Shari'ah Supervisory Board (SSB) for the whole system consisting of scholars from different disciplines, including shari'ah, economics, finance, and commercial law, to ensure that rules are defined and enforced so that economic agents comply fully with their contractual obligations to all stakeholders (Greuning and Iqbal 2008).

ISSUES IN ISLAMIC WINDOWS

In the 1980s, Islamic banks, during the period of its growth, were faced with a lack of quality investment opportunities, which created business opportunities for conventional Western banks. Western banks acted as intermediaries by utilizing Islamic funds according to Islamic banking guidelines and principles. They supported Islamic banks to place funds in commerce and trade-related activities by arranging a trade to buy goods and resell them on behalf of the Islamic bank at a markup. Subsequently, as conventional banks in Western Europe, the United States, and the rest of the world recognized the emergence of the Islamic financial market and the increase in demand for shari'ah-compliant banking products and services, they were encouraged to begin offering such products and services to their clients and to attract new clients through dedicated divisions within the conventional bank in so-called Islamic windows.

Corporate governance issues in Islamic windows raise more serious and complicated concerns than in pure shari'ah-compliant banks. In the treatment of IAH, Islamic windows not only face the issues of fairness and transparency like pure Islamic banks, but also have the issue of balance-sheet segregation, as the funds cannot be mingled with those of the bank's other activities. Another major concern in Islamic windows is to what extent they should be treated as a "bank within a bank" (Fiennes 2007). According to Fiennes, there are three points that need to be considered in order to address the compliance and the financial protection issues:

1. There must be separate accounts for the Islamic operations in order to provide transparency for the stakeholders. It must be very clear how Islamic widows raise funds and how they utilize them.
2. The need for a governing body, which, for convenience, can take the form of a shadow board of directors that has no legal status, but has control of a segregated balance sheet and is able to implement many of the governance requirements, such as an independent audit committee, a structure that ensures full segregation, and an SSB. This should be

considered a necessary cost of establishing a firewall between the Islamic window and the parent conventional bank.

3. The best way to ensure clarity and rigid separation is a separate legal entity. In some countries, like Malaysia, it is a regulatory authority's requirement. This will ensure that the principles of corporate governance needed for sound Islamic banking are implemented.

In addition, there are two main points that need to be embedded in the governance structure in order to ensure that the interests of consumers are safeguarded: (1) the IAH should have full and timely disclosure of the financial position and the performance of the Islamic operation, and (2) they should be aware of the legal position in case the bank as a whole becomes insolvent. The corporate governance structure needs to ensure that risks of contagion are clear to all stakeholders. There is one contradiction in the issue of Islamic banking windows, which is partly from a shari'ah perspective; Islamic windows should be as financially separate as possible. On the other hand, from the perspective of fairness to the consumer, it is vital that the bank should make it clear that the Islamic window is a legal part of the whole bank, because this will give comfort to the consumer, particularly in the case of sound international banks (Fiennes 2007).

SHARI'AH GOVERNANCE SYSTEM

As was mentioned earlier, Islamic finance regulations are still in a premature stage; therefore, continuous improvement, elaboration, and clarity is needed to enhance the framework. In order to enhance the soundness and stability of the IIFS, there was a need to set additional guidelines for corporate governance, which would complement the existing principles and prudential standards. The new guidelines aimed to elaborate and re-emphasize the important of competency, independence, confidentiality, and consistency of the shari'ah boards. They also intended to provide tools to stakeholders to exercise their rights in verifying the existence of an effective shari'ah governance system and a transparent process of audit for shari'ah compliance. The IFSB has issued guiding principles on shari'ah-compliant governance systems to complement the existing governance control and compliance function within the IIFS. The IFSB (2009b) defines the Shari'ah Governance System as follows:

The set of institutional and organizational arrangements through which an IIFS ensures that there is effective independent oversight of Shari'ah *compliance over each of the following structures and processes:*

- *Issuance of relevant* Shari'ah *pronouncements/resolutions that govern the whole of its operation.*
- *Dissemination of information on such* Shari'ah *pronouncements/ resolutions to the operative personnel of the IIFS who monitor the day-to-day compliance with the* Shari'ah *pronouncements/ resolutions vis-à-vis every level of operations and each trans-action.*
- *An internal* Shari'ah *compliance review/audit for verifying that* Shari'ah *compliance has been satisfied during which may incident for non-compliance will be recorded and reported and as far as possible addressed and rectifies.*
- *An annual* Shari'ah *compliance review/audit for verifying that the internal* Shari'ah *compliance review/audit has been appropriately carried out and its finding have been duly noted by the* Shari'ah *board.*

In a well-elaborated and clearly detailed fashion, the definition sets the objectives of an effective corporate governance system. It ensures the existence of an effective and independent shari'ah-compliance oversight at each stage in the process, starting from the first stage. This first stage involves the issuance of the resolutions that govern the operations in the next stage, which is the application and the day-to-day operations of the individuals regarding the third stage. The third stage involves the internal audit and review to ensure and verify that the operations are in shari'ah compliance with regard to the last stage, which is the annual shari'ah review to ensure that the internal control is satisfied and that findings have been rectified.

The guidelines, which consist of nine principles, pertain to the requirements of the SSB members in five areas: general, competence, independence, confidentiality, and professionalism. The objective in and role of each of the five parts is explained in more detail in the following paragraphs.

General Approach

The first part sets the ground for the initial stage, which is the development of the governance model that will be adopted and the roles and responsibilities of the shari'ah board. Adopting the logic off the OECD, which is "no single model" and "no single cure," supervisors in each jurisdiction should have the liberty and wisdom to design and tailor the governance structure and model to its specific needs and requirements. While developing the model, supervisors should take into consideration the maturity of the IIFS and the prevailing market conditions. The second principle explains and states

TABLE 11.5 General Approach to the Shari'ah Governance System

Principle 1.1	The shari'ah governance structure adopted by the IIFS should be commensurate and proportionate with the size, complexity, and nature of its business.
Principle 1.2	Each IIFS must ensure that the shari'ah board has 1. a clear frame of reference regarding its mandates and responsibilities. 2. well-defined operating procedures and lines of reporting. 3. good understanding of, and familiarity with, professional ethics and conduct.

Source: Islamic Financial Services Board (2009b).

the requirements for the shari'ah board to effectively perform its roles and responsibilities. One would say that this first approach is the road map for effective corporate governance system. Table 11.5 shows the IFSB principles related to the general approach to the Shari'ah Governance System.

Competence

After setting the roles and responsibilities of the shari'ah board, the second approach of the objective is to ensure the competence and effectiveness of the shari'ah board members through setting a proper mechanism to assign the members of the board. This includes examining the qualifications of the board members and ensuring that as a whole, it meets the necessary requirements for the job. A clear development plan for the members must also be in place to ensure that they are undergoing professional development. Furthermore, an assessment mechanism to evaluate the efficiency of the shari'ah board and the individual contributions of its members must be established. Table 11.6 shows the IFSB principles related to competence.

TABLE 11.6 Competence in the Shari'ah Governance System

Principle 2.1	The IIFS shall ensure that any person mandated with overseeing the Shari'ah Governance System fulfils acceptable fit and proper criteria.
Principle 2.2	The IIFS shall facilitate continuous professional development of persons serving on its shari'ah board, as well as its ISCU and ISRU, if applicable.
Principle 2.3	There should be a formal assessment of the effectiveness of the shari'ah board as a whole and of the contributions of each member to the effectiveness of the board.

Source: Islamic Financial Services Board (2009b).

TABLE 11.7 Independence in the Shari'ah Governance System

Principle 3.1	The shari'ah board should play a strong and independence oversight role, with adequate capability to exercise objective judgment on the shari'ah-related matters. No individual or group of individuals shall be allowed to dominate the shari'ah board's decision making.
Principle 3.2	In order to fulfill their responsibilities, the shari'ah board should be provided with complete, adequate, and timely information prior to all meetings and on an ongoing basis.

Source: Islamic Financial Services Board (2009b).

Independence

The objective of the principles of the third area is twofold; one is to ensure that while making decisions, the shari'ah board is operating as a fully capable and independent entity. Equally important is the elimination of any existing domination over the decision-making process. Another essential component is to ensure that institutions have in place effective and efficient systems to provide the shari'ah board with sufficient, reliable, and timely information to enable them to make decisions. Table 11.7 shows the IFSB principles related to independence.

Confidentiality

Bearing in mind that each board member has access to sensitive and confidential information, it is essential to re-emphasize the importance of information confidentiality. Table 11.8 shows the IFSB principles related to confidentiality.

Consistency

In order to maintain and improve consistency across the jurisdiction and to support the shari'ah pronouncements and resolutions issuance, it's important to be fully aware and knowledgeable about the legal and regulatory framework. Table 11.9 shows the IFSB principles related to consistency.

TABLE 11.8 Confidentiality in the Shari'ah Governance System

Principle 4.1	Shari'ah board members should ensure that internal information obtained in the course of their duties is kept confidential.

Source: Islamic Financial Services Board (2009b).

TABLE 11.9 Consistency in the Shari'ah Governance System

Principle 5.1	The IIFS should fully understand the legal and regulatory framework for issuance of shari'ah pronouncements and resolutions in the jurisdiction where it operates. It should ensure that its shari'ah board strictly observes the said framework and, wherever possible, promotes convergence of the shari'ah governance standards.

Source: Islamic Financial Services Board (2009b).

SUMMARY

The landmark of the issue of corporate governance is the work of the Organisation for Economic Co-operation and Development (OECD). In 2004, the OECD released the revised principles of corporate governance, which included six guideline principles. The guidelines are considered to be the major source and reliable reference for governments, organizations, and corporations. They are to be used while evaluating and developing the regulatory framework for corporate governance within these institutions. There are two major models to corporate governance:

1. The first model is the Anglo-American approach, which adopts the view that the creation of value for shareholders should be given priority over the interests of other stakeholders.

2. The second model is the Continental European approach, which adopts the view that equal attention is to be given to the interests of the other stakeholders in the organization, as well as to the interests of the shareholders.

In the past few years, the issue of corporate governance has gained large attention. This is mainly attributed to the poor control and monitoring of large public corporations, particularly in the United States and United Kingdom, which has resulted in poor economic and social development.

Corporate governance in Islamic banking aims to promote social justice and order among all members of society. The corporate governance principles issued by the IFSB in 2006 aim to encourage IIFS to effectively use their resources and comply with shari'ah rules and principles. There are two major issues in corporate governance that are unique to Islamic banks: (1) the IAH governance right, which is considered the most complicated issue in Islamic banking; and (2) compliance with shari'ah rules and principles as the primary objective of IIFS. Another issue of concern is the transparency and disclosure of financial information, which to some extent, needs improvement. In addition to the issues of corporate governance in pure Islamic banks, the issue of balance sheet segregation is considered unique to Islamic windows. It is mandatory that funds related to Islamic windows are not commingled with the funds related to conventional activities.

In an endeavor to further strengthen and improve upon the existing governance system, the IFSB in December 2009 has issued new guideline principles on shari'ah governance systems to complement the existing governance control and compliance function within the IIFS. The objective of the new standard is to ensure the existence of an effective and independent shari'ah-compliance oversight at each stage in the operations cycle. The nine principles of the guidelines covers five the general approach, competence, independence, confidentiality, and professionalism.

CHAPTER 12

Market Discipline and Transparency in Islamic Banking

T he Basel Committee has stated that "the purpose of pillar three (Market Discipline) is to complement the Minimum Capital Requirements (Pillar 1) and the Supervisory Review Process (Pillar 2)." (BCOBS 2004)

The committee, in order to enforce market discipline, has developed a set of disclosure requirements to enable market participants to assess key pieces of information on the scope of application, capital, risk exposure, and risk assessment processes to reach to the capital adequacy of the institution. Banks under Pillar 1 measure the various types of risks they face and the resulting capital requirements by applying specific methodologies and approaches. The purpose of Pillar 3 is to share and inform the market participants and stakeholders about the bank's exposure to those risks in order to enhance comparability and transparency through a common, consistent, and understandable disclosure framework. It is important to note that the disclosure framework should be consistent with how senior management and the board of directors assess and manage the risk of the bank.

The IFSB (2007a) has issued a standard to promote disclosure and transparency for Islamic banks based mainly on the principles of Pillar 3 of Basel Accord II. The objectives of the standard are:

- To support and complement the IFSB to implement standards to regulate capital adequacy, risk management, supervisory review, and corporate governance through the actions of the market participants in the market.
- To improve and enhance the monitoring capability of the market participants in general, and by investment account holders in particular, by facilitating the access to relevant, reliable, and timely information.

It is important to note here that the nature of the relationship between the IIFS and the IAHs gives transparency and disclosure of information a much higher role than in conventional banks. The fact that IAHs carry all the risk makes it crucial for IIFS to provide accurate, reliable, and timely information in order for IAH and all market participants to assess the risk and reward and to make their investment decisions and to exercise close monitoring. Such disclosure is also important for the stability of the financial system as a whole.

There are four key issues that need to be considered in order to have effective disclosure framework:

1. With regard to the accounting disclosures, the disclosure framework is designed to complement the Basel II framework and the internationally accepted accounting standards; therefore, it should not conflict with the requirements under any of these standards that are broader in scope. In addition, the framework needs to include specific information that is necessary for the IAH and shareholders due to the unique futures of the IIFS.
2. IIFS and Islamic windows should disclose all relevant information considered as material. Information is regarded as material if its omission or misstatement could influence anyone who depends on that information for the purpose of making economic and legitimate assessments or decisions in accordance with shari'ah requirements.
3. With regard to frequency and timeliness, disclosures should be made on a semiannual basis for information that is periodical in nature. However, qualitative disclosure that provides a general summary of a bank's risk-management objectives and policies, reporting system, and definitions may be published on an annual basis. IIFS should disclose on a quarterly basis information that is risk-sensitive in nature such as tier one capital, total capital adequacy ratio, and their components.
4. With respect to proprietary and confidential information, IIFS need to maintain an appropriate balance between the need for meaningful disclosure and the protection of proprietary and confidential information that is competition-sensitive in nature (IFSB 2007a).

THE DISCLOSURE FRAMEWORK FOR IIFS

The disclosure framework sets the principles and guidance for the IIFS approach to determine their disclosure policy and the internal control over this policy. It is important to note that, while having Pillar 3 of Basel II as a base, the framework was designed to cater for the unique nature and risk characteristic of the Islamic finance. The framework consists of four major parts that cover the following areas: (1) general principles which include corporate information, capital structure and capital adequacy, (2) investment account holders both restricted and unrestricted, (3) risk management which include credit risk, credit risk mitigation, liquidity risk, market risk, operational risk, equities, rate of return risk, displaced commercial risk, and (4) governance and Shari'ah Governance.

In this section, we briefly examine the principles of the framework.

1. **Corporate information:** to give details on the qualitative and quantitative disclosure requirements to allow the market to assess how Basel II applies to a banking group and how the different entities within the group are treated for capital adequacy purpose.
2. **Capital structure:** a qualitative disclosure that gives summary information on the terms and conditions of the main features of all capital and equity related capital instruments and unrestricted investment accounts. A quantitative disclosure to give detailed capital components and detailed PER and IRR. Such disclosures provide market participants with necessary information about a bank's ability to absorb financial losses.
3. **Capital adequacy:** a qualitative disclosure to give a summary discussion of the bank's approach to assessing the adequacy of its capital to support current and future activities. And description of the policy applied to identify the RWA funded by unrestricted investment accounts. A quantitative disclosure for (a) capital requirements for credit, market, and operational risk, (b) capital adequacy ratio, and (c) displaced commercial risk. It is important that banks disclose information about its capital adequacy as well as about the capital allocation process to provide market participants with a link between the disclosure of capital and risk exposure and assessment, and to gain a better understanding of the risks and rewards inherent in the bank's activities.
4. **Investment Accounts—unrestricted and restricted:** a qualitative disclosure that includes (a) procedure and policies applicable to the investment accounts, (b) funds are invested and managed in accordance to Shari'ah, (c) products information, (d) the basis of allocation of expenses and profit in relation to the IAH funds, (e) policies governing the management of restricted and unrestricted IAH funds. A quantitative disclosure that includes (a) the ratios of PER to PSIA, IRR to PSIA, ROA and ROE, (b) ratios of profit distributed to PSIA by type of IAH, and (c) ratios of financing to PSIA by type of IAH. There are additional sets of qualitative and quantitative disclosures to both unrestricted and restricted investment account.
5. **General disclosure for risk management:** a qualitative disclosure that includes (a) description of the risk management objectives, strategies, policies, and procedures, (b) structure and organizations supporting the

risk management framework, (c) risk management scope and nature and reporting system, and (d) risk mitigation policies and procedures. A quantitative disclosures that includes (a) range and measures of risk facing each restricted IAH fund, (b) treatment of assets financed by the restricted and unrestricted IAH separately in the calculation of RWA, and (c) percentage of financing for each category of counterpart to total financing.

6. **Credit risk:** to provide general disclosure for all banks from both a qualitative and quantitative perspective in order to give an overview of the size and nature of the bank's credit risk exposure and to provide the necessary information on how a bank assesses and manages that risk. This allows the market to assess asset quality by providing a breakdown of the bank's exposure in the standardized framework. In addition, it provides market participants with a sense of suitability of the Standardized Approach for the bank and provides a basis for a comparative analysis of banks. A qualitative disclosure that includes (a) credit risk management and objectives, (b) risk management structure, (c) name of the external credit assessment institutions, and (d) definition of past due receivable and impaired financial assets and policies and practices for loan loss provisions. A quantitative disclosure that includes (a) total gross credit exposure and average gross credit exposure over the period in terms of geographical area, counterparty, and industry and rating categories, (b) amount and changes in loss provisions, and (c) any penalties charged to customers for default and the treatment of such.

7. **Credit-risk mitigation:** to provide disclosure for the approaches used for credit-risk mitigation in order to enable market participants to assess the types of mitigation techniques employed and their impact on risk and regulatory capital levels. A qualitative disclosure that includes (a) the use of collateral and other shari'ah-compliant risk mitigation techniques along with the related policies for assets leased under *ijarah muntahiyah bittamlik*, (b) the main types of collateral and other shari'ah-compliant risk mitigation techniques acquired by the IIFS, (c) policies and procedures for valuation of collateral and for leased assets under *ijarah muntahiyah bittamlik* and also policies for disposition of assets, and (d) risk weight applicable to guarantors in case of third party guarantee. A quantitative disclosure that includes the total carrying amounts by type of collateral and assets owned and leased under *ijarah muntahiyah bittamlik*.

8. **Liquidity risk:** A qualitative disclosure that includes (a) the liquidity risk management framework, and (b) liquidity risk policies including the accessibility to shari'ah-compliant funds and the diversification of the resources of funds. A quantitative disclosure that includes (a) indicators

of exposures to liquidity risk, and (b) maturity analysis of various types of funding.

9. **Market risk:** A qualitative disclosure of the market risk management framework including reporting of all assets held for sale and all assets that difficult to sell or exposed to high price volatility. A quantitative disclosure that includes (a) indicators of exposure to market risk, (b) total amount of assets exposed to market risk by type of asset, and (c) measures of value-at-risk or other sensitivity analysis for different types of market risk.

10. **Operational risk:** A qualitative disclosure of policies on (a) processes that help track loss events, reporting of such losses, reviewing of reports by line management, and risk management and ensuring shari'ah compliance, (b) how operational risk is incorporated into the management framework, and (c) loss mitigation processes. A quantitative disclosure that includes (a) RWA equivalent to operational risk, and (b) indicators of operational risk exposures such as gross income and shari'ah noncompliant income.

11. **Equities:** disclosure for banking book position. In Islamic banking, equity position includes assets resulting from financing made by the bank based on musharakah or mudarabah contracts.

12. **Rate of return risk:** In conventional banking, interest-rate risk is dealt with under Pillar 2, the supervisory review process, as it does not require minimum regulatory capital charge under Pillar 1. The disclosed information enables market participants to assess the current and potential level of interest-rate risk in the banking book, by which the bank identifies, measures, monitors, and controls the risks and results of this process (BCOBS 2004). For Islamic banks, there is no such interest-rate risk. Instead, there is a rate-of-return risk, which is the major contribution to the displaced commercial risk. Displaced commercial risk is dealt with under Pillar 1 in the Capital Adequacy Standard (CAS) issued by the Islamic Financial Services Board. A qualitative disclosure that includes (a) factors affecting rate of return and benchmark rates and the possible reflect on pricing, and (b) process and system for monitoring and measuring elements that give rise to rate of return risk. A quantitative disclosure that includes (a) indicators of exposure to rate of return risk, and (b) sensitivity analysis of profit and rate of return to movement in the market price.

13. Displaced commercial risk is partially covered under the disclosure to IAHs. In this part it should cover (a) the IIFS policy on DCR, (b) historical data about the performance of the *mudarabah* over the last five years, and (c) five years historical comparison of rate of return of return to IAH and the benchmark in the market, the profit paid to shareholders.

14. Corporate governance: a qualitative disclosure that includes (a) corporate governance arrangement and practices, (b) any related party transactions, (c) investors and customer education programs conducted, and (d) social functions and charitable contributions.
15. Shari'ah Governance: A qualitative disclosure that includes (a) arrangements, systems, and control in place to ensure shari'ah compliance and how it meets the national and international standards, (b) how shari'ah non compliance earning occurs and the treatment of such income, and (c) how mandatory is shari'ah ruling. A quantitative disclosure that includes (a) nature, size, and number of violation of shari'ah compliance during the year, (b) the annual *zakat* contribution, and (c) shari'ah board annual remuneration.

MARKET DISCIPLINE ISSUES

According to Crocket (2001), there are four prerequisites for effective market discipline: (1) market participants need to have sufficient *information* to reach informed judgments; (2) they need to have the *ability* to process it correctly; (3) they need to have the right incentives; and (4) they need to have the right *mechanism* to exercise discipline. The four prerequisites have been discussed in many Islamic banking books.

According to Archer and Abdel Karim, prior to the implementation of the IFSB standards on disclosure, the Islamic banking industry had witnessed a severe lack of disclosure. This may be attributed to the fact that Islamic banks were hardly required to disclose any information related to IAH funds, such as

- The type of assets in which the funds are invested.
- The risks to which they are exposed and how they are managed.
- The bases of allocation of profit between the bank and IAH, including the type and amount of expenses that the bank charges to their accounts.
- Whether the IAH or shareholders are given priority in placing liquid funds available for investment.
- The smoothing of returns to IAH and the basis for the calculation and utilization of the Profit Equalization Reserve and the Investment Risk Reserve.

In addition, the accounting treatment of the IAH funds in the balance sheet was a debatable issue. Some banks reported unrestricted IAH funds under liabilities, while others reported them as equity, and other banks reported all IAH funds as off-balance sheet items. This issue was due to the different approaches adopted to regulate Islamic banks in different countries (Abdel Karim 2001).

This lack of transparency resulted in information asymmetry between IAH and the management of the bank. While preventing IAH from being adequately informed about the performance of their investments, it gave freedom to management to favor shareholders at the expense of IAH through the board of directors and the general assembly. Despite the guideline principles standards on corporate governance and the Shari'ah Governance System that were prepared and issued by IFSB and the AAOIFI to regulate and created awareness among regulatory authorities and Islamic banks, very few countries have adopted these standards, which resulted in serious limitations to their impact (Mustafa 2003). In order to improve corporate governance for IAH through disclosure, there needs to be a cross-sector approach that draws upon securities regulations to regulate Islamic banks that accept investment accounts, in order to give more attention to investor protection and interest. This should provide investors and prospective investors with adequate timely information to better assess the potential risk and rewards of their investment and to protect their interests.

Regarding the second prerequisite, which is the ability to process information, there are two main concerns:

1. The complexity of Islamic banking operations and mode of finance, which makes them difficult to clearly understand. The inherent risks of the contracts used in Islamic banking in both activities of mobilization and utilization of funds are not familiar or clearly understood by many.
2. The inability to attract market participants such as analysts, brokers, rating agencies, and institutional investors who have the knowledge and ability to process the information, due to the small size of the Islamic financial industry as a whole.

Regarding the third prerequisite, which focuses on incentives, one of the concerns is that the existence of an IRR represents some sort of a safety net effect, which reduces the incentive for IAH to monitor the performance of management. In addition, some countries, such as Bahrain and Sudan, enjoy a formal system of *shari'ah*-compliant deposit insurance based on *Takaful*. PER also tends to reduce the incentives of IAH to withdraw their funds due to a low rate of return, which in turn weakens the market discipline.

Finally, with regard to the fourth prerequisite, which revolves around the right mechanism to exercise discipline, IAH lack a mechanism whereby they can contribute to effective market discipline. In the case of subordinated debts, bonds are tradable in the financial markets, and their yields provide the market's assessment of the risks taken by the banks. Supervisors receive early warning signals either through a higher required risk premium by the investors or through trouble when issuing new bonds. IAH investments are not tradable in the capital market; therefore, they lack the mechanisms whereby they can send signals to the market about their assessment of the risks taken by the banks, in order to pressurize the management of Islamic banks (Archer and Abdel Karim 2007).

According to Abdullah, the four prerequisites need to be further developed. However, extreme focus should be placed on the first two, as they are considered necessary to be able to achieve the next two. This is due to several reasons.

First, there is a need to develop the informational infrastructure of the industry in order to promote transparency to enhance the understanding of the operations of Islamic financial institutions. Second, transparency facilitates decision-making, and hence, improves the allocation of resources. Third, the small size of the Islamic financial industry does not attract capable market participants such as brokers, rating agencies, and institutional investors. Such market participants have the ability to correctly process the information disclosed by Islamic financial institutions.

The concept of *Virtuous Cycle of Transparency*, developed by Abdullah, is a cycle that embraces all aspects of regulations, disclosure, transparency, corporate governance, market discipline, and the growth of the Islamic banking industry. The three major players in this cycle are: (1) the regulators, (2) the board of directors and the senior management, and (3) the market participants. After setting the guidelines and principles, the role of regulators in this cycle is:

- To develop regulatory disclosure requirements, which are useful to the market on a national and international basis.
- To enforce regulations by monitoring the implementation and compliance of Islamic financial institutions with the disclosure requirements.
- To be vigilant about negative signals sent by the market, as this may be an early warning of distress in individual institutions.
- Timely involvement to prevent or minimize the occurrence of bank failure.

The second player is the board of directors and the senior management and their role in providing both quantitative and qualitative information that enhances and promotes transparency. Such information needs to meet the following criteria:

- First, the usefulness of information depends on what the market discipline needs to achieve. There are different types of information that are required to demonstrate different activities of the bank, such as satisfactory performance and adequate profitability, good risk management, shari'ah compliance, and resolution of the conflict regarding IAH and shareholders.

- Second, the information needs to be accurate, which may be verified through external parties.
- Third, information needs to be material and provided on a timely basis.
- Fourth, it should not be proprietary in that it could endanger the competitive position of the bank.

The third player is the market participants. There are two main roles that can be performed by the market participants: (1) disciplining institutions, where each market develops a system of rewards and punishments for banks based on information disclosure; and (2) soliciting information, whereby the market relays the information needed to the financial institutions. The implementation of this role by the market participants will produce several benefits, such as:

- Providing Islamic banks with an incentive to address the issues of corporate governance.
- It prevents or at least reduces the possibility of bank failure through market reactions and early regulatory intervention to the early signals of distress in individual institutions.
- Transparency of operations as a prerequisite to market discipline will ultimately lead to low-risk premium in the market.
- It saves time and cost for regulators.

The drawback to this approach, however, is the possible conflict of interest between regulators and the market. In situations where the market reacts severely to banks with a weak position, which may result in bank failure, regulators may try to avoid this in order to maintain the soundness and stability of the financial sector. This is because loss of confidence in one bank may lead to loss of confidence in the whole banking system through the contagion effect (Abdullah 2007).

SUMMARY

Disclosure framework is the backbone of market discipline. A common, consistent, and understandable disclosure framework plays a crucial role in informing the market and stakeholders about the banks' exposure to those risks and in enhancing comparability.

The disclosure framework for Islamic banks aims to achieve two objectives:

1. To support and complement the IFSB in the implementation of standards to regulate capital adequacy, risk management, supervisory review, and corporate governance through the actions of the market participants in the market.
2. To improve and enhance the monitoring capability of the market participants, and by investment account holders in particular. This is facilitated by providing access to relevant, reliable, and timely information. The IFSB disclosure framework sets the principles and guidance for the 13 major areas that need to be covered in the disclosure regime.

There are four key elements to ensure effective market discipline:

1. Information that is sufficient to reach informed judgments.
2. Ability to process the information correctly.
3. The need for right incentives.
4. The right mechanism to exercise discipline.

There are major concerns in applying the four elements to Islamic banking that can be summarized as follows:

- The lack of sufficient information due to many reasons, for example, the ambiguity surrounding the way management utilizes the IAH funds and the level of risk associated with this. Also, the existence of several different approaches to regulating Islamic banks in different countries raises serious issues regarding the basis for the calculation and utilization of the Profit Equalization Reserve and the Investment Risk Reserve, as well as the different treatment of the IAH in the balance sheet.
- The ability to process information is affected by the complexity of Islamic banking operations and mode of finance, which makes it difficult for customers to understand. Also, it is affected by the inability to attract market participants such as analysts, brokers, rating agencies, and institutional investors who have the knowledge and ability to process the information, due to the small size of the Islamic financial industry.
- The practice of maintaining PER and IRR in some countries as a risk-mitigation and formal system of shari'ah-compliant deposit insurance based on *takaful*. In some countries, this reduces the incentive for IAH to monitor the performance of management and subsequently weakens the market discipline.

- IAH lack a mechanism whereby they can contribute to effective market discipline because their investments are not tradable in the capital market. Therefore, there is no mechanism in place to enable them to send signals to the market about their assessment of the risks taken by Islamic banks.

Virtuous Cycle of Transparency is a concept that was developed to provide a complete and effective framework for market discipline. The framework is developed based on three major players: (1) the regulators, (2) the board of directors and the senior management, and (3) the market participants. The role of the regulators is to develop, enforce, and monitor the regulatory disclosure requirements. Also, their role is to prevent or minimize the occurrence of bank failure by interfering at the appropriate time. The role of the board of directors and the senior management is to provide timely quantitative and qualitative information that enhances and promotes transparency. The role of the market participants is to solicit information and discipline institutions by setting a rewards and punishments system for banks based on the quality and timeliness of the information disclosure.

CHAPTER 13

Challenges Facing Islamic Banking and Recommendations

This book was designed to investigate and examine the effectiveness and adequacy of the regulatory framework of the Islamic Banks with regard to capital adequacy requirements, the supervisory review process, transparency and market discipline, and corporate governance. The book aims to shed light on the obstacles and challenges that face the development of the Islamic financial industry and to also provide some recommendations necessary to overcome these challenges and obstacles. The book commences with an overview of the Islamic principles and the history and development of Islamic banks. As a prerequisite to understanding the regulatory framework of Islamic banks, it is necessary to first understand four issues:

1. The nature of risk that faces the Islamic banks.
2. The unique characteristic, futures and risk associated with the *shari'ah* compliance products.
3. The important role and function of bank capital and the necessity of regulations.
4. The regulatory framework for a conventional banking system as being the foundation and main source of the regulatory framework for Islamic banking.

The book explores the nature of risk in Islamic banks and the special risk characteristics that are associated with Islamic banks, as well as the unique risk characteristics implied in each of the Islamic financial instruments. A literature review on the definition, role, and functions of the capital in both conventional and Islamic banking were presented. This section is extremely important to show the differences in the capital structure, roles, and functions, and in the calculation of capital requirements between Islamic and conventional banks. The Basel Capital Adequacy Accord of 1988, the amendments of 1996 and 2005 to incorporate market risk, and the revised Basel II Accord of 2004 were also discussed. Criticisms for the first accord resulted in the revised framework, the two major ones being that it encouraged banks to place their assets in higher risk categories and it did not take operational risk into consideration.

The book provides a descriptive analysis and examination of the Islamic standards that regulates capital adequacy and its three pillars. It also elaborates on each of the three pillars, namely the minimum capital adequacy requirements, the supervisory review process, and market discipline, and explained in detail their respective regulatory requirements and challenges. Corporate governance as one of the 12 Key Standards for Sound Financial Systems and one of the major concerns in the Islamic financial industry, was also discussed in detail. Finally, the book explores the issues and concerns of corporate governance in Islamic banks, particularly the relationship between the IAH and the banks themselves with regard to their governance rights.

CONCLUSIONS

The results and healthy growth of the Islamic financial industry compared to the conventional banking industry during the recent global economic crisis that commenced in 2007 are clear evidence that the principles and rules representing the foundation of Islamic banks are solid and valid. The profit and loss sharing principles and the asset-packed nature of the Islamic finance modes being at the core of the Islamic financial industry has proven to be a sound banking practice. Ultimately, it has resulted in the Islamic banking system being the least affected by the global banking crisis. The Islamic financial industry is a fairly new player in the global financial industry, and thus, is faced with many challenges. And there is a future set of challenges facing regulators and supervisors, the Islamic financial institutions, and governments and authorities.

The challenges facing regulators and supervisors are as follows:

- The lack of standard practices and the different interpretations to the same issue due to the existence of different shari'ah boards for each bank.
- Market discipline and transparency are serious issues of concern in Islamic banks. Despite the disclosure to promote transparency and market discipline issued by the IFSB in 2007, the majority of banks are not adhering to it.
- Corporate governance issues arise from the nature of the relationship between the IAH and the Islamic bank, which is based on profit sharing and loss bearing arrangement.

- In some countries where Islamic banks operate, supervisors lack the power to enforce compliance.

The challenges to the Islamic financial institutions can be summarized as follows:

- The need to develop shari'ah-compliant products and services as alternatives to the existing conventional tools, which are interest-based. This has to take into consideration the fact that the conventional Western banking industry has developed over three centuries, whereas the Islamic financial industry has only been around for a few decades. The challenge to Islamic banks is to develop such alternatives while meeting the internationally accepted standards of risk management and corporate governance.
- The industry is faced with a shortage in expertise in *fiqh al muamalat*, which is the shari'ah commercial jurisprudence. The development of the industry depends to a large extent on their opinions, which is a key issue in establishing the legitimacy of modern Islamic finance.
- The liquidity constraint due to the lack of liquidity tools, such as derivatives, and tools for hedging risk.

And finally, the challenges to governments and authorities are as follows:

- To provide an effective legal infrastructure and framework for the Islamic financial industry. Overcoming the legal challenges and issues are of great importance to the development of the Islamic financial industry. The fact that Islamic commercial law is in a premature stage makes this challenge especially difficult. Governments and authorities must develop Islamic commercial law that meets the requirement and needs of the Islamic financial industry, and at the same time keeps abreast of the conventional financial industry law. Issues such as creating liquidity instruments like derivatives, traded bills, and notes, as well as instruments for hedging risk that comply with shari'ah principles, represent major obstacles to the development of the Islamic financial industry.
- To provide supervisors and regulators with enough power to perform their duties effectively.

RECOMMENDATIONS

The book puts forward the following recommendations to regulators and supervisors, Islamic banks, and governments and authorities:

1. It is important to ensure uniformity and harmonization of shari'ah standards and practices across the board. Therefore, there is a need to have

one shari'ah board to support the system. This will also help in enhancing the credibility and confidence in the Islamic financial system.

2. In today's world it is important to put safety first. Therefore, there is a need to adjust the capital adequacy formula—both the standard and the supervisory—to take into consideration the interest of both the restricted and unrestricted PSIA. As explained in Chapter 9, this will: (a) strengthen the safety and soundness of the financial system by further strengthening our capital adequacy measurements; (b) provide a cushion against loss of the PSIA capital; (c) eliminate the moral hazard issue, which arises from the perception that management may tend to take excessive risk aiming for higher returns; and (d) provide additional comfort to PSIA, particularly unrestricted PSIA, and enhance overall confidence in the Islamic banking system.

3. To ensure that Islamic banks manage liquidity issues through establishing a supporting system that includes a lender of last resort, a liquidity management system. It is equally important to broaden and enlarge the scope of the secondary market.

4. Enhancing and enforcing the standards for effective corporate governance to protect and safeguard customers, as well as for effective market discipline and transparency, to provide timely and reliable information to IAH. The enforcement of these standards will help in enhancing industry credibility and will create confidence among all stakeholders.

5. To continuously develop upon the Islamic legal infrastructure and framework to cater for the ever developing needs and requirements of Islamic finance and to face the challenges of today's and the future's modern world. It is also important to ensure harmony with the conventional legal framework. From a human resource perspective, an extreme focus, attention, and generous investment should be given and allocated to develop and train a new generation of experts in Islamic banking regulations and laws.

6. It is crucial to revive and widely open the gates of *ijtihad*; in light of today's issues and concerns that faces Muslims, we need to reread and reinterpret both the Quran and the sunnah. This should not only include the commercial and financial part but all aspects of Muslims lives. It is important to note that financial aspect cannot be interpreted in isolation to the other aspects of their lives. This will not only help Muslims but will also help non Muslims to understand Islam in the right and genuine prospective.

Abbreviations

Following is a list of abbreviations and acronyms used throughout this book and the Islamic banking industry.

AAOIFI	Accounting and Auditing Organization for Islamic Financial Institutions
BCOBS	Basel Committee on Banking Supervision
BIS	Bank for International Settlements
CAR	Capital adequacy ratio
EAD	Exposure at default
ECAI	External credit assessment institution
FSA	Financial Services Authority
HJ	Hamish jiddiyyah
HSBC	Hong Kong and Shanghai Banking Corporation
IAH	Investment account holder
IASB	International Accounting Standards Board
IBJ	Industrial Bank of Japan
IDB	Islamic Development Bank
IFRO	International financial regulatory organization
IFSB	Islamic Financial Services Board
IIFM	International Islamic Financial Market
IIFS	Institution offering Islamic financial services
IIRA	Islamic International Rating Agency
IRB	Internal rating-based approach
IRR	Investment risk reserve
ISCU	Internal shari'ah compliance unit
ISRU	Internal shari'ah review/audit unit
FRC	Financial Reporting Council
FSA	Financial Services Authority
LGD	Loss given default
OECD	Organization for Economic Cooperation and Development
OIC	Organization of Islamic Conferences
PBUH	Peace be upon him
PD	Probability of default
PER	Profit equalization reserve

PL	Promise to lease
PP	Promise to purchase
PSIA	Profit-sharing investment account
SSB	Shari'ah Supervisory Board
UBS	Union Bank of Switzerland
VAR	Value at risk
WIP	Work-in-process

Glossary

This Glossary defines the finance instruments and terminology most commonly used in Islamic banking. Definitions have been adapted from publications by the Islamic Financial Services Board (www.ifsb.org).

diminishing *musharakah* A form of partnership in which one of the partners promises to buy the equity share of the other partner gradually until the title to the equity is completely transferred to the buying partner. The transaction starts with the formation of a partnership, after which buying and selling of the other partner's equity take place at market value or the price agreed upon at the time of entering into the contract. The buying and selling are independent of the partnership contract and should not be stipulated in the partnership contract, since the buying partner is only allowed to give a promise to buy. It is not permitted that one contract be entered into as a condition for concluding the other.

hamish al jiddiyya An amount of security deposit held as collateral by the IIFS at the point of entering into a contract, to confirm seriousness in an undertaking. The IIFS will take the amount of actual damage from the *Hamish al jiddiyya* in case the customer breaches his undertaking.

ijarah An *ijarah* contract refers to an agreement made by an institution offering Islamic financial services (IIFS) to lease to a customer an asset specified by the customer for an agreed period against specified installments of lease rental. It commences with a promise to lease that is binding on the part of the potential lessee prior to entering the contract.

ijarah muntahia bittamleek* or *ijarah wa iqtina A form of lease contract that offers the lessee an option to own the asset at the end of the lease period either by purchase of the asset through a token consideration or payment of the market value or by means of a gift contract.

investment *wakalah* An agency contract, where the investment account holder appoints the IIFS to carry out on behalf of the principal the investment for a fee or for no fee, as the case may be.

istisna A contract that refers to an agreement to sell a customer a nonexistent asset, which is to be manufactured or built according to the buyer's specifications and is to be delivered on a specified future date at a predetermined selling price.

mudarabah A contract between the capital provider and the bank, whereby the capital provider would contribute capital to an enterprise or activity, which is to be managed by the entrepreneur as *mudarib*. Profit generated by that enterprise or activity is shared in accordance with the terms of the *mudarabah* agreement, whereas losses are to be borne solely by the capital provider, unless the losses are due to the *mudarib*'s misconduct, negligence, or breach of contracted terms.

murabahah A contract that refers to a sales contract whereby the IIFS sells to a customer at cost, plus an agreed profit margin, a specified kind of asset that is already in its possession.

murabahah **for the purchase orderer (MPO)** An MPO contract refers to a sales contract whereby the IIFS sells to a customer at cost, plus an agreed profit margin, a specified kind of asset that has been purchased and acquired by the IIFS based on a promise to purchase from the customer. This promise can be binding or nonbinding.

musharakah A contract between the IIFS and a customer to contribute capital to an enterprise, whether existing or new, or to ownership of a real state or movable asset, on either a temporary or a permanent basis. Profit generated by the enterprise or real estate/asset is shared in accordance with the terms of the *musharakah* agreement, whereas losses are shared in proportion to each partner's share of capital.

parallel *istisna* A second *istisna* contract, where a third party will be manufacturing for the IIFS a specified kind of asset that corresponds to the kind of commodity specified in the first contract.

parallel *salam* A contract that refers to a second *salam* contract, with a third party acquiring from the IIFS a specified kind of commodity that corresponds to the kind of commodity specified in the first *salam* contract.

qard A non-interest-bearing loan intended to allow the borrower to use the loaned funds for a period, with the understanding that the same amount of the loan funds will be repaid at the end of the period.

rab al-mal The capital or funds provider

rahn A pledge to pawn a specific asset whereby the debtor (*rahin*) is entitled to hold custody of the asset. In the event of default by the creditor (*mrtahin*), the debtor may sell the asset.

restricted investment accounts The account holders authorize the IIFSs to invest their funds based on *mudarabah* or agency contracts with certain restrictions as to where, how, and for what purpose these are to be invested.

salam A contract that refers to an agreement to purchase at a predetermined price a specified kind of commodity not available with the seller and that is to be delivered on a specified future date in a specified quantity and quality. As buyers, the IIFSs make full payment of the purchase price upon execution of a *salam* contract. This contract is similar to conventional banks forward contracts but requires full payment at the time of the contract. This contract is used generally in financing agriculture activities where the IIFS pay the full value of the crops in advance and receives the commodities later at the time of harvest. The commodity may or may not be traded over the counter or on an exchange.

sukuk The Islamic bond representing the holder's proportionate ownership in an undivided part of underlying assets, where the holder assumes all rights and obligations to such assets.

unrestricted investment accounts   The account holders authorize the IIFSs to invest their funds based on *mudarabah* or *wakalah* (agency) contracts without laying any restrictions. The IIFSs can commingle these funds with their own funds and invest them in a pooled portfolio.

urbun   An amount of security deposit held as collateral by the IIFS at the point of entering into a contract to guarantee contract performance. The IIFS holds the right to obtain the dissolution of the contract during a certain period, otherwise, it will be considered as partial payment by the customer.

wadiah   An amount deposited for safe-keeping, whereby the depositor is guaranteed the funds in full.

References

Abdel Karim, R. 2001. International accounting harmonization, banking regulations and Islamic banks. *International Journal of Accounting* 36 (2): 169–193.

Abdullah, D. 2007. Transparency and market discipline: Basel pillar three. In *Islamic finance: The regulatory challenge*, ed. S. Archer and R. A. Karim. Singapore: John Wiley & Sons.

Accounting and Auditing Organization for Islamic Financial Institutions. 2008. *AAOIFI overview and objectives*. www.aaoifi.com/overview.html; www.aaoifi.com/objectives.html.

Accounting and Auditing Organization for Islamic Financial Institutions (AAOIFI), Bahrain. n.d. AAOIFI Shari'ah Standard No. 17. Investment sukuk.

Ainley, M., A. Mashayekhi, R. Hicks, A. Rahman, and A. Ravalia. 2007. *Islamic finance in the UK: Regulation and challenges*. United Kingdom: Financial Services Authority (FSA).

Akhtar, Shamshad. 2007. Islamic banking: Past, present and future outlook. State Bank of Pakistan, September 11.

Alfriend, Malcolm C. 1988. Risk-based capital standard: History and explanation. *Economic Review* (November/December).

Al Omar, F., and M. Abdel Haq. 1996. *Islamic banking: Theory, practice and challenges*. London: Zed Books.

Archer, S., and R. Abdel Karim. 2007. Measuring risk for capital adequacy: The issue of profit-sharing investment accounts. In *Islamic finance: The regulatory challenge*, ed. S. Archer and R. Abdel Karim. Singapore: John Wiley & Sons.

Archer, S., and A. Haron. 2007. Operational risk exposure of Islamic banks. In *Islamic finance: The regulatory challenge*, ed. S. Archer and R. Abdel Karim. Singapore: John Wiley & Sons.

Association of Supervisors of Banks of the Americas (ASBA). Consolidated Supervision-Work Group No 3Aziz, Zeti Akhtar. 2004. Current issues and developments in Islamic banking and finance. ASLI's Conference on Developing Islamic Banking and Capital Market: "New Opportunities, New Market and New Frontier in Islamic Banking and Finance," Kuala Lumpur, August 25.

Aziz, Zeti Akhtar. 2007. The challenge for a global Islamic capital market—Strategic development in Malaysia. The Sukuk Summit—London, June 20.

The Banker. 2009. Has Islamic finance reached a significant size and maturity to genuinely compete with conventional banking services? Can Islamic banking be more than a niche industry? (October 28).

Bank for International Settlements. 2003. www.bis.org/about/index.htm.

Bartels, J. 2002. Basel II and the survival of the SME: Are lenders and borrowers ready to comply with Basel II? *Business Credit* 104, no. 10 (November/December): 49.

Basel Committee on Banking Supervision. 1988. International convergence of capital measurement and capital standards.

Basel Committee on Banking Supervision. 1996. Amendment to the capital accord to incorporate market risk. January 1996.

Basel Committee on Banking Supervision. 2000. Consolidated Supervision.Seminar for senior bank supervisors. Washington. October 20, 2000.

Basel Committee on Banking Supervision. 2001. Consultative document.

Basel Committee on Banking Supervision. 2004. *International convergence of capital measurement and capital standards: A revised framework.* (June). www.bis.org/publ/bcbs107.htm.

Basel Committee on Banking Supervision. 2005. Amendment to the capital accord to incorporate market risk. November 2005.

Bashir, Abdel-Hameed M. 1999. Risk and profitability measures in Islamic banks: The case of two Sudanese banks. *Islamic Economic Studies* 6, no. 2 (May).

Bauerle, J. 2001. Double-edged sword: Technology and operational risk under the new Basel capital accord. *Business Credit* 103, no. 9 (October).

Benink, H., and C. Wihlborg. 2001. An unlevel playing field. *The Banker* (April).

Bhambra, H. 2007. Supervisory implications of Islamic finance in the current regulatory environment. In *Islamic finance: The regulatory challenge*, ed. S. Archer and R. Abdel Karim. Singapore: John Wiley & Sons.

Caprio, G., Jr. and R. Levine. 2002. Corporate governance of banks: Concepts and international observations. Paper presented at the conference, Building the Pillars of Financial Sector Governance: The Roles of Public and Private Sectors. Organized by the World Bank, International Monetary Fund, and Brookings Institution, Washington, D.C.

C. G. Weeramantry. 1988. *Islamic jurisprudence: An international perspective.* Vishva Lekha.

Charkham, J. 2003. *Guidance for the directors of banks.* Global Corporate Governance Forum, Focus group two, World Bank, Washington, D.C.

Crockett, A. 2001. Market discipline and financial stability. Paper presented at the Banks and Systemic Risk Conference, Bank of England, May 22–25, London, 1–9. Available at www.bis.org/cgi-bin/print.cgi.

Davis, H. 1999. A positive step: Financial Services Authority's view of the revisions to the Basel accord. *The Banker* (July): 149.

Delorenzo, Y., and M. McMillen. 2007. Law and Islamic finance: An interactive analysis. In *Islamic finance: The regulatory challenge*, ed. S. Archer and R. Abdel Karim. Singapore: John Wiley & Sons.

Divanna, J. 2007. From emergence to innovation. *The Banker* (November 1).

Dowd, K. 1999. Does asymmetric information justify bank capital adequacy regulation? *CATO Journal* 19, no. 1 (Spring/Summer): 39–47.

El-Gamal, M. 2006. Overview of Islamic finance. U.S. Department of Treasury, Office of International Affairs, Occasional Paper No. 4 (August).

El-Hawary, Grais, and Iqbal. 2004. Regulating Islamic financial institutions: The nature of the regulated. World Bank research paper 3227.

El-Hawary, Grais, and Iqbal. 2007. Diversity in the regulation of Islamic financial institutions. *The Quarterly Review of Economics and Finance* 46 (2007): 778–800.

Ervin, W., and J. Seidel. 2002. Basel capital accord must leave some room for human judgment. *American Banker* 167 (August 30): 61–62.

Fiennes, T. 2007. Supervisory implications of Islamic banking: A supervisor's perspective. In *Islamic finance: The regulatory challenge*, ed. S. Archer and R. Abdel Karim. Singapore: John Wiley & Sons.

Gardner, M., and D. L. Mills. 1988. *Managing financial institutions: An asset/liability approach*. Hinsdale, IL: Dryden Press.

Gomaa, Ali, Grand Mufti of Egypt. 2006. Questions from America. *Al Ahram Newspaper*, March–April.

Goodman, G., and R. Becker. 2003. Guide for banks in evaluating risk. *Law Journal* (January).

Governance system for institutions offering Islamic financial services. www.ifsb.org.

Grais, W., and A. Kulathunga. 2007. Capital structure and risk in Islamic financial services. In *Islamic finance: The regulatory challenge*, ed. S. Archer and R. Abdel Karim. Singapore: John Wiley & Sons.

Grais, W., and M. Pellegrini. 2006. Corporate governance in institutions offering Islamic financial services: Issues and options. World Bank research paper 4052.

Grais, W., and M. Pellegrini. 2006a. Corporate governance and stakeholders' financial interests in institutions offering Islamic financial services. World Bank research paper 4053.

Grais, W., and M. Pellegrini. 2006b. Corporate governance and shariah compliance in institutions offering Islamic financial services. World Bank research paper 4054.

Greuning, H. V., and S. B. Bratanovic. 1999. *Analyzing banking risk*. Washington, DC: International Bank for Reconstruction and Development, World Bank.

Greuning, H. V., and Z. Iqbal. 2008. *Risk analysis for Islamic banks*. Washington, DC: International Bank for Reconstruction and Development, World Bank.

Gulf Cooperation Council. 2003. Soaring interest: Islamic banking is moving increasingly into the mainstream in the GCC, and global heavyweights are beginning to take note. *Middle East Economic Digest*, 27, no. 5 (December 12).

Hallaq, Wael B. 1984. Was the gate of ijtihad closed? *International Journal of Middle East Studies* 16, no. 1 (March). Cambridge University Press.

Hallock, M., and J. Heintz. 2001. Measuring operational risk: Bank accounting and finance. *Euromoney Publications* 14, no. 4 (Summer).

Haron, A., and J. Hock. 2007. Inherent risk: Capital and market risks. In *Islamic finance: The regulatory challenge*, ed. S. Archer and R. Abdel Karim. Singapore: John Wiley & Sons.

Haron, S., and B. Shanmugam. 1997. *Islamic banking system: Concepts and applications*. Malaysia: Pelanduk Publications.

Heffernan, S. 1996. *Modern banking in theory and practice.* Singapore: John Wiley & Sons.

Heikal, Mohamed Hassanain. 1983. Kharif al-ghadab:qissat Bidayat wa-nihayat asr Anwar al-Sadat. The print company for publishing and distribution. Beirut, Lebanon. The Translation of Autumn of Fury: The assassination of Sadat

International Islamic Financial Market. 2008. www.iifm.netprofile.php.

Iqbal, Z., and A. Mirakhor. 2007. *An introduction to Islamic finance: Theory and practice.* Singapore: John Wiley & Sons.

Islamic Financial Services Board. 2005a. *Capital adequacy standard for institutions (other than insurance institutions) offering only Islamic financial services.* (December). www.ifsb.org.

Islamic Financial Services Board. 2005b. *Guiding principles of risk management for institutions (other than insurance institutions) offering only Islamic financial services.* (December). www.ifsb.org.

Islamic Financial Services Board. 2006. *Guiding principles on corporate governance for institutions offering only Islamic financial services (excluding Islamic insurance, takaful institutions, and Islamic mutual funds).* (December). www.ifsb.org.

Islamic Financial Services Board. 2007a. *Disclosure to promote transparency and market discipline for institutions offering Islamic financial services (excluding Islamic insurance, takaful institutions, and Islamic mutual funds).* (December). www.ifsb.org.

Islamic Financial Services Board. 2007b. *Guidance on key elements in the supervisory review process of institutions offering Islamic financial services (excluding Islamic insurance, takaful institutions, and Islamic mutual funds).* (December). www.ifsb.org.

Islamic Financial Services Board. 2008a. *Exposure draft—Guiding principles on conduct of business for institutions offering Islamic financial services.* (December). www.ifsb.org.

Islamic Financial Services Board. 2008c. www.ifsb.org/index.php.

Islamic Financial Services Board. 2009a. *Capital adequacy requirements for sukuk, securitizations and real estate investment.* (January). www.ifsb.org.

Islamic Financial Services Board. 2009b. *Guiding principles on shari'ah governance system* (December).

Islamic Financial Services Board. www.ifsb.org.

Islamic International Rating Agency. www.irating.com.

JCR-VIS Credit Rating Company Limited. 2005. Developing Islamic capital market instruments. Luxembourg, November 9.

Kamali, Mohammad Hashim. 2006. A collective ijtihad for solving society's problems. *Common Ground News (CGNews),* March 14.

Khasawna, A. 2008. *Al Masaref Al Islamia.* Jordan: Alam Alkotob Al Hadeeth and Arbed and Gedar Lilkotob Al Alamiya.

Levin, R. 2003. The corporate governance of banks: A concise discussion of concepts and evidence. Discussion paper No. 3, presented at the Global Corporate Governance Forum, Paris.

Lewis, M. K., and L. M. Algaoud. 2001. *Islamic banking.* United Kingdom and United States: Edward Elgar Publishing Limited.

Lopez, J. A. 1999. The Basel proposal for a new capital adequacy framework. *FRBSF Economic Letter* Vol 99, issue 23, no. 23 (July 30): 1–2.

Macy, J. R., and M. O'Hara. 2003. The corporate governance of banks. *Economic Policy Review* (April): 91–107.

Mahmoud, A. M. 1996. *Moadal kefayet rasalmal li albonok wefqan li ittifaqeit Basel wa al tatbeeq fe gomhoriat Misr Al Arabia.* Working Paper No. 18, Banking Institute—CBE, Cairo.

Mayer Brown. 2009. Background information to the new IFSB standards (IFSB7). Mayer Brown International LLP (April).

Meenai, S. A. 1989. *The Islamic development bank: A case study of Islamic cooperation.* London and New York: Kegan Paul International.

Mideast & N. Africa Encyclopedia. Fiqh. www.answers.com/topic/fiqh.

Mirakhor, A. 1990. The progress of Islamic banking: The case of Iran and Pakistan. In *Islamic law and finance,* ed. C. Mallat, 91–115. London: Graham and Trotman.

Mohamed, I. H. 2002. *Basel wa al salama al masrafia.* Paper, Union of Arab Banks, Cairo.

Mustafa, B. G. 2003. The implementation of accounting standards for Islamic banks: A study of preparers' and auditors' opinions in Sudan. Unpublished doctoral dissertation, University of Surrey, United Kingdom.

Nasser, El Gharib. 2001. *Osool al masrafia al Islamia wa qadaya al tashgiel.* Cairo: Union of Arab Banks.

Omar, M. 1995. *Lagnat Basel bein al qadima wa al hadetha.* Working Paper No. 17, Banking Institute—CBE, Cairo.

O'Sullivan, D. 1996. A sector with everything still to play for. *Middle East Economic Digest* 40, no. 28 (July 12): 7.

Organization for Economic Cooperation and Development. 2004. OECD principles of corporate governance.

Oxford Islamic Studies Online, Hanbali School of Law. "Hanbali School of Law" n.d. The Oxford dictionary of Islam. www.oxfordislamicstudies.com/article/opr/t125/e799.

Oxford Islamic Studies Online, Hanafi School of Law. "Hanafi School of Law" n.d. The Oxford dictionary of Islam. www.oxfordislamicstudies.com/article/opr/t125/e798.

Oxford Islamic Studies Online Maliki School of Law. "Maliki School of Law" n.d. The Oxford Dictionary of Islam. www.oxfordislamicstudies.com/article/opr/t125/e1413.

Oxford Islamic Studies Online, Shafii School of Law. "Shafii School of Law" n.d. The Oxford dictionary of Islam. www.oxfordislamicstudies.com/article/opr/t125/e2148.

Paglia, J. K., and J. K. Phlegar. 2001. The new Basel capital accord: What will be the impact on small banks and consumers? *Bank Accounting and Finance* 15: 63.

Reed, E. W., R. V. Cotter, E. Gill, and R. Smith. 1984. *Commercial banking.* 3rd ed. Upper Saddle River, NJ: Prentice Hall.

Roussakis, E. N. 1984. *Commercial banking: An era of deregulation.* New York: Praeger.

Salhani, Claude. 2006. Open the gates of ijtihad. *Common Ground News Services (CGNews)*, March 7.

Schacht, Joseph. 1964. An Introduction to Islamic law. Oxford: Clarendon Press.

Schuler, K. 1992. The world history of free banking: An overview. In *The experience of free banking*, ed. K. Dowd, 4–47. London: Routledge.

Shaker, F. 2002. *Al itar al gadeed al mouktarah le kefayet ras al mal wa al qadaya al matrouha amam al gehat al reqabia wa al masrafia al Arabia.* Cairo: Union of Arab Banks.

Shoaib, N. 2007. Top 500 Islamic financial institutions: From niche to mainstream. *The Banker* (November 1).

State Bank of Pakistan. 2003. Islamic Banking Department. *www*.sbp.org.pk.

Stevens, E. 2000. Evolution in banking supervision. *Economic Commentary* (March): 1–4.

Stewart, J. 2001. Lack of methodology in the madness. *The Banker* (April).

Sundararajan, V. 2007. Risk characteristics of Islamic products: Implications for risk measurement and supervision. In *Islamic finance: The regulatory challenge*, ed. S. Archer and R. Abdel Karim. Singapore: John Wiley & Sons.

Tarbert, H. P. 2000. Are international capital adequacy rules adequate? The Basel accord and beyond. *University of Pennsylvania Law Review* 148, no. 5 (May): 77–79.

Timewell, S., and J. Divanna. 2007. How fast is the Islamic finance industry growing? *The Banker* (November).

Tiner, W., and S. Kingsley. 2001. Basel and risk: The new requirements. *The Banker* (April 1).

Usmani, Taqi. n.d. Principles of shari'ah governing Islamic investment funds. Albalagh. www.albalagh.net/Islamic_economics/finance.shtml.

Venardos, M. Angelo. 2007. *Islamic banking and finance in South-East Asia: Its development and future.* Singapore: World Scientific Publishing Co. Pte. Ltd.

Vikor, Knut S. 1995. The development of ijtihad and Islamic reform. Third Nordic Conference on Middle Eastern Studies: Ethnic Encounter and Culture Change, Joensuu, Finland, June 19–22.

Yunis, H. 2007. Corporate governance for banks. In *Islamic finance: The regulatory challenge*, ed. S. Archer and R. Abdel Karim. Singapore: John Wiley & Sons.

Zaher, T., and M. K. Hassan. 2001. A comparative literature survey of Islamic finance and banking. *Financial Market, Institutions, and Instruments* 10, no. 4 (November).

About the Author

Amr Mohamed El Tiby has 27 years of banking experience in the Middle East and Gulf region and currently serves as a bank vice president. After earning a bachelor's degree in faculty in commerce at Cairo University in 1980, El Tiby went on to earn a degree in finance from the same university in 1985. He also holds a master's degree in economics (2003) from the American University in Cairo with focus on the regulatory framework of conventional banks and a PhD in economics with a focus on Islamic finance (2009) from the American University in London.

He writes extensively on the topic of risk and regulations of Islamic finance. His articles have been widely published in the United Arab Emirates as well as the United States by the Global Association of Risk Professionals (GARP), CPI Financial (www.cpifinancial.net), and the Emirates Institute for Banking and Finance Studies (EIBFS).

Index